CHENG & TSUI
"Bringing Asia to the World"™



中文听说读写

# INTEGRATED CHINESE

Simplified Characters

# 1

## Textbook

4th Edition

Yuehua Liu and Tao-chung Yao
Nyan-Ping Bi, Liangyan Ge, Yaohua Shi

Original Edition by Tao-chung Yao and Yuehua Liu
Liangyan Ge, Yea-fen Chen, Nyan-Ping Bi, Xiaojun Wang, Yaohua Shi

CHENG & TSUI

"Bringing Asia to the World"™



Fourth Edition

Fifth Printing 2022

24 23 22 5 6 7

ISBN 978-1-62291-133-2
[Fourth Edition, Simplified Characters, Hardcover]

ISBN 978-1-62291-135-6
[Fourth Edition, Simplified Characters, Paperback]

Library of Congress Cataloging-in-Publication Data [Third Edition]

Integrated Chinese = [Zhong wen ting shuo du xie]. Traditional character edition. Level 1, part 1/ Yuehua Liu . . . [et. al]. – 3rd. ed.

p. cm.

Chinese and English.

Includes indexes.

Parallel title in Chinese characters.

ISBN 978-0-88727-645-3 – ISBN 978-0-88727-639-2 (pbk.) – ISBN 978-0-88727-644-6 – ISBN 978-0-88727-638-5 (pbk.) 1. Chinese language–Textbooks for foreign speakers–English. I. Liu, Yuehua. II. Title: Zhong wen ting shuo du xie.

PL1129.E5I683 2008

495.1–dc22

Printed in Canada

The *Integrated Chinese* series includes textbooks, workbooks, character workbooks, teacher's resources, audio, video, and more. Visit chengtsui.co for more information on the other components of *Integrated Chinese*.

**Publisher**
JILL CHENG

**Editorial Manager**
BEN SHRAGGE

**Editors**
LEI WANG with LIJIE QIN, MIKE YONG, RANDY TELFER, and SHUWEN ZHANG

**Creative Director**
CHRISTIAN SABOGAL

**Illustrator/Designer**
KATE PAPADAKI

**Images**
© Adobe Stock
© Cheng & Tsui

**Cheng & Tsui Company, Inc.**
25 West Street
Boston, MA 02111-1213 USA
Phone (617) 988-2400 / (800) 554-1963
Fax (617) 426-3669
chengtsui.co

This Fourth Edition of *Integrated Chinese* is dedicated to the memory of our dearest colleague and friend Professor Tao-chung (Ted) Yao.

# Publisher's Note

When *Integrated Chinese* was first published in 1997, it set a new standard with its focus on the development and integration of the four language skills (listening, speaking, reading, and writing). Today, to further enrich the learning experience of the many users of *Integrated Chinese* worldwide, Cheng & Tsui is pleased to offer this revised and updated Fourth Edition of *Integrated Chinese*. We would like to thank the many teachers and students who, by offering their valuable insights and suggestions, have helped *Integrated Chinese* evolve and keep pace with the many positive changes in the field of Chinese language instruction. *Integrated Chinese* continues to offer comprehensive language instruction, with many new features, including a new and innovative web application, as detailed in the Preface.

The Cheng & Tsui Chinese Language Series is designed to publish and widely distribute quality language learning materials created by leading instructors from around the world. We welcome readers' comments and suggestions concerning the publications in this series. Please contact the following members of our Editorial Board, in care of our Editorial Department (e-mail: editor@cheng-tsui.com).

# Contents

# Preface

The *Integrated Chinese* (IC) series is an internationally acclaimed Mandarin Chinese language course that delivers a cohesive system of print and digital resources for highly effective teaching and learning. First published in 1997, it is now the leading series of Chinese language learning resources in the United States and beyond. Through its holistic focus on the language skills of listening, speaking, reading, and writing, IC teaches novice and intermediate students the skills they need to function in Chinese.

## What's New

It has been eight years since the publication of the Third Edition of IC. We are deeply grateful for all the positive feedback, as well as constructive suggestions for improvement, from IC users. In the meantime, China and the world have seen significant transformations in electronic communications, commerce, and media. Additionally, the technology available to us is transforming the way teachers and students interact with content. The teaching of Chinese as a second language needs to keep pace with these exciting developments. Therefore, the time seems right to update IC across delivery formats.

In developing this latest edition of IC, we have consulted the American Council on the Teaching of Foreign Languages (ACTFL) *21st Century Skills Map for World Languages*. The national standards for foreign language learning in the 21st century focus on goals in five areas—communication, cultures, connections, comparisons, and communities. In addition to classifying the applicable **Language Practice** activities by communication mode (interpersonal, interpretive, and presentational), we have added a host of materials that address the 5 Cs. The delivery of IC via the new ChengTsui Web App elevates the teaching and learning experience by presenting multimedia and interactive content in a truly blended and integrated way.

New, visually rich supplementary modules that recur in each lesson have been introduced. These can be taught in any sequence to serve as prompts for classroom discussion and student reflection:

- **Get Real with Chinese** draws on realia to situate language learning in real-life contexts. Students are required to analyze, predict, and synthesize before coming to conclusions about embedded linguistic and cultural meaning. Photos and questions connect the classroom to authentic Chinese experiences.
- **Chinese Chat** provides opportunities for language practice in the digital environment. Realistic texting, microblogging, and social media scenarios show students how the younger generation has adapted Chinese to new communication technologies.
- **Characterize It!** encourages students to approach Chinese characters analytically. The exercises in the first five lessons introduce a major pattern to teach character structure; then a major radical to teach characters' meanings. The remaining lessons introduce two major radicals each to allow students to continue to expand their knowledge strategically. Additional activities are provided on the ChengTsui Web App.
- While not a new segment, **How About You?** has been revamped for the Fourth Edition. This module encourages students to personalize their study of vocabulary and learn words and phrases that relate to their own interests and background. Questions now appear in both Chinese and English, while visual cues, which typically correspond to possible answers, promote vocabulary expansion and retention. Vocabulary items corresponding to the visual cues are listed in a separate index.

Moreover, to promote students' awareness of cultural diversity in a world of rapid globalization, we have included **Compare & Contrast** activities in the **Cultural Literacy** (formerly Culture Highlights) section. This section as a whole has been given a lavishly illustrated, magazine-style treatment to better engage students. Users who subscribe to the ChengTsui Web App will have access to additional cultural content related to the lesson themes.

We have also updated the **Grammar** section to include exercises tailored to each grammar point, so students can immediately put into practice the language forms they have just learned. Additional practice exercises for each grammar point are accessible via the ChengTsui Web App.

The **Basics** (formerly Introduction) section has been completely redesigned to emphasize its foundational importance in the book. More information on its pedagogical function can be found on page 1. **Keeping It Casual** (formerly That's How the Chinese Say It!) remains a review of functional expressions after Lessons 5 and 10 that encourages students to build their own personalized list of useful expressions.

Finally, the new **Lesson Wrap-Up** section includes context-based tasks that prepare students to communicate with native Chinese speakers. Also in this section are **Make It Flow!** exercises, which help students develop and apply strategies to organize information coherently and cohesively in written and spoken discourse. We created this activity to address the common phenomenon of novice and intermediate students speaking in choppy, isolated sentences. The ultimate purpose of acquiring a language is communication, and a hallmark of effective communication is the ability to produce continuous discourse. The **Lesson Wrap-Up** activities are intended as assessment instruments for the **Can-Do Checklist**, which encourages students to measure their progress at the end of the lesson.

As previous users of IC will note, we have renamed the four-volume series. The new sequencing of Volumes 1 to 4 better reflects the flexibility of the materials and the diversity of our user groups and their instructional environments.

As with the Third Edition, the Fourth Edition of IC features both traditional and simplified character versions of the Volume 1 and 2 textbooks and workbooks, and a combination of traditional and simplified characters in the Volume 3 and 4 textbooks and workbooks. However, in response to user feedback, we have updated the traditional characters to ensure they match the standard set currently used in Taiwan. For reference, we have consulted the Taiwan Ministry of Education's *Revised Chinese Dictionary*.

The most significant change in the Fourth Edition is the incorporation of innovative educational technology. Users of the print edition have access to audio (at chengtsui.co/resources), while subscribers to the ChengTsui Web App have access to streaming audio plus additional, interactive content.

Users who choose to subscribe to the *Basic Edition* of the ChengTsui Web App will have access to:

- Audio (Textbook and Workbook)
- Video of the lesson texts
- Vocabulary flashcards
- Additional grammar exercises
- Additional character practice
- Additional cultural content

Users who choose to subscribe to the *Essential Edition* of the ChengTsui Web App will, in addition to the above, have access to the Workbook with auto-grading and the Character Workbook as a download.

In addition to the student editions, the ChengTsui Web App is available in an *Educator Edition*. The *Educator Edition* web-application overlay suggests teaching tips and strategies and conveniently makes connections between the Textbook and the additional resources provided in the Teacher's Resources, such as video activity sheets, quizzes, and answer keys.

A key feature of the ChengTsui Web App is coherence. The innovative instructional design provides an integrated user experience. Learners can move seamlessly between the transmission, practice, application, and evaluation stages, navigating the content to suit their particular learning needs and styles. For more information and a free trial, please visit chengtsui.co.

Both in its print and digital versions, the new IC features a contemporary layout that adds clarity and rigor to our instructional design. Rich new visuals complement the text's revised, user-friendly language and up-to-date cultural content. We hope that students and teachers find the many changes and new features timely and meaningful.

## Organizational Principles

In the higher education setting, the IC series of four volumes often covers two years of instruction, with smooth transitions from one level to the next. The lessons first cover topics from everyday life, then gradually move to more abstract subject matter. The materials do not follow one pedagogical methodology, but instead blend several effective teaching approaches. Used in conjunction with the ChengTsui Web App, incorporating differentiated instruction, blended learning, and the flipped classroom is even easier. Here are some of the features of IC that distinguish it from other Chinese language resources:

### Integrating Pedagogy and Authenticity

We believe that students should be taught authentic materials even in their first year of language instruction. Therefore, most of our pedagogical materials are simulated authentic materials. Authentic materials (produced by native Chinese speakers for native Chinese speakers) are also included in every lesson.

## Integrating Traditional and Simplified Characters

We believe that students should learn both traditional and simplified Chinese characters. However, we also realize that teaching students both forms from day one could be overwhelming. Our solution is for students to focus on one form during their first year of study, and to acquire the other during their second. Therefore, the first two volumes of IC are available in separate traditional and simplified versions, with the alternative character forms of the texts included in the Appendix.

By their second year of study, we believe that all students should be exposed to both forms of written Chinese. Accordingly, the final two volumes of IC include both traditional and simplified characters. Students in second-year Chinese language classes come from different backgrounds, and should be allowed to write in their preferred form. However, it is important that the learner write in one form only, and not a hybrid of both.

## Integrating Teaching Approaches

Because no single teaching method can adequately train a student in all language skills, we employ a variety of approaches in IC. In addition to the communicative approach, we also use traditional methods such as grammar-translation and the direct method.

Users of the ChengTsui Web App can employ additional teaching approaches, such as differentiated learning and blended learning. Students can self-pace their learning, which is a very powerful instructional intervention. The product also facilitates breaking down direct instruction into more engaging "bites" of learning, which improves student engagement. Moreover, the ChengTsui Web App allows students to interact with the content at home and practice and apply their learning in the classroom with corrective teacher feedback, which has the potential to improve student outcomes. Additionally, teachers and learners do not need to follow the instructional flow of the underlying book. They can navigate using multiple pathways in flexible and customized ways and at varying paces for true individualized learning.

# Acknowledgments

We would like to thank users around the world for believing in IC. We owe much of the continued success of IC to their invaluable feedback. Likewise, we would be remiss if we did not acknowledge the University of Notre Dame for sponsoring and inviting us to a one-day workshop on IC on April 9, 2016. Leading Chinese language specialists from across the country shared their experiences with the IC authors. We are especially indebted to Professor Yongping Zhu, Chair of the Department of East Asian Languages and Cultures at Notre Dame, and his colleagues and staff for organizing the workshop.

Professors Fangpei Cai and Meng Li of the University of Chicago took time out from their busy teaching schedules to compile a detailed list of comments and suggestions. We are profoundly touched by their generosity. In completing this Fourth Edition, we have taken into consideration their and other users' recommendations for revision. Indeed, many of the changes are in response to user feedback. The authors are naturally responsible for any remaining shortcomings and oversights.

For two summers in a row, Professor Liangyan Ge's wife, Ms. Yongqing Pan, warmly invited the IC team to their home to complete the bulk of the work of revising the IC series. Words are inadequate to express our thanks to Ms. Pan for her warm hospitality and her superb cooking day in and day out.

We are deeply grateful to our publisher Cheng & Tsui Company and to Jill Cheng in particular for her unswerving support for IC over the years. We would also like to express our heartfelt appreciation to our editor Ben Shragge and his colleagues for their meticulous attention to every aspect of this new edition.

As we look back on the evolution of IC, one person is never far from our thoughts. Without Professor Tao-chung Yao's commitment from its inception, IC would not have been possible. Sadly, Professor Yao passed away in September 2015. Throughout that summer, Professor Yao remained in close contact with the rest of the team, going over each draft of IC 1 with an eagle eye, providing us with the benefit of his wisdom by phone and email. This Fourth Edition of IC is a living tribute to his vision and guidance.

*Note: Prefaces to the previous editions of IC are available at chengtsui.co.*

# Series Structure

The IC series has been carefully conceptualized and developed to facilitate flexible delivery options that meet the needs of different instructional environments.

| Component per Volume | Description | Print/Other Formats | ChengTsui Web App |
|---|---|---|---|
| **Textbook** | • Ten engaging lessons per volume, each with readings, grammar explanations, communicative exercises, and culture notes | • Paperback or Hardcover<br>• Simplified or Traditional Characters (Volumes 1 and 2)<br>• Simplified with Traditional Characters (Volumes 3 and 4) | • *Basic*, *Essential*, and *Educator Editions* |
| **Workbook** | • Wide range of integrated activities covering the three modes of communication (interpersonal, interpretive, and presentational) | • Paperback<br>• Simplified or Traditional Characters (Volumes 1 and 2)<br>• Simplified with Traditional Characters (Volumes 3 and 4) | • *Essential* and *Educator Editions* |
| **Character Workbook** | • Radical- and character-writing and stroke order practice | • Paperback<br>• Simplified with Traditional Characters | • *Essential* and *Educator Editions* |
| **Audio** | • Audio for Textbook vocabulary, lesson texts, and pronunciation exercises, plus pronunciation and listening exercises from the Workbook<br>• Normal and paused versions | • Audio available to print users at chengtsui.co/resources | • *Basic*, *Essential*, and *Educator Editions* |
| **Video** | • Volumes 1 and 2: acted dialogues and narratives presented in the Textbooks; also includes theme-related Culture Minutes sections in authentic settings<br>• Volumes 3 and 4: documentary-style episodes correlating to the lesson themes in authentic settings | • One DVD per volume. The 4th Edition of IC continues to use the 3rd Edition DVDs. | • *Basic*, *Essential*, and *Educator Editions*<br>• Streaming video |
| **Teacher's Resources** | • Comprehensive implementation support, teaching tips, syllabi, tests and quizzes, answer keys, and supplementary resources | • Downloadable resources that include core lesson guides along with ancillary materials previously on the companion website | • *Educator Edition* |

# Lesson Structure

All components of IC (Textbooks, Workbooks, and Teacher's Resources) are considered core and are designed to be used together to enhance teaching and learning. Recurrent lesson subsections are highlighted in the Textbook Elements column. Note that Supplementary Modules do not compose a separate section, but are rather discrete entities that appear throughout each lesson.

| Section | Textbook Elements | Interactive Content | Workbooks | Teacher's Resources |
|---|---|---|---|---|
| **Lesson Opener** | • Learning Objectives state what students will be able to do by the end of the lesson<br>• Relate & Get Ready helps students reflect on similarities and differences between Chinese culture and their own | | • Opportunity for students to revisit learning objectives and self-assess | • Overview of language functions, vocabulary, grammar, pronunciation, and characters taught in the lesson<br>• Sequencing recommendations and teaching aids |
| **Lesson Text** | • Two Chinese lesson texts demonstrate practical vocabulary and grammar usage<br>• *Pinyin* versions of the lesson texts provide pronunciation support<br>• Language Notes elaborate on important structures and phrases in the lesson texts | • Audio builds receptive skills<br>• Video provides insight into non-verbal cues and communication plus context through authentic settings | • Listening comprehension and speaking exercises based on the lesson texts<br>• Reading comprehension | • Strategies for teaching the lesson texts, plus question prompts<br>• Pre- and post-video viewing activity worksheets and scripts |
| **Vocabulary** | • Vocabulary lists define and categorize new words from the lesson texts (proper nouns are listed last) | • Audio models proper pronunciation<br>• Flashcards assist with vocabulary acquisition | • Handwriting and stroke order practice is provided in the Character Workbook<br>• All exercises use lesson vocabulary to support acquisition | • Explanations, pronunciation tips, usage notes, and phrasal combinations<br>• Vocabulary slideshows |
| **Grammar** | • Grammar points, which correspond to numbered references in the lesson texts, explain and model language forms<br>• Exercises allow students to practice the grammar points immediately | • Additional exercises deepen knowledge of the language | • Writing and grammar exercises based on grammar introduced in the lesson | • Explanations, pattern practice, and additional grammar notes<br>• Grammar slideshows |
| **Language Practice** | • Role-plays, pair activities, contextualized drills, and colorful cues prompt students to produce language<br>• Pronunciation exercises in the first three lessons | • Audio accompanies pronunciation exercises in the first three lessons | • Exercises and activities spanning the three modes of communication (interpersonal, interpretive, and presentational), plus *pinyin* and tone practice, to build communication and performance skills | • Student presentations, integrative practice, and additional practice activities<br>• Additional activities categorized by macro-skill |

| Section | Textbook Elements | Interactive Content | Workbooks | Teacher's Resources |
|---|---|---|---|---|
| **Cultural Literacy** | • Culture notes provide snapshots of contemporary and traditional Chinese-speaking cultures<br>• Compare & Contrast draws connections between cultures | • Additional content further develops cultural literacy of the lesson theme | • Authentic materials to develop predictive skills | • Background notes expand on the section and offer additional realia |
| **Lesson Wrap-Up** | • Make It Flow! develops students' ability to produce smooth discourse<br>• Projects encourage review and recycling of lesson materials through different text types<br>• Can-Do Checklist allows students to assess their fulfillment of the learning objectives | | | • Teaching tips for implementing self-diagnostic activities, answer keys for Make it Flow!, and additional sample quizzes and tests<br>• Slideshows that summarize content introduced in the lesson |
| **Supplementary Modules** | • How About You? encourages students to personalize their vocabulary<br>• Get Real with Chinese teaches students to predict meaning from context<br>• Characterize It! explores the structure of Chinese characters<br>• Chinese Chat demonstrates how language is used in text messaging and social media | • Additional Characterize It! exercises and slideshows increase understanding of characters | • Pattern exercises to build radical and character recognition | • Teaching tips and strategies for fully exploiting and implementing these new elements |

# Scope and Sequence

| Lesson | Learning Objectives | Grammar | Cultural Literacy |
|---|---|---|---|
| **Basics** | • Learn about Chinese and its dialects<br>• Become familiar with syllabic structure, *pinyin*, and pronunciation<br>• Gain an understanding of the writing system and basic grammatical features<br>• Use common expressions in the classroom and daily life | | |
| **1 Greetings** | • Exchange basic greetings<br>• Ask for a person's family name and full name and provide your own<br>• Determine whether someone is a teacher or a student<br>• Ask where someone's from | 1. The verb 姓 (*xìng*)<br>2. Questions ending with 呢 (*ne*)<br>3. The verb 叫 (*jiào*)<br>4. Subject + verb + object<br>5. The verb 是 (*shì*) (to be)<br>6. Questions ending with 吗 (*ma*)<br>7. The negative adverb 不 (*bù*) (not, no)<br>8. The adverb 也 (*yě*) (too, also) | • Family names<br>• Full names |
| **2 Family** | • Use basic kinship terms for family members<br>• Describe a family photo<br>• Ask about someone's profession<br>• Name some common professions | 1. The particle 的 (*de*) (I)<br>2. Measure words (I)<br>3. Question pronouns<br>4. Indicating possession using 有 (*yǒu*)<br>5. Indicating existence using 有 (*yǒu*)<br>6. Using 二 (*èr*) and 两 (*liǎng*)<br>7. The adverb 都 (*dōu*) (both, all) | • Kinship terms<br>• Family structure |
| **3 Time and Date** | • Discuss times and dates<br>• Talk about ages and birthdays<br>• Arrange a dinner date with someone | 1. Numbers up to 100<br>2. Dates<br>3. Time<br>4. Pronouns as modifiers and the particle 的 (*de*) (II)<br>5. The sentence structure of 我请你吃饭 (*wǒ qǐng nǐ chī fàn*)<br>6. Alternative questions<br>7. Affirmative + negative (A-not-A) questions (I)<br>8. The adverb 还 (*hái*) (also, too, as well) | • Calendars<br>• Age<br>• Birthday traditions |
| **4 Hobbies** | • Name common hobbies<br>• Ask about someone's hobbies<br>• Make plans for the weekend with friends | 1. Word order<br>2. Affirmative + negative (A-not-A) questions (II)<br>3. The conjunction 那（么） (*nà [me]*) (then, in that case)<br>4. 去 (*qù*) (to go) + action<br>5. Questions with 好吗 (*hǎo ma*) (OK?)<br>6. The modal verb 想 (*xiǎng*) (want to, would like to)<br>7. Verb + object as a detachable compound | • Mahjong<br>• Chinese chess<br>• Go<br>• Feasting |

| Lesson | Learning Objectives | Grammar | Cultural Literacy |
|---|---|---|---|
| **5 Visiting Friends** | • Welcome a visitor<br>• Introduce one person to another<br>• Be a gracious guest<br>• Ask for beverages as a guest<br>• Offer beverages to a visitor<br>• Briefly describe a visit to a friend's place | 1. Moderating tone of voice: 一下 *(yí xià)* and （一）点儿 *(yì) diǎnr)*<br>2. Adjectives as predicates using 很 *(hěn)*<br>3. The preposition 在 *(zài)* (at, in, on)<br>4. The particle 吧 *(ba)*<br>5. The particle 了 *(le)* (I)<br>6. The adverb 才 *(cái)* (not until) | • Tea<br>• Greetings<br>• Etiquette |
| **Keeping It Casual (L1–L5)** | • Review functional expressions | 1. 算了 *(suàn le)* (forget it, never mind)<br>2. 谁呀 *(shéi ya)* (who is it?)<br>3. 是吗 *(shì ma)* (really, is that so?) | |
| **6 Making Appointments** | • Answer a phone call and initiate a phone conversation<br>• Set up an appointment with a teacher on the phone<br>• Ask a favor<br>• Ask someone to return your call | 1. The preposition 给 *(gěi)* (to, for)<br>2. The modal verb 要 *(yào)* (will, be going to) (I)<br>3. The adverb 别 *(bié)* (don't)<br>4. Time expressions<br>5. The modal verb 得 *(děi)* (must, have to)<br>6. Directional complements (I) | • Phone etiquette<br>• Cell phones<br>• Terms for Mandarin |
| **7 Studying Chinese** | • Discuss your exam performance<br>• Comment on your character writing<br>• Discuss your experience learning Chinese<br>• Talk about your study habits<br>• Describe typical classroom situations | 1. Descriptive complements (I)<br>2. The adverbs 太 *(tài)* (too), 真 *(zhēn)* (really), and 很 *(hěn)* (very)<br>3. The adverb 就 *(jiù)* (I)<br>4. Double objects<br>5. Ordinal numbers<br>6. 有（一）点儿 *(yǒu[yì]diǎnr)* (somewhat, rather, a little bit)<br>7. Question pronoun: 怎么 *(zěnme)* (how, how come)<br>8. The 的 *(de)* structure (I)<br>9. Connecting sentences in continuous discourse | • Simplified vs. traditional characters<br>• Writing conventions<br>• Four treasures of the study |
| **8 School Life** | • Describe a student's daily routine<br>• Write a simple diary entry or blog post<br>• Write a brief letter or formal email applying appropriate conventions<br>• Update a friend on recent activities<br>• Express hope that a friend will accept your invitation | 1. The position of time-when expressions<br>2. The adverb 就 *(jiù)* (II)<br>3. Describing simultaneity using 一边...一边... *(yìbiān . . . yìbiān . . . )*<br>4. Series of verbs/verb phrases<br>5. The particle 了 *(le)* (II)<br>6. The particle 的 *(de)* (III)<br>7. The 正在 v structure *(zhèngzài)* (be doing. . . )<br>8. Indicating inclusiveness: 除了...以外，还/也... *(chúle . . . yǐwài, hái/yě . . . )* (in addition to, also)<br>9. Comparing 能 *(néng)* and 会 *(huì)* (I)<br>10. The conjunctions 要是 *(yàoshi)* and 因为 *(yīnwèi)* and the adverb 就 *(jiù)* (III) | • Semesters<br>• Letter-writing conventions |

| Lesson | Learning Objectives | Grammar | Cultural Literacy |
|---|---|---|---|
| 9 Shopping | • Describe the color, size, and price of a purchase<br>• Recognize Chinese currency<br>• Pay in cash or with a credit card<br>• Determine the proper change you should receive<br>• Ask for merchandise in a different size or color<br>• Exchange merchandise | 1. The modal verb 要 *(yào)* (want to do) (II)<br>2. Measure words (II)<br>3. The 的 *(de)* structure (II)<br>4. Using 多 *(duō)* interrogatively<br>5. Denominations of currency<br>6. Comparing using 跟/和. . . （不）一样 *(gēn/hé . . . [bù] yíyàng)* ([not] the same as . . . )<br>7. The conjunctions 虽然. . . ，可是/但是. . . *(suīrán . . . , kěshì/dànshì . . . )* (although . . . yet . . . ) | • Traditional clothes<br>• Prices<br>• Forms of address |
| 10 Transportation | • Discuss different means of transportation<br>• Explain how to transfer from one subway or bus line to another<br>• Navigate public transit<br>• Express gratitude after receiving a favor<br>• Offer New Year wishes | 1. Topic-comment sentences (I)<br>2. Indicating alternatives: 或者 *(huòzhě)* (or) and 还是 *(háishi)* (or)<br>3. Indicating sequence: 先. . .再. . . *(xiān . . . zài)* (first . . . , then . . . )<br>4. Pondering alternatives: 还是. . . （吧） *(háishi . . . [ba])* (had better)<br>5. Indicating totality: 每. . .都. . . *(měi . . . dōu)* (every)<br>6. Indicating imminence: 要. . .了 *(yào . . . le)* (soon) | • High-speed rail<br>• Taxi drivers<br>• New Year traffic |
| Keeping It Casual (L6–L10) | • Review functional expressions | 1. 喂 *(wéi)* (hello [on the phone])<br>2. 没问题 *(méi wèntí)* (no problem)<br>3. Expressions of gratitude<br>4. 哪里，哪里 *(nǎli, nǎli)* (I'm flattered) or 是吗？ *(shì ma)* (is that so?)<br>5. 就是它吧 *(jiù shì tā ba)* (let's go with that) or 就是他/她了 *(jiù shì tā le)* (we'll go with him/her)<br>6. 祝 *(zhù)* (I wish . . . ) | |

# Abbreviations of Grammatical Terms

| | |
|---|---|
| **adj** | adjective |
| **adv** | adverb |
| **conj** | conjunction |
| **interj** | interjection |
| **m** | measure word |
| **mv** | modal verb |
| **n** | noun |
| **nu** | numeral |
| **p** | particle |
| **pn** | proper noun |
| **pr** | pronoun |
| **prefix** | prefix |
| **prep** | preposition |
| **qp** | question particle |
| **qpr** | question pronoun |
| **t** | time word |
| **v** | verb |
| **vc** | verb plus complement |
| **vo** | verb plus object |

# Legend of Digital Icons

The icons listed below refer to interactive content. Audio is available at chengtsui.co/resources to readers who have purchased the print edition. All other digital content is available exclusively to ChengTsui Web App subscribers.

| | |
|---|---|
| Audio | **Lesson Text, Vocabulary** |
| Video | **Lesson Text** |
| Flashcards | **Vocabulary** |
| More characters | **Characterize It!** |
| More exercises | **Grammar** |
| 文化 Continue to explore | **Cultural Literacy** |

# Cast of Characters

## Wang Peng
王朋

A Chinese freshman from Beijing. He has quickly adapted to American college life and likes to play and watch sports.

## Li You
李友

Amy Lee, an American student from New York State. She and Wang Peng meet each other on the first day of class and soon become good friends.

## Gao Wenzhong
高文中

Winston Gore, an English student. His parents work in the United States. Winston enjoys singing, dancing, and Chinese cooking. He has a secret crush on Bai Ying'ai.

## Gao Xiaoyin
高小音

Jenny Gore, Winston's older sister. She has already graduated from college, and is now a school librarian.

## Bai Ying'ai
白英爱

Baek Yeung Ae, an outgoing Korean student from Seoul. She finds Wang Peng very "cool" and very "cute."

## Chang Laoshi
常老师

Chang Xiaoliang, originally from China and in her forties. She has been teaching Chinese in the United States for ten years.

# BASICS

## Learning Objectives

This section gives students the fundamentals they need to begin studying Chinese. Background is provided on the language's syllabic structure, *pinyin*, and pronunciation; writing system; and important grammatical features. Practice exercises, along with accompanying audio recordings (indicated by 🔊), are provided to help students learn proper pronunciation. Lists of useful expressions are also included. Classes may devote three or four sessions to this core material before starting Lesson 1.

# Mandarin and Dialects

China is roughly the same size as the United States. There are numerous regional dialects of Chinese. These dialects, most of which are mutually unintelligible, are often divided into eight groups: Mandarin, Wu, Hakka, Southern Min, Northern Min, Cantonese, Xiang, and Gan.

Conventional terms for Modern Standard Chinese include *Putonghua* ("common language") in Mainland China; *Guoyu* ("national language") in Taiwan; and *Huayu* ("language spoken by ethnic Chinese people") in other Chinese-speaking communities, such as those in Singapore and Malaysia. It is the *lingua franca* of intra-ethnic (among different Chinese dialect speakers) as well as inter-ethnic (among Han Chinese and non-Han minority groups) communication in China. Its grammar is codified from the modern Chinese literary canon, while its pronunciation is based on the Beijing dialect. Modern Standard Chinese is usually referred to as Mandarin in English.

China officially recognizes fifty-six ethnic groups. The Han, the largest group, accounts for over 90% of China's population. Many of the other fifty-five ethnic groups speak their own distinct languages.

# Syllabic Structure, Pinyin, and Pronunciation

A Modern Standard Chinese syllable typically has three parts: an initial consonant, a final consisting of a vowel or a vowel and the ending consonant *-n* or *-ng*, and a tone. The tone is superimposed on the entire syllable. A syllable may also have no initial consonant.

**syllable = (initial) + final/tone**

In this book, Chinese sounds are represented by *Hanyu Pinyin,* or *pinyin* for short. The *pinyin* system uses twenty-five of the twenty-six letters of the English alphabet. Although *pinyin* symbols are thus the same as English letters, the actual sounds they represent can vary widely from their English counterparts. This section is designed to raise your awareness of these distinctions. Over time, you will acquire a more nuanced understanding of Chinese pronunciation and improve your skills through listening and practice.

## A Simple Finals

Audio

There are six simple finals in *pinyin*: *a, o, e, i, u, ü*

*a* is a central vowel when pronounced by itself. Keep your tongue in a relaxed position to pronounce it. *a* sounds similar to the "a" in "fa la la."

*o* is a rounded semi-high back vowel. Round your lips when pronouncing it. *o* seldom appears as a syllable by itself. Usually it compounds with the initials *b, p, m,* and *f,* and should be practiced with them. Because of the bilabial or labiodental nature of *b, p, m,* and *f, o* sounds almost like a diphthong or the double vowel *uo*. It glides from a brief *u* to *o*.

*e* is an unrounded semi-high back vowel. To pronounce it, first position your tongue as if you are about to pronounce *o*, then unround your mouth. At the same time, spread your lips apart as if you were smiling. This vowel is different from "e" in English, which is pronounced with the tongue raised slightly forward.

*i* is an unrounded high front vowel. To pronounce it, smile tightly and pull the corners of your mouth straight back. It is similar to the long vowel in "sheep." When pronouncing it, however, you raise your tongue higher.

*u* is a rounded high back vowel. Pucker up your lips when pronouncing it. *u* is similar to the long vowel in "coop," but, when pronouncing it, you raise your tongue higher and retract it more.

*ü* is a rounded high front vowel. To produce this vowel, first position your tongue as if you are about to pronounce *i*, then round your lips.

In the *pinyin* system, *i* represents two special vowels in addition to the high front vowel. One is a front apical vowel, the other a back apical vowel—that is to say, they are articulated with the front and back part of the tongue, respectively. Both of these vowels are homorganic with the very limited sets of initials with which they can co-occur (see *z*, *c*, *s* and *zh*, *ch*, *sh*, *r*). In other words, they are pronounced in the same area of the vocal tract as those consonants. You will learn how to pronounce *i* simply by prolonging the sounds of these two groups of consonants.

B

## Initials

There are twenty-one initial consonants in *pinyin*. They are grouped as follows:

Audio

| | |
|---|---|
| 1. *b p m f* | 4. *j q x* |
| 2. *d t n l* | 5. *z c s* |
| 3. *g k h* | 6. *zh ch sh r* |

### B.1 *b, p, m, f*

*b* is different from its English counterpart. It is not voiced, as the vocal cords do not vibrate upon its pronunciation, and sounds more like the "p" in "speak."

*p* is aspirated. In other words, there is a strong puff of breath when this consonant is pronounced. It is also voiceless, and sounds like the "p" in "pork."

*m* is produced in the same manner as the English "m." It is voiced.

Pronounce *f* as you would in English.

Only the simple finals *a*, *o*, *i*, and *u* and compound finals that start with *a*, *o*, *i*, or *u* can be combined with *b*, *p*, and *m*; only the simple finals *a*, *o*, and *u* and compound finals that start with *a*, *o*, or *u* can be combined with *f*. When these initials are combined with *o*, there is actually a short *u* sound in between. For instance, the syllable *bo* actually includes a very short *u* sound between *b* and *o*: it is pronounced *b(u)o*.

Practice your pronunciation with the audio exercises below:

Audio

| B.1.a | (Initial-Final Combinations) | | |
|---|---|---|---|
| *ba* | *bi* | *bu* | *bo* |
| *pa* | *pi* | *pu* | *po* |
| *ma* | *mi* | *mu* | *mo* |
| *fa* | *fu* | *fo* | |

| B.1.b | *b* vs. *p* | | |
|---|---|---|---|
| *ba* | *pa* | *bu* | *pu* |
| *po* | *bo* | *pi* | *bi* |

| B.1.c | *m* vs. *f* | | |
|---|---|---|---|
| *ma* | *fa* | *mu* | *fu* |

| B.1.d | *b, p, m, f* | | |
|---|---|---|---|
| *bo* | *po* | *mo* | *fo* |
| *fu* | *mu* | *pu* | *bu* |

## B.2 *d, t, n, l*

When pronouncing *d*, *t*, and *n*, touch your upper gum with the tip of your tongue. The tongue is raised more to the back than it would be to pronounce their English counterparts. *d* and *t* are voiceless. Roughly, *d* sounds like the "t" in "stand," and *t* sounds like the "t" in "tea." When pronouncing *l*, touch your palate with the tip of your tongue. *n* is nasal.

Only the simple finals *a*, *i*, *e*, and *u* and compound finals that start with *a*, *i*, *e*, or *u* can be combined with *d*, *t*, *n*, and *l*; *n* and *l* can also be combined with *ü* and the compound finals that start with *ü*.

Practice your pronunciation with the audio exercises below:

Audio

**B.2.a** (Initial-Final Combinations)

| | | | | |
|---|---|---|---|---|
| *da* | *di* | *du* | *de* | |
| *ta* | *ti* | *tu* | *te* | |
| *na* | *ni* | *nu* | *ne* | *nü* |
| *la* | *li* | *lu* | *le* | *lü* |

**B.2.b** *d* vs. *t*

| | | | |
|---|---|---|---|
| *da* | *ta* | *di* | *ti* |
| *du* | *tu* | *de* | *te* |

**B.2.c** *l* vs. *n*

| | | | |
|---|---|---|---|
| *lu* | *lü* | *nu* | *nü* |
| *lu* | *nu* | *lü* | *nü* |

**B.2.d** *d, t, n, l*

| | | | |
|---|---|---|---|
| *le* | *ne* | *te* | *de* |
| *du* | *tu* | *lu* | *nu* |

## B.3 *g, k, h*

*g* is unaspirated and voiceless, whereas *k* is aspirated and voiceless. When pronouncing *g* and *k*, raise the back of your tongue against your soft palate. Roughly, *g* sounds like the "k" in "sky," and *k* sounds like the "k" in "kite."

*h* is voiceless. When pronouncing *h*, raise the back of your tongue towards your soft palate. Unlike the pronunciation of its English counterpart, the friction is noticeable.

Only the simple finals *a*, *e*, and *u* and the compound finals that start with *a*, *e*, or *u* can be combined with *g*, *k*, and *h*.

Practice your pronunciation with the audio exercises below:

Audio

**B.3.a** (Initial-Final Combinations)

| | | |
|---|---|---|
| *gu* | *ge* | *ga* |
| *ku* | *ke* | *ka* |
| *hu* | *he* | *ha* |

**B.3.b** *g* vs. *k*

| | | | |
|---|---|---|---|
| *gu* | *ku* | *ge* | *ke* |

**B.3.c** *g* vs. *h*

| | | | |
|---|---|---|---|
| *gu* | *hu* | *ge* | *he* |

**B.3.d** *k* vs. *h*

| | | | |
|---|---|---|---|
| *ke* | *he* | *ku* | *hu* |

**B.3.e** *g, k, h*

| | | |
|---|---|---|
| *gu* | *ku* | *hu* |
| *he* | *ke* | *ge* |

## B.4 *j, q, x*

To make the *j* sound, first raise the flat center of your tongue to the roof of your mouth and position the tip of your tongue against the back of your bottom teeth; then loosen your tongue and let the air squeeze out through the channel you've made. It is unaspirated and the vocal cords do not vibrate. The *pinyin j* is similar to the "j" in "jeep," but it is unvoiced and articulated with the tip of the tongue resting behind the lower incisors. You also need to pull the corners of your mouth straight back to pronounce it.

*q* is pronounced in the same manner as *j*, but it is aspirated. The *pinyin q* is similar to the "ch" in "cheese," except that it is articulated with the tip of the tongue resting behind the lower incisors. When pronouncing *q*, don't forget to pull the corners of your mouth straight back.

To make the *x* sound, first raise the flat center of your tongue toward (but not touching) the hard palate and then let the air squeeze out. The vocal cords do not vibrate. *x*, like *j* and *q*, is articulated with the tip of the tongue resting behind the lower incisors. To pronounce *x* correctly, you also need to pull the corners of your mouth straight back, as if making a tight smile.

The finals that can be combined with *j*, *q*, and *x* are limited to *i* and *ü* and compound finals that start with *i* or *ü*. When *j*, *q*, and *x* are combined with *ü* or a compound final starting with *ü*, the umlaut is omitted and the *ü* appears as *u*.

Practice your pronunciation with the audio exercises below:

Audio

| B.4.a | (Initial-Final Combinations) |
|---|---|
| *ji* | *ju* |
| *qi* | *qu* |
| *xi* | *xu* |

| B.4.b | *j* vs. *q* | | |
|---|---|---|---|
| *ji* | *qi* | *ju* | *qu* |

| B.4.c | *q* vs. *x* | | |
|---|---|---|---|
| *qi* | *xi* | *qu* | *xu* |

| B.4.d | *j* vs. *x* | | |
|---|---|---|---|
| *ji* | *xi* | *ju* | *xu* |

| B.4.e | *j, q, x* | |
|---|---|---|
| *ji* | *qi* | *xi* |
| *ju* | *qu* | *xu* |

## B.5 *z, c, s*

*z* is similar to the English "ds" sound, as in "lids."

*c* is similar to the English "ts" sound, as in "students." It is aspirated.

*s* is similar to the English "s" sound.

To pronounce these sounds, touch the back of your upper teeth with your tongue.

The simple finals that can be combined with *z*, *c*, and *s* are *a*, *e*, *u*, and the front apical vowel *i* (not the regular palatal high front vowel *i*).

When pronouncing the syllables *zi*, *ci*, and *si*, hold your tongue in the same position; relax it slightly as the articulation moves from the voiceless initial consonant to the voiced vowel.

Practice your pronunciation with the audio exercises below:

Audio

| B.5.a | (Initial-Final Combinations) | | |
|---|---|---|---|
| *za* | *zu* | *ze* | *zi* |
| *ca* | *cu* | *ce* | *ci* |
| *sa* | *su* | *se* | *si* |

| B.5.b | *s* vs. *z* | | |
|---|---|---|---|
| *sa* | *za* | *su* | *zu* |
| *se* | *ze* | *si* | *zi* |

| B.5.c | *z* vs. *c* | | |
|---|---|---|---|
| *za* | *ca* | *zi* | *ci* |
| *ze* | *ce* | *zu* | *cu* |

| B.5.d | *s* vs. *c* | | |
|---|---|---|---|
| *sa* | *ca* | *si* | *ci* |
| *su* | *cu* | *se* | *ce* |

| B.5.e | *z, c, s* | |
|---|---|---|
| *sa* | *za* | *ca* |
| *su* | *zu* | *cu* |
| *se* | *ze* | *ce* |
| *si* | *zi* | *ci* |
| *za* | *cu* | *se* |
| *ci* | *sa* | *zu* |
| *su* | *zi* | *ce* |

## B.6 *zh, ch, sh, r*

To make the *zh* sound, first curl up the tip of your tongue against your hard palate, then loosen it and let the air squeeze out through the channel you've made. It is unaspirated and the vocal cords do not vibrate. *zh* sounds rather like the first sound in "jerk," but it is unvoiced.

*ch* is pronounced like *zh*, but *ch* is aspirated. *ch* sounds rather like the "ch" in "chirp."

To make the *sh* sound, turn the tip of your tongue up toward (but not touching) the hard palate and then let the air squeeze out. The vocal cords do not vibrate. *sh* sounds rather like the "sh" in "shirt" and "Shirley."

*r* is pronounced in the same manner as *sh*, but it is voiced; therefore, the vocal cords vibrate. Pronounce it simply by prolonging *sh*, making sure your lips are not rounded.

The finals that can be combined with *zh*, *ch*, *sh*, and *r* are *a*, *e*, *u*, and the back apical vowel *i*, as well as compound finals that start with *a*, *e*, or *u*. When pronouncing the syllables *zhi*, *chi*, *shi*, and *ri*, hold your tongue in the same position; relax it slightly as the articulation moves from the initial consonant to the vowel.

Practice your pronunciation with the audio exercises below:

Audio

| B.6.a | (Initial-Final Combinations) | | |
|---|---|---|---|
| *zha* | *zhu* | *zhe* | *zhi* |
| *cha* | *chu* | *che* | *chi* |
| *sha* | *shu* | *she* | *shi* |
| *ru* | *re* | *ri* | |

| B.6.b | *zh* vs. *sh* | | |
|---|---|---|---|
| *sha* | *zha* | *shu* | *zhu* |

| B.6.c | *zh* vs. *ch* | | |
|---|---|---|---|
| *zha* | *cha* | *zhu* | *chu* |

| B.6.d | *ch* vs. *sh* | | |
|---|---|---|---|
| *chu* | *shu* | *sha* | *cha* |

| B.6.e | *zh, ch, sh* | | |
|---|---|---|---|
| *shi* | *zhi* | *chi* | *shi* |
| *she* | *zhe* | *che* | *she* |

| B.6.f | *sh* vs. *r* | | |
|---|---|---|---|
| *shu* | *ru* | *shi* | *ri* |

| B.6.g | *r* vs. *l* | | |
|---|---|---|---|
| *lu* | *ru* | *li* | *ri* |

| B.6.h | *sh, r, l* | | |
|---|---|---|---|
| *she* | *re* | *le* | *re* |

| B.6.i | *zh, ch, r* | | |
|---|---|---|---|
| *zhe* | *re* | *che* | *re* |

| B.6.j | *zh, ch, sh, r* | | |
|---|---|---|---|
| *sha* | *cha* | *zha* | |
| *shu* | *zhu* | *chu* | *ru* |
| *zhi* | *chi* | *shi* | *ri* |
| *che* | *zhe* | *she* | *re* |

## Reference Chart for Initials

| Place of Articulation \ Manner of Articulation | Stop | | Affricative | | Fricative | Nasal | Lateral | Approximant |
|---|---|---|---|---|---|---|---|---|
| | Unaspirated | Aspirated | Unaspirated | Aspirated | | | | |
| Bilabial | *b* | *p* | | | | *m* | | |
| Labiodentals | | | | | *f* | | | |
| Apical-toothback | | | *z* | *c* | *s* | | | |
| Apical-alveolar | *d* | *t* | | | | *n* | *l* | |
| Apical-postalveolar | | | *zh* | *ch* | *sh* | | | *r* |
| Alveolo-palatal | | | *j* | *q* | *x* | | | |
| Velar | *g* | *k* | | | *h* | | | |

C

# Compound Finals

Consonant finals in *pinyin* are grouped as follows:

Audio

1. *ai ei ao ou*
2. *an en ang eng ong*
3. *ia iao ie iu* ian in iang ing iong*
4. *ua uo uai ui** uan un*** uang ueng*
5. *üe üan ün*
6. *er*

* The main vowel *o* is omitted in the spelling of the final *iu* (*iu* = *iou*). Therefore, *iu* represents the sound *iou*. The *o* is especially conspicuous in third- and fourth-tone syllables.

** The main vowel *e* is omitted in the final *ui* (*ui* = *uei*). Like *iu* above, it is quite conspicuous in third- and fourth- tone syllables.

*** The main vowel *e* is omitted in *un* (*un* = *uen*).

In *pinyin*, compound finals are composed of a main vowel and one or two secondary vowels, or a main vowel and one secondary vowel followed by the nasal ending *-n* or *-ng*. When the initial vowels are *a*, *e*, or *o*, they are stressed. The vowels following are soft and brief. When the initial vowels are *i*, *u*, or *ü*, the main vowels come after them. *i*, *u*, and *ü* are transitional sounds. If there are vowels or nasal consonants after the main vowels, they should be unstressed as well. In a compound final, the main vowel can be affected by the phonemes before and after it. For instance, the *a* in *ian* is pronounced with a lower degree of aperture and a higher position of the tongue than the *a* in *ma*; and to pronounce the *a* in *ang*, the tongue has to be positioned more to the back of the mouth than is usually the case with *a*.

When pronouncing the *e* in *ei*, the tongue must be positioned a bit toward the front and a bit higher than it would be if pronouncing the simple vowel *e* alone. The *e* in *ie* is pronounced with a lower position of the tongue than the *e* in *ei*. When pronouncing the *e* in *en* and the *e* in a neutral tone like the second syllable of *gēge*, you should position your tongue in the center of your mouth, as with the pronunciation of the "e" in "the."

As noted above, in *pinyin* orthography some vowels are omitted for the sake of economy, e.g., *i(o)u*, *u(e)i*. However, when pronouncing such sounds, these vowels must not be omitted.

*Pinyin* spelling rules are as follows:

1. If there is no initial consonant before *i*, *i* is written as a semi-vowel, *y*. Thus *ia*, *ie*, *iao*, *iu*, *ian*, and *iang* become *ya*, *ye*, *yao*, *you* (note that the *o* cannot be omitted here), *yan*, and *yang*. Before *in* and *ing*, add *y*, e.g., *yin* and *ying*.
2. If there is no initial consonant before *ü*, add a *y* and drop the umlaut: *yu*, *yuan*, *yue*, *yun*.
3. *u* becomes *w* if it is not preceded by an initial, e.g., *wa*, *wai*, *wan*, *wang*, *wei*, *wen*, *weng*, *wo*. *u* by itself becomes *wu*.
4. *ueng* is written as *ong* if preceded by an initial, e.g., *tong*, *dong*, *nong*, *long*. Without an initial, it is *weng*.
5. To avoid confusion, an apostrophe is used to separate two syllables with connecting vowels, e.g., *nǚ'ér* (daughter) and the city *Xī'ān* (*nǚ* and *ér*, *Xī* and *ān* are separate syllables). Sometimes an apostrophe is also needed even if the two syllables are not connected by vowels, e.g., *fáng'ài* (to hinder) and *fāng'àn* (plan, scheme).

Practice your pronunciation with the audio exercises below:

Audio

**C.1** *ai ei ao ou*

| | | | |
|---|---|---|---|
| *pai* | *lei* | *dao* | *gou* |
| *cai* | *mei* | *sao* | *shou* |

**C.2** *an en ang eng ong*

| C.2.a | *an* vs. *ang* | | |
|---|---|---|---|
| *tan* | *tang* | *chan* | *chang* |
| *zan* | *zhang* | *gan* | *gang* |

| C.2.b | *en* vs. *eng* | | |
|---|---|---|---|
| *sen* | *seng* | *shen* | *sheng* |
| *zhen* | *zheng* | *fen* | *feng* |

| C.2.c | *eng* vs. *ong* | | |
|---|---|---|---|
| *cheng* | *chong* | *deng* | *dong* |
| *zheng* | *zhong* | *keng* | *kong* |

**C.3** *ia iao ie iu ian in iang ing iong*

| C.3.a | *ia* vs. *ie* | | |
|---|---|---|---|
| *jia* | *jie* | *qia* | *qie* |
| *xia* | *xie* | *ya* | *ye* |

| C.3.b | *ian* vs. *iang* | | |
|---|---|---|---|
| *xian* | *xiang* | *qian* | *qiang* |
| *jian* | *jiang* | *yan* | *yang* |

| C.3.c | *in* vs. *ing* | | |
|---|---|---|---|
| *bin* | *bing* | *pin* | *ping* |
| *jin* | *jing* | *yin* | *ying* |

| C.3.d | *iu* vs. *iong* | | |
|---|---|---|---|
| *xiu* | *xiong* | *you* | *yong* |

| C.3.e | *ao* vs. *iao* | | |
|---|---|---|---|
| *zhao* | *jiao* | *shao* | *xiao* |
| *chao* | *qiao* | *ao* | *yao* |

| C.3.f | *an* vs. *ian* | | |
|---|---|---|---|
| *chan* | *qian* | *shan* | *xian* |
| *zhan* | *jian* | *an* | *yan* |

| C.3.g | *ang* vs. *iang* | | |
|---|---|---|---|
| *zhang* | *jiang* | *shang* | *xiang* |
| *chang* | *qiang* | *ang* | *yang* |

## C.4 *ua uo uai ui uan un uang*

**C.4.a** *ua* vs. *uai*

| | | | |
|---|---|---|---|
| *shua* | *shuai* | *wa* | *wai* |

**C.4.b** *uan* vs. *uang*

| | | | |
|---|---|---|---|
| *shuan* | *shuang* | *chuan* | *chuang* |
| *zhuan* | *zhuang* | *wan* | *wang* |

**C.4.c** *un* vs. *uan*

| | | | |
|---|---|---|---|
| *dun* | *duan* | *kun* | *kuan* |
| *zhun* | *zhuan* | *wen* | *wan* |

**C.4.d** *uo* vs. *ou*

| | | | |
|---|---|---|---|
| *duo* | *dou* | *zhuo* | *zhou* |
| *suo* | *sou* | *wo* | *ou* |

**C.4.e** *ui* vs. *un*

| | | | |
|---|---|---|---|
| *tui* | *tun* | *zhui* | *zhun* |
| *dui* | *dun* | *wei* | *wen* |

## C.5 *üe üan ün*

**C.5.a** *ün* vs. *un*

| | | | |
|---|---|---|---|
| *jun* | *zhun* | *yun* | *wen* |

**C.5.b** *üan* vs. *uan*

| | | | |
|---|---|---|---|
| *xuan* | *shuan* | *juan* | *zhuan* |
| *quan* | *chuan* | *yuan* | *wan* |

**C.5.c** *üe*

| | | |
|---|---|---|
| *yue* | *que* | *jue* |

## C.6 *er*

*ger* (*er* with a first tone does not exist in Mandarin, but the word "*ger*" [*ge* with the *r* ending] contains the final *er* in first tone. See D.1 Practice III for more examples.)

D

# Tones

Every Chinese syllable has a tone.

## D.1 Four Tones and Neutral Tone

There are four tones in Modern Standard Chinese.

The first tone is a high-level tone with a pitch value of 55 (see chart below); its tone mark is " ˉ ".

The second tone is a rising tone with a pitch value of 35; its tone mark is " ˊ ".

The citation form of the third tone has a pitch value of 214. However, in normal speech it almost always occurs as a "half third tone" with a pitch value of 21. Its tone mark is " ˇ ". Please see D.2. Tone Sandhi for a discussion of how to pronounce third-tone syllables in succession.

The fourth tone is a falling tone with a pitch value of 51; its tone mark is " ˋ ".

In addition to the four tones, there is also a neutral tone in Modern Standard Chinese. Neutral tone words include those that do not have fundamental tones (e.g., the question particle *ma*), and those which do have tones when pronounced individually, but are not stressed in certain compounds (e.g., the second *ba* in *bàba*, "father"). There are no tone marks for neutral tone syllables. A neutral tone syllable is pronounced briefly and softly, and its pitch value is determined by the stressed syllable immediately before it. A neutral tone following a first-tone syllable, as in *māma* (mother), carries a pitch tone of 2. When it follows a second-tone syllable, a third-tone syllable, or a fourth-tone syllable, its pitch tone will be 3, 4, and 1 respectively.

Tones are crucial in Chinese. The same initial-final combination with different tones may have different meanings. For instance, *mā* is "mother," *má* is "hemp," *mǎ* is "horse," *mà* is "to scold," and *ma* is an interrogative particle. The four tones can be diagrammed as follows:

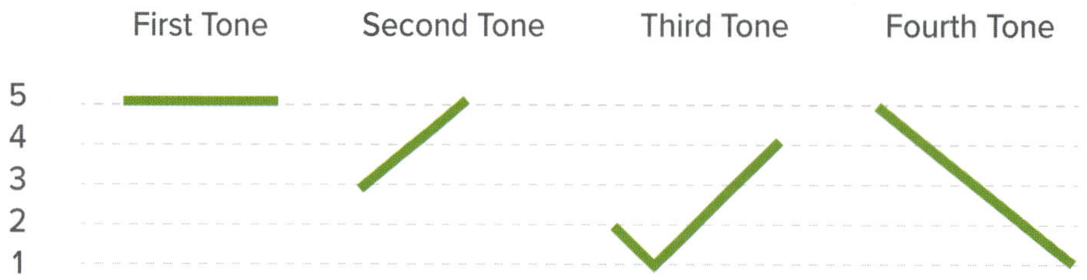


Tone marks are written above the main vowel of a syllable. The main vowel can be identified according to the following sequence: *a-o-e-i-u-ü*. For instance, in *ao* the main vowel is *a*. In *ei* the main vowel is *e*. There is one exception: when *i* and *u* are combined into a syllable, the tone mark is written on the second vowel: *iù*, *uì*.

## D.1 Practice I: Monosyllabic Words

Audio

| 1.a | Four Tones | | |
|---|---|---|---|
| *bī* | *bí* | *bǐ* | *bì* |
| *pū* | *pú* | *pǔ* | *pù* |
| *dà* | *dǎ* | *dá* | *dā* |
| *shè* | *shě* | *shé* | *shē* |
| *tí* | *tī* | *tǐ* | *tì* |
| *kè* | *kě* | *kē* | *ké* |
| *jǐ* | *jí* | *jì* | *jī* |
| *gú* | *gù* | *gū* | *gǔ* |

| 1.b | 1st vs. 2nd | | |
|---|---|---|---|
| *zā* | *zá* | *hē* | *hé* |
| *chū* | *chú* | *shī* | *shí* |

| 1.c | 1st vs. 3rd | | |
|---|---|---|---|
| *tū* | *tǔ* | *xī* | *xǐ* |
| *mō* | *mǒ* | *shā* | *shǎ* |

| 1.d | 1st vs. 4th | | |
|---|---|---|---|
| *fā* | *fà* | *qū* | *qù* |
| *dī* | *dì* | *kē* | *kè* |

| 1.e | 2nd vs. 1st | | |
|---|---|---|---|
| *hú* | *hū* | *zhé* | *zhē* |
| *xí* | *xī* | *pó* | *pō* |

| 1.f | 2nd vs. 3rd | | |
|---|---|---|---|
| *gé* | *gě* | *jú* | *jǔ* |
| *tí* | *tǐ* | *rú* | *rǔ* |

| 1.g | 2nd vs. 4th | | |
|---|---|---|---|
| *lú* | *lù* | *cí* | *cì* |
| *mó* | *mò* | *zhé* | *zhè* |

| 1.h | 3rd vs. 1st | | |
|---|---|---|---|
| *tǎ* | *tā* | *gǔ* | *gū* |
| *mǐ* | *mī* | *chě* | *chē* |

| 1.i | 3rd vs. 2nd | | |
|---|---|---|---|
| *chǔ* | *chú* | *xǐ* | *xí* |
| *kě* | *ké* | *qǔ* | *qú* |

| 1.j | 3rd vs. 4th | | |
|---|---|---|---|
| *bǒ* | *bò* | *chǔ* | *chù* |
| *nǐ* | *nì* | *rě* | *rè* |

| 1.k | 4th vs. 1st | | |
|---|---|---|---|
| *jì* | *jī* | *sù* | *sū* |
| *là* | *lā* | *hè* | *hē* |

| 1.l | 4th vs. 2nd | | |
|---|---|---|---|
| *nà* | *ná* | *jù* | *jú* |
| *zè* | *zé* | *lǜ* | *lǘ* |

| 1.m | 4th vs. 3rd | | |
|---|---|---|---|
| *sà* | *sǎ* | *kù* | *kǔ* |
| *zì* | *zǐ* | *zhè* | *zhě* |

## D.1 Practice II: Bisyllabic Words

Audio

| | Tones | Examples | | |
|---|---|---|---|---|
| 2.a | 1st+1st: | *chūzū* | *tūchū* | *chūfā* |
| 2.b | 1st+2nd: | *chātú* | *xīqí* | *chūxí* |
| 2.c | 1st+3rd: | *shēchǐ* | *gēqǔ* | *chūbǎn* |
| 2.d | 1st+4th: | *chūsè* | *hūshì* | *jīlǜ* |
| 2.e | 2nd+1st: | *shíshī* | *qíjī* | *shíchā* |
| 2.f | 2nd+2nd: | *jíhé* | *shépí* | *pígé* |
| 2.g | 2nd+3rd: | *jítǐ* | *bóqǔ* | *zhélǐ* |
| 2.h | 2nd+4th: | *qítè* | *fúlì* | *chíxù* |
| 2.i | 3rd+1st: | *zǔzhī* | *zhǔjī* | *lǐkē* |
| 2.j | 3rd+2nd: | *pǔjí* | *zhǔxí* | *chǔfá* |
| 2.k | 3rd+4th: | *lǚkè* | *gǔlì* | *tǐzhì* |
| 2.l | 4th+1st: | *zìsī* | *qìchē* | *lǜshī* |
| 2.m | 4th+2nd: | *fùzá* | *dìtú* | *shìshí* |
| 2.n | 4th+3rd: | *zìjǐ* | *bìhǔ* | *dìzhǐ* |
| 2.o | 4th+4th: | *mùdì* | *xùmù* | *dàdì* |

## D.1 Practice III: Words with "*er*" sound

Audio

| | | |
|---|---|---|
| 3.a | *érzi* | *érqiě* |
| 3.b | *ěrduo* | *mù'ěr* |
| 3.c | *shí'èr* | *èrshí* |

## D.2 Tone Sandhi

Audio

If two third-tone syllables are spoken in succession, the first third tone becomes second tone (a tone change that linguists call tone sandhi), e.g.:

| | | | |
|---|---|---|---|
| *xǐlǐ* | ➡ | *xílǐ* | (baptism) |
| *chǐrǔ* | ➡ | *chírǔ* | (shame) |
| *qǔshě* | ➡ | *qúshě* | (accept or reject) |

Note: Following standard *pinyin* practice, we do not change the tone marks from third to second tone. Initially, the student has to consciously remember to pronounce the first syllable in the second tone; but through practice and imitation, it will soon become habit.

Practice your pronunciation with the audio exercises below:

Audio

| | | | | | |
|---|---|---|---|---|---|
| *chǔlǐ* | → | *chúlǐ* | *jǔzhǐ* | → | *júzhǐ* |
| *gǔpǔ* | → | *gúpǔ* | *zǐnǚ* | → | *zínǚ* |
| *bǐnǐ* | → | *bínǐ* | *zhǐshǐ* | → | *zhíshǐ* |

## D.3 Neutral Tone

Audio

The neutral tone occurs in unstressed syllables, typically following a syllable with one of the four tones. It is unmarked, e.g.:

*chēzi* (car), *māma* (mom), *chúzi* (cook), *shūshu* (uncle), *lǐzi* (plum), *shìzi* (persimmon)

Practice your pronunciation with the audio exercises below:

Audio

| | | | | |
|---|---|---|---|---|
| **1st+neutral** | *māma* | *gēge* | *shīfu* | *chūqu* |
| **2nd+neutral** | *dízi* | *bóbo* | *bízi* | *chúle* |
| **3rd+neutral** | *lǐzi* | *qǐzi* | *dǐzi* | *fǔshang* |
| **4th+neutral** | *bàba* | *dìdi* | *kèqi* | *kùzi* |

## E Combination Exercises

Audio

1.

| | | |
|---|---|---|
| *shān* | *xiān* | *sān* |
| *cháng* | *qiáng* | *cáng* |
| *zhǐ* | *jǐ* | *zǐ* |
| *lüè* | *nüè* | *yuè* |
| *kè* | *lè* | *rè* |

2.

| | | | |
|---|---|---|---|
| *Zhōngguó* | *xīngqī* | *lǜshī* | *zhàopiàn* |
| *zàijiàn* | *tóngxué* | *xǐhuan* | *diànshì* |
| *yīnyuè* | *kělè* | *yǎnlèi* | *shàngwǔ* |
| *cèsuǒ* | *chūntiān* | *xiàwǔ* | *bànyè* |
| *gōngkè* | *kāishǐ* | *rìjì* | *cāntīng* |
| *zuìjìn* | *xīwàng* | *yīsheng* | *chūzū* |
| *zhōumò* | *guānxi* | *dòufu* | *jiéhūn* |
| *liúxué* | *nǚ'ér* | *shénme* | *suīrán* |
| *wǎngqiú* | *xǐzǎo* | *niánjí* | *yóuyǒng* |

# Writing System

## A Formation of Characters

Unlike English, Chinese is written in characters, each of which represents a syllable. Two sets of Chinese characters are in use: simplified characters and traditional characters. Simplified characters typically have fewer strokes than their traditional counterparts, though many characters are shared between the two sets. Characters have historically been divided into the following six categories:

### A.1 象形 (*xiàngxíng*) (pictographs, pictographic characters), e.g.:

 人 (*rén*) person

 山 (*shān*) mountain

 日 (*rì*) sun

 月 (*yuè*) moon

 木 (*mù*) tree

### A.2 指事 (*zhǐshì*) (simple ideograms), e.g.:

 上 (*shàng*) above

 下 (*xià*) below

### A.3 会意 (*huìyì*) (compound ideograms), e.g.:

 明 (*míng*) bright

 休 (*xiū*) rest

### A.4 形声 (*xíngshēng*) (pictophonetic characters [with one element indicating meaning and the other sound]), e.g.:

江，河，饭，姑

### A.5 转注 (*zhuǎnzhù*) (mutually explanatory characters), e.g.:

老，考

### A.6 假借 (*jiǎjiè*) (phonetic loan characters), e.g.:

来，我

A popular myth is that Chinese writing is pictographic, and that each Chinese character represents a picture. In fact, only a small proportion of Chinese characters evolved from pictures. The vast majority are pictophonetic characters consisting of a radical and a phonetic element. The radical often suggests the meaning of a character, and the phonetic element indicates its original pronunciation, which may or may not represent its modern pronunciation.

B

# Basic Radicals

Although there are more than fifty thousand Chinese characters, you only need to know two or three thousand to be considered literate. Mastering two or three thousand characters is, of course, still a rather formidable task. However, the learning process is easier if you grasp the basic components of Chinese characters. Traditionally, Chinese characters are grouped according to their common components, known as radicals, 部首 (*bùshǒu*). The 214 Kangxi radicals have been the standard set of radicals since the publication of the great *Kangxi Dictionary* (《康熙字典》) (《*Kāngxī Zìdiǎn*》) in 1716; although some contemporary dictionaries, which treat simplified characters as primary forms, have reduced that number to 189. If you know the radicals and other basic components well, you will find recognizing, remembering, and reproducing characters much easier. Knowing the radicals is also a must when using dictionaries that arrange characters according to their radicals. The following is a selection of forty radicals that everybody starting to learn characters should know. As you review the chart, identify where the radicals appear in the examples.

| No. | Radical | Pinyin | English | Examples |
|---|---|---|---|---|
| 1. | 人 (亻) | *rén* | person | 今，他 |
| 2. | 刀 (刂) | *dāo* | knife | 分，到 |
| 3. | 力 | *lì* | power | 加，助 |
| 4. | 又 | *yòu* | right hand, again | 友，取 |
| 5. | 口 | *kǒu* | mouth | 叫，可 |
| 6. | 囗* | *wéi* | enclose | 回，因 |
| 7. | 土 | *tǔ* | earth | 在，坐 |
| 8. | 夕 | *xī* | sunset | 外，多 |
| 9. | 大 | *dà* | big | 天，太 |
| 10. | 女 | *nǚ* | woman | 婆，好 |
| 11. | 子 | *zǐ* | child | 字，孩 |
| 12. | 寸 | *cùn* | inch | 寺，封 |
| 13. | 小 | *xiǎo* | small | 少，尖 |
| 14. | 工 | *gōng* | labor, work | 左，差 |
| 15. | 幺 | *yāo* | tiny, small | 幻，幼 |
| 16. | 弓 | *gōng* | bow | 引，弟 |
| 17. | 心 (忄) | *xīn* | heart | 想，忙 |
| 18. | 戈 | *gē* | dagger-axe | 我，或 |
| 19. | 手 (扌) | *shǒu* | hand | 拿，打 |
| 20. | 日 | *rì* | sun | 早，明 |

| No. | Radical | Pinyin | English | Examples |
|---|---|---|---|---|
| 21. | 月 | *yuè* | moon | 期，朗 |
| 22. | 木 | *mù* | wood | 李，杯 |
| 23. | 水（氵） | *shuǐ* | water | 汞，洗 |
| 24. | 火（灬） | *huǒ* | fire | 烧，热 |
| 25. | 田 | *tián* | field | 男，留 |
| 26. | 目 | *mù* | eye | 看，睡 |
| 27. | 示（礻） | *shì* | show | 票，社 |
| 28. | 糸（纟） | *mì* | fine silk | 素，红 |
| 29. | 耳 | *ěr* | ear | 聋，聊 |
| 30. | 衣（衤） | *yī* | clothing | 袋，衫 |
| 31. | 言（讠） | *yán* | speech | 誓，话 |
| 32. | 贝 | *bèi* | cowrie shell | 贵，财 |
| 33. | 走 | *zǒu* | walk | 趣，起 |
| 34. | ⻊ | *zú* | foot | 跳，跑 |
| 35. | 金（钅） | *jīn* | gold | 鉴，银 |
| 36. | 门 | *mén* | door | 间，闷 |
| 37. | 隹 | *zhuī* | short-tailed bird | 难，集 |
| 38. | 雨 | *yǔ* | rain | 雪，雷 |
| 39. | 食（饣） | *shí* | eat | 餐，饭 |
| 40. | 马 | *mǎ* | horse | 骑，骂 |

* Used as a radical only, not as a character by itself.

| | |
|---|---|
| 弓 | 弓字旁 |
| 子 | 子字旁 |
| 女 | 女字旁 |
| 纟 | 绞丝旁 |

| | |
|---|---|
| 马 | 马字旁 |
| 扌 | 提手旁 |
| 艹 | 草字头 |
| 大 | 大字头 |

Two Chinese radical charts.

# Basic Character Structures

To help you learn Chinese characters, we present the major structures for Chinese characters below. However, this list is not intended to be exhaustive. Less common structures are not covered here, and some of the components can be further divided into subcomponents. For example, by our classification, 照 is in the Top-Bottom structure, but its top component can be seen as a combination of 日 on the left and 召 on the right. Teachers are encouraged to explain the structures of individual characters whenever appropriate, and to emphasize that it is much easier to memorize a character by component than by individual stroke.

| No. | Pattern | | Examples |
|---|---|---|---|
| 1. | Unitary |  | 上 水 人 女 山 长 东 |
| 2. | Left-Right | 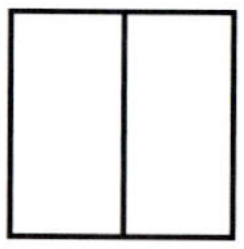 | 忙 唱 便 汉 都 找 汤 |
| 3. | Top-Bottom | 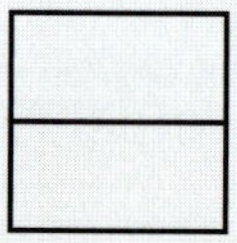 | 李 字 念 想 笔 花 紧 |
| 4. | Semi-Enclosing | 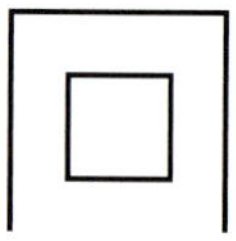 | 同 周 问 间 风 |
| 5. | Enclosing | 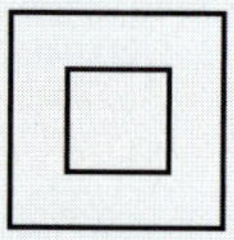 | 回 因 国 图 圆 |
| 6. | Horizontal Trisection | 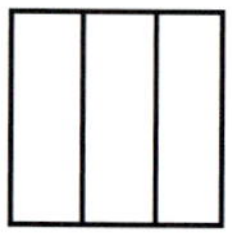 | 班 街 掰 粥 |
| 7. | Vertical Trisection | 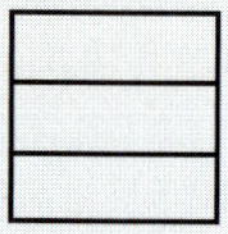 | 鼻 幕 曼 |
| 8. | Left-Bottom Enclosing | 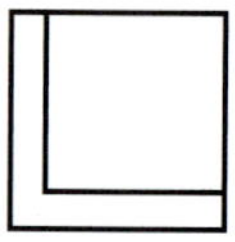 | 这 起 过 道 适 题 |
| 9. | Left-Top Enclosing | 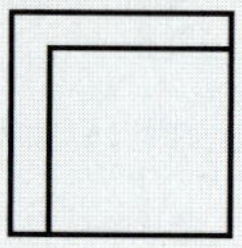 | 床 麻 病 历 屋 |

**D**

## Basic Strokes

As you review the chart, identify where the strokes appear in the examples.

| Basic Stroke | Chinese | Pinyin | English | Examples |
|---|---|---|---|---|
| ㇔ | 点 | *diǎn* | dot | 小，六 |
| ㇐ | 横 | *héng* | horizontal | 一，六 |
| ㇑ | 竖 | *shù* | vertical | 十，中 |
| ㇒ | 撇 | *piě* | downward left | 人，大 |
| ㇏ | 捺 | *nà* | downward right | 八，人 |
| ㇀ | 提 | *tí* | upward | 我，江 |
| ㇖ | 横钩 | *hénggōu* | horizontal hook | 你，字 |
| ㇚ | 竖钩 | *shùgōu* | vertical hook | 小，你 |
| ㇂ | 斜钩 | *xiégōu* | slanted hook | 戈，我 |
| ㇕ | 横折 | *héngzhé* | horizontal bend | 五，口 |
| ㇗ | 竖折 | *shùzhé* | vertical bend | 七，亡 |

Note: With the exception of the "*tí*" stroke (which moves upward to the right) and the "*piě*" stroke (which moves downward to the left), all Chinese strokes move from top to bottom, left to right.

Do you know the names of the strokes below? Can you write them properly?

㇔　　㇐　　㇏　　㇑　　㇒

**E**

## Stroke Order

Following these stroke order rules will make it easier for you to accurately count the number of strokes in a character. Knowing the exact number of strokes in a character will help you find the character in a radical-based dictionary. Finally, your Chinese characters will look better if you write them in the correct stroke order!

1. From left to right 川，人
2. From top to bottom 三
3. Horizontal before vertical 十
4. From outside to inside 月
5. Middle before two sides 小
6. Inside before closing 日，回

Note: Learn the correct stroke order of the characters introduced in this book by using the associated Character Workbook.

# Important Grammatical Features

Chinese grammar is relatively simple, since Chinese contains virtually no significant inflectional changes. However, beginners of Chinese should frequently review some fundamental characteristics of the language, even though not all these characteristics are unique to Chinese.

1. The most basic sentence structure in Chinese is:

   **Subject + Verb + Object**

   王朋 喜欢 打球。

   *Wang Peng like play ball*

   Wang Peng likes to play ball.

2. In Chinese, modifiers of nouns go before the nouns.

   姐姐 给 我 买 的 衬衫。

   *older sister for me buy shirt*

   The shirt that my older sister bought me.

3. In Chinese, adverbials, which modify verbs, go before verbs. Adverbials typically follow the subject or the topic of the sentence.

   王朋 昨天 看 了 一个 中国 电影。

   *Wang Peng yesterday see one China movie*

   Wang Peng watched a Chinese movie yesterday.

   Unlike in English, adverbials in Chinese never appear at the end of the sentence.

4. In general, Chinese nouns do not directly follow numerals; there must be a measure word in between.

   一 个 人

   *a person*

   三 本 书

   *three books*

5. If a sentence has multiple clauses with the same subject, the subject in the ensuing clauses is typically omitted. If two consecutive sentences have the same subject, the subject of the second sentence is typically represented by a pronoun.

   李友 在 商店 买 衣服。 她 买 了 一件 衬衫，

   *Li You at store buy clothes she buy one shirt*

   还 买 了 一条 裤子，花 了 六十 块 钱。

   *also buy one pants spend sixty dollar money*

   Li You went shopping for clothes. She bought a shirt. She bought a pair of pants as well. She spent sixty dollars.

6. When the "recipient" of an action becomes known information to both interlocutors, the "recipient" of the action often appears at the beginning of the sentence as the "topic," and the rest of the sentence functions as a "comment." So the sentence structure becomes: Topic-Comment.

| | | | | | | | | | | | |
|---|---|---|---|---|---|---|---|---|---|---|---|
| 爸爸 | 昨天 | 给 | 了 | 我 | 一个 | 手机， | 那个 | 手机 | 我 | 不 | 喜欢。 |
| *Dad* | *yesterday* | *give* | | *I* | *one* | *cell phone,* | *that* | *cell phone* | *I* | *not* | *like* |

Dad bought me a cell phone yesterday, and I don't like it.

# Useful Expressions

## A Classroom Expressions

You will hear these expressions every day in Chinese class.

Audio

| | | |
|---|---|---|
| 1. | *Nǐ hǎo!* | How are you? How do you do? Hello. |
| 2. | *Lǎoshī hǎo!* | How are you, teacher? |
| 3. | *Shàng kè.* | Let's begin the class. |
| 4. | *Xià kè.* | The class is over. |
| 5. | *Dǎ kāi shū.* | Open the book. |
| 6. | *Wǒ shuō, nǐmen tīng.* | I'll speak, you listen. |
| 7. | *Kàn hēibǎn/báibǎn.* | Look at the blackboard/whiteboard. |
| 8. | *Duì bu duì?* | Is it right? |
| 9. | *Duì!* | Right! Correct! |
| 10. | *Hěn hǎo!* | Very good! |
| 11. | *Qǐng gēn wǒ shuō.* | Please repeat after me. |
| 12. | *Zài shuō yí biàn.* | Say it again. |
| 13. | *Dǒng bu dǒng?* | Do you understand? |
| 14. | *Dǒng le.* | Yes, I/we understand; I/we do. |
| 15. | *Zàijiàn!* | Goodbye! |

## B Survival Expressions

Audio

These expressions will help you survive in a Chinese language environment. A good language student constantly learns new words by asking questions. Learn the following expressions and start to acquire Chinese on your own.

| | | |
|---|---|---|
| 1. | *Duìbuqǐ!* | Sorry! |
| 2. | *Qǐng wèn . . .* | Excuse me . . . May I ask . . . |
| 3. | *Xièxie!* | Thanks! |
| 4. | *Zhè shì shénme?* | What is this? |
| 5. | *Wǒ bù dǒng.* | I don't understand. |
| 6. | *Qǐng zài shuō yí biàn.* | Please say it one more time. |
| 7. | *" . . . " Zhōngwén zěnme shuō?* | How do you say " . . . " in Chinese? |
| 8. | *" . . . " shì shénme yìsi?* | What does " . . . " mean? |
| 9. | *Qǐng nǐ gěi wǒ . . .* | Please give me . . . |
| 10. | *Qǐng nǐ gàosu wǒ . . .* | Please tell me . . . |

## C Numerals

Knowing Chinese numerals will help you with basic tasks like shopping and asking for the time. You can get a head start by memorizing 0 to 10 now. After you've memorized them, try saying your telephone number in Chinese.

Audio

| | | | | | |
|---|---|---|---|---|---|
| 〇 (*líng*) | 一 (*yī*) | 二 (*èr*) | 三 (*sān*) | 四 (*sì*) | 五 (*wǔ*) |
| zero | one | two | three | four | five |
| 六 (*liù*) | 七 (*qī*) | 八 (*bā*) | 九 (*jiǔ*) | 十 (*shí*) | |
| six | seven | eight | nine | ten | |

# Lesson 1

## 第一课

*Dì yī kè*

# 问好

*Wèn hǎo*

# GREETINGS

## Learning Objectives

**In this lesson, you will learn to:**

- Exchange basic greetings
- Ask for a person's family name and full name and provide your own
- Determine whether someone is a teacher or a student
- Ask where someone's from

## Relate & Get Ready

**In your own culture/community:**

- How do people greet each other when meeting for the first time?
- Which do people say first, their given name or family name?
- How do acquaintances or close friends address each other?

# Exchanging Greetings

## Dialogue 1

At school, Wang Peng and Li You meet each other for the first time.

Audio

Video

你好[a]！

你好！

请问[b]，你[c]贵姓？

我姓[1]*李。你呢[2]？

我姓王。李小姐[d]，你叫[3]什么名字？

我叫李友。王先生，你叫什么名字？

我叫王朋[4]。

### Pinyin Dialogue

*Nǐ hǎo*[a]*!*

*Nǐ hǎo!*

*Qǐng wèn*[b]*, nǐ*[c] *guì xìng?*

*Wǒ xìng*[1] *Lǐ. Nǐ ne*[2]*?*

*Wǒ xìng Wáng. Lǐ xiǎojiě*[d]*, nǐ jiào*[3] *shénme míngzi?*

*Wǒ jiào Lǐ Yǒu. Wáng xiānsheng, nǐ jiào shénme míngzi?*

*Wǒ jiào Wáng Péng*[4]*.*

* Here and throughout the book, the blue lesson text and numbers correspond to explanations in the **Grammar section.**

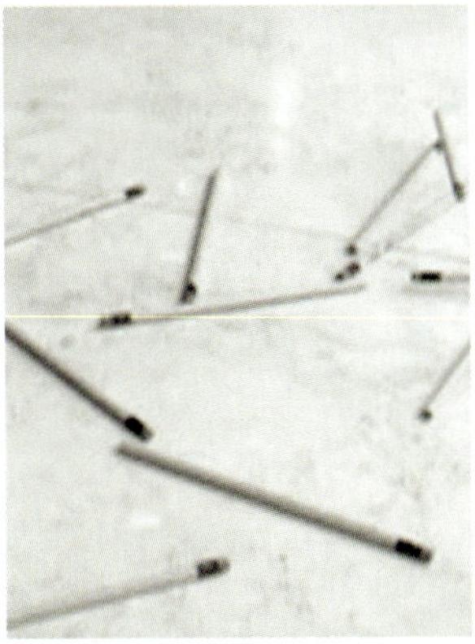

**a 你好! *(Nǐ hǎo!)***

This common greeting is used to address strangers as well as old acquaintances. To respond, simply repeat the same greeting.

**b 请问 *(qǐng wèn)***

This is a polite phrase used to get someone's attention before asking a question or making an inquiry, similar to "excuse me, may I ask" in English.

**c 你 *(nǐ)* vs. 您 *(nín)***

To be more polite and respectful, replace 你 *(nǐ)* with its honorific form, 您 *(nín)*. [See Language Note A, Dialogue 1, Lesson 6.]

**d 小姐 *(xiǎojiě)***

This is a word with two third-tone syllables. The tone sandhi rule applies, thus making the first third tone, 小 *(xiǎo)*, a second tone. The second syllable, 姐 *(jiě)*, can also be pronounced in the neutral tone.

# Vocabulary

Audio

Flashcards

| No. | Word | Pinyin | Part of Speech | Definition |
|---|---|---|---|---|
| 1 | 你 | *nǐ* | pr | you |
| 2 | 好 | *hǎo* | adj | fine, good, nice, OK, it's settled |
| 3 | 请 | *qǐng* | v | please (polite form of request), to treat or to invite (somebody) |
| 4 | 问 | *wèn* | v | to ask (a question) |
| 5 | 贵 | *guì* | adj | honorable, expensive |
| 6 | 姓 | *xìng* | v/n | (one's) family name is . . . ; family name [See Grammar 1.] |
| 7 | 我 | *wǒ* | pr | I, me |
| 8 | 呢 | *ne* | qp | (question particle) [See Grammar 2.] |
| 9 | 小姐 | *xiǎojiě* | n | Miss, young lady |
| 10 | 叫 | *jiào* | v | to be called, to call [See Grammar 3.] |
| 11 | 什么 | *shénme* | qpr | what |
| 12 | 名字 | *míngzi* | n | name |
| 13 | 先生 | *xiānsheng* | n | Mr., husband, teacher |
| 14 | 李友 | *Lǐ Yǒu* | pn | (a personal name) |
| | 李 | *lǐ* | pn/n | (a family name); plum |
| 15 | 王朋 | *Wáng Péng* | pn | (a personal name) |
| | 王 | *wáng* | pn/n | (a family name); king |

## How About You?

你叫什么名字？

*Nǐ jiào shénme míngzi?*

What is your name?

我叫 ________。

*Wǒ jiào* ________.

# Grammar

## 1 The verb 姓 *(xìng)*

姓 *(xìng)* is both a noun and a verb. When it is used as a verb, it must be followed by an object.

**A**

Q: 你姓什么？

*Nǐ xìng shénme?*

What is your family name?

A: 我姓李。

*Wǒ xìng Lǐ.*

My family name is Li.

姓 *(xìng)* is usually negated with 不 *(bù)*. [See Grammar 7.]

**B**

Q: 你姓李吗？

*Nǐ xìng Lǐ ma?*

Is your family name Li?

A: 我不姓李。 [✗ 我不姓。]

*Wǒ bú xìng Lǐ.*

My family name is not Li.

The polite way to ask for and give a family name is as follows.

**C**

Q: 你贵姓？ [✗ 你贵姓什么？]

*Nǐ guì xìng?*

What is your family name?
(Lit. Your honorable family name is . . . ?)

Remember to drop the honorific 贵 *(guì)* when you reply.

A: 我姓王。 [✗ 我贵姓王。]

*Wǒ xìng Wáng.*

My family name is Wang.

You can also respond to 你贵姓 *(nǐ guì xìng)* by saying 免贵姓王 *(miǎn guì xìng Wáng)*, 免贵姓李 *(miǎn guì xìng Lǐ)*. (Lit. Dispense with "honorable." [My] family name is Wang/Li.)

### EXERCISES

Complete these exchanges with your own family name.

1 Q: 请问，你贵姓？ A: 我姓________。

2 Q: 你姓什么？ A: 我姓________。

## 2 Questions ending with 呢 *(ne)*

呢 *(ne)* often follows a noun or pronoun to form a question when the content of the question is already clear from the context.

**A**

Q: 请问，你贵姓？

*Qǐng wèn, nǐ guì xìng?*

What's your family name, please?

A: 我姓李，你呢？

*Wǒ xìng Lǐ, nǐ ne?*

My family name is Li. How about you?

**B**

Q: 你叫什么名字？

*Nǐ jiào shénme míngzi?*

What's your name?

A: 我叫王朋，你呢？

*Wǒ jiào Wáng Péng, nǐ ne?*

My name is Wang Peng. How about you?

When 呢 *(ne)* is used in this way, there must be some context. In each of the two examples above, the context is provided by the preceding sentence: 我姓李 *(wǒ xìng Lǐ)* in (A), and 我叫王朋 *(wǒ jiào Wáng Péng)* in (B).

**GET Real WITH CHINESE**

*You're at the first meeting of your college's Chinese Student Association. What is this sophomore's name?*

### EXERCISES

In pairs, ask and give your name and family name.

1 Q: 我姓________，你呢？ A: 我姓________。

2 Q: 我叫________，你呢？ A: 我叫________。

## 3 The verb 叫 (*jiào*)

While 叫 (*jiào*) has several meanings, it means "to be called" in this lesson. Like 姓 (*xìng*), it must be followed by an object, which can be either a full name or a given name, but seldom a given name that consists only of one syllable.

**A**

Q: 你叫什么名字？

*Nǐ jiào shénme míngzi?*

What is your name?

A: 我叫王小朋。

*Wǒ jiào Wáng Xiǎopéng.*

My name is Wang Xiaopeng.

叫 (*jiào*) is usually negated with 不 (*bù*). [See Grammar 7.]

**B**

Q: 你叫李生吗？

*Nǐ jiào Lǐ Shēng ma?*

Is your name Li Sheng?

A: 我不叫李生。

*Wǒ bú jiào Lǐ Shēng.*

My name is not Li Sheng.

### EXERCISES

Take turns answering the questions below.

1 Q: 请问，你叫什么名字？ A: 我叫________。

2 Q: 你叫李好吗？ A: 我不叫________。

## 4 Subject + verb + object

From the examples in the previous Grammar Points, we can see that the basic word order in a Chinese sentence is subject + verb + object.

The word order remains the same in statements and questions. You don't place the question word at the beginning of a question as you do in English, unless that question word is the subject. [See also Grammar 3, Lesson 2, and Grammar 1, Lesson 4.]

# Language Practice

## A Mix and mingle

INTERPERSONAL

Introduce yourself to your classmates using the outline below.

**Student A** 你好！

*Nǐ hǎo!*

**Student B** ____________。

____________.

**Student A** 请问，你贵姓？

*Qǐng wèn, nǐ guì xìng?*

**Student B** 我姓 ____________。你呢？

*Wǒ xìng ____________. Nǐ ne?*

**Student A** 我姓 ____________，我叫 ____________。你叫什么名字？

*Wǒ xìng ____________, wǒ jiào ____________. Nǐ jiào shénme míngzi?*

**Student B** 我叫 ____________。

*Wǒ jiào ____________.*

### Characterize it!

Unitary

1 小 2 请 3 王 4 生 5 贵

Which of these characters are formed with the pattern on the left?

More characters

## B Getting acquainted

INTERPERSONAL

Complete the following exchange between two people who have never met before. Do a role-play based on the prompts.

**Student A** 你好！

*Nǐ hǎo!*

**Student B** ________。

________.

**Student A** 我姓 ________，请问，你贵姓？

*Wǒ xìng ________, qǐng wèn, nǐ guì xìng?*

**Student B** ________。

________.

**Student A** ________，你叫什么名字？

________, *nǐ jiào shénme míngzi?*

**Student B** 我叫 ________。

*Wǒ jiào ________.*

**Chinese Chat**

You want to add Wang Peng and Li You to a group text message. From this contact list, which names would you select?

# Where Are You From?

## Dialogue 2

Wang Peng and Li You start chatting after bumping into each other on campus.

Audio

Video

王先生，你是[5]老师吗[6]？

我不[7][a]是老师，我是学生。李友，你呢？

我也[8]是学生。你是中国人吗？

是[b]，我是北京人。你是美国人吗？

是，我是纽约人。

### Pinyin Dialogue

*Wáng xiānsheng, nǐ shì[5] lǎoshī ma[6]?*

*Wǒ bú[7][a] shì lǎoshī, wǒ shì xuésheng. Lǐ Yǒu, nǐ ne?*

*Wǒ yě[8] shì xuésheng. Nǐ shì Zhōngguó rén ma?*

*Shì[b], wǒ shì Běijīng rén. Nǐ shì Měiguó rén ma?*

*Shì, wǒ shì Niǔyuē rén.*

China has the fastest growing air passenger market in the world. Based on his boarding pass, identify this traveler's flight plan.

**GET Real WITH CHINESE**

## Language Notes

### a 不

The original tone of 不 is the falling or fourth tone, "bù." However, when followed by another fourth tone syllable, 不 changes to second tone, as in 不是 *(bú shì)*.

### b 是 *(shì)*/不是 *(bú shì)*

These are not universal equivalents of "yes" and "no." One does not always need to introduce an affirmative answer to a yes/no question with 是 *(shì)* or a negative answer with 不是 *(bú shì)*. For instance, to answer the question 你姓王吗? *(Nǐ xìng Wáng ma?)* (Is your family name Wang?) affirmatively, one can reply, 对，我姓王 *(Duì, wǒ xìng Wáng)* (Yes, my family name is Wang) or simply, 我姓王 *(Wǒ xìng Wáng)*. To answer the question negatively, say 不，我不姓王 *(Bù, wǒ bú xìng Wáng)* (No, my family name is not Wang), or simply, 我不姓王 *(Wǒ bú xìng Wáng)*.

# Vocabulary

Audio

Flashcards

| No. | Word | Pinyin | Part of Speech | Definition |
|---|---|---|---|---|
| 1 | 是 | *shì* | v | to be [See Grammar 5.] |
| 2 | 老师 | *lǎoshī* | n | teacher |
| 3 | 吗 | *ma* | qp | (question particle) [See Grammar 6.] |
| 4 | 不 | *bù* | adv | not, no [See Grammar 7.] |
| 5 | 学生 | *xuésheng* | n | student |
| 6 | 也 | *yě* | adv | too, also [See Grammar 8.] |
| 7 | 人 | *rén* | n | people, person |
| 8 | 中国 | *Zhōngguó* | pn | China |
| 9 | 北京 | *Běijīng* | pn | Beijing |
| 10 | 美国 | *Měiguó* | pn | America |
| 11 | 纽约 | *Niǔyuē* | pn | New York |

## How About You?

你是美国人吗？

*Nǐ shì Měiguó rén ma?*

Are you American?

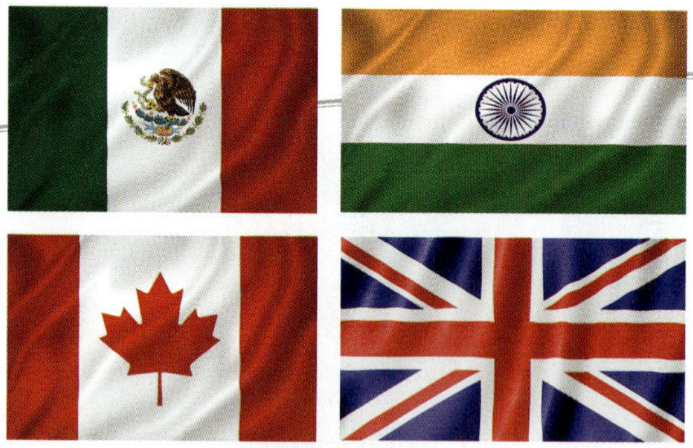

（不）是，我是＿＿＿＿＿＿人。

*(Bú) shì, wǒ shì ＿＿＿＿＿＿ rén.*

See index for corresponding vocabulary or research another term.

# Grammar

## 5 The verb 是 (*shì*) (to be)

是 (*shì*) (to be) is a verb that can be used to link two things that are in some way equivalent. These two things can be nouns, pronouns, or noun phrases, e.g.:

**A** Q: 你是老师吗?

*Nǐ shì lǎoshī ma?*

Are you a teacher?

A: 我是老师。

*Wǒ shì lǎoshī.*

I am a teacher.

**B** 李友是学生。

*Lǐ Yǒu shì xuésheng.*

Li You is a student.

是 (*shì*) is negated with 不 (*bù*). [See also Grammar 7.]

**C** 王朋不是美国人。

*Wáng Péng bú shì Měiguó rén.*

Wang Peng is not American.

### EXERCISES

Form questions and affirmative answers based on the information below. Use exercise 1 as an example.

More exercises

1 王朋 学生

→ Q: 王朋是学生吗? A: 王朋是学生。

2 李友 美国人

3 王朋 北京人

## 6 Questions ending with 吗 *(ma)*

When 吗 *(ma)* is added to the end of a declarative statement, that statement turns into a question. To answer the question in the affirmative, drop 吗 *(ma)* from the end of the question. To answer the question in the negative, drop 吗 *(ma)*, and insert a negative adverb—usually 不 *(bù)*—before the verb. [See Grammar 7.]

**A**

Q: 你是老师吗？

*Nǐ shì lǎoshī ma?*

Are you a teacher?

A: 我是老师。

*Wǒ shì lǎoshī.*

I am a teacher. (affirmative)

A: 我不是老师。

*Wǒ bú shì lǎoshī.*

I am not a teacher. (negative)

**B**

Q: 你姓王吗？

*Nǐ xìng Wáng ma?*

Is your family name Wang?

A: 我姓王。

*Wǒ xìng Wáng.*

My family name is Wang. (affirmative)

A: 我不姓王。

*Wǒ bú xìng Wáng.*

My family name is not Wang. (negative)

## 7 The negative adverb 不 (bù) (not, no)

In Chinese, there are two main negative adverbs. One of the two, 不 *(bù)* (not, no), occurs in this lesson.

**A** 我不是北京人。

*Wǒ bú shì Běijīng rén.*

I am not from Beijing.

**B** 李友不是中国人。

*Lǐ Yǒu bú shì Zhōngguó rén.*

Li You is not Chinese.

**C** 老师不姓王。

*Lǎoshī bú xìng Wáng.*

The teacher's family name is not Wang.

**D** 我不叫李中。

*Wǒ bú jiào Lǐ Zhōng.*

My name is not Li Zhong.

### EXERCISES

Give negative answers to these questions. Use exercise 1 as an example.

1 Q: 李友是中国人吗？

→ A: 李友不是中国人。

2 Q: 王朋是老师吗？

3 Q: 李友是北京人吗？

More exercises

## 8 The adverb 也 (*yě*) (too, also)

The adverb 也 (*yě*) basically means "too" or "also." In Chinese, adverbs, especially one-syllable adverbs, normally appear after subjects and before verbs. The adverb 也 (*yě*) cannot be put before the subject or at the very end of a sentence.

**A** 我也是学生。

*Wǒ yě shì xuésheng.*

I'm a student, too.

**B** 王朋是学生，李友也是学生。

*Wáng Péng shì xuésheng, Lǐ Yǒu yě shì xuésheng.*

Wang Peng is a student. Li You is a student, too.

**C** 你是中国人，我也是中国人。

*Nǐ shì Zhōngguó rén, wǒ yě shì Zhōngguó rén.*

You are Chinese. I am Chinese, too.

[⊗ ……我是中国人也。]

[⊗ ……也我是中国人。]

When the adverb 也 (*yě*) is used together with the negative adverb 不 (*bù*) (not, no), 也 (*yě*) is placed before 不 (*bù*).

**D** 王朋不是老师，李友也不是老师。

*Wáng Péng bú shì lǎoshī, Lǐ Yǒu yě bú shì lǎoshī.*

Wang Peng is not a teacher. Li You is not a teacher, either.

**E** 你不是纽约人，我也不是纽约人。

*Nǐ bú shì Niǔyuē rén, wǒ yě bú shì Niǔyuē rén.*

You are not from New York. I am not from New York, either.

## EXERCISES

Use these sentences to form question-and-answers, inserting 也 where appropriate.

Use exercise 1 as an example.

More exercises

1 王朋是学生。

→ Q: 王朋是学生，你呢？ A: 我也是学生。

2 李友是美国人。

3 李友不是老师。

### Chinese Chat

A friend you just met online is chatting with you on Google Hangouts. How would you reply?

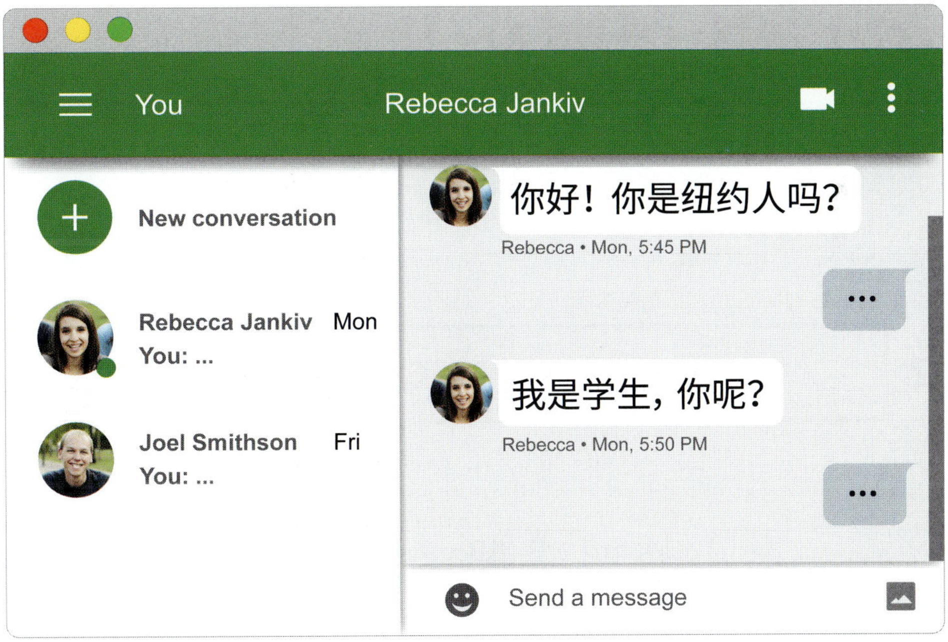

# Language Practice

## C Getting to know you

INTERPERSONAL

In pairs, form a question-and-answer, inserting 是 *(shì)* in the ◇ and 吗 *(ma)* when needed, e.g.:

王朋 ◇ 学生

*Wáng Péng ◇ xuésheng*

| | | |
|---|---|---|
| Q: | 王朋是学生吗? | *Wáng Péng shì xuésheng ma?* |
| A: | 王朋是学生。 | *Wáng Péng shì xuésheng.* |

| | | |
|---|---|---|
| 1 | 李友◇美国人 | *Lǐ Yǒu ◇ Měiguó rén* |
| 2 | 王朋◇中国人 | *Wáng Péng ◇ Zhōngguó rén* |
| 3 | 李友◇美国学生 | *Lǐ Yǒu ◇ Měiguó xuésheng* |
| 4 | 王朋◇北京人 | *Wáng Péng ◇ Běijīng rén* |
| 5 | 李友◇纽约人 | *Lǐ Yǒu ◇ Niǔyuē rén* |
| 6 | 你◇学生 | *nǐ ◇ xuésheng* |

## D On the contrary

INTERPERSONAL

In pairs, ask and answer the following questions, using 不 *(bú)* where appropriate, e.g.:

| | | |
|---|---|---|
| Q: | 李小姐叫李朋吗? | *Lǐ xiǎojiě jiào Lǐ Péng ma?* |
| A: | 李小姐不叫李朋。 | *Lǐ xiǎojiě bú jiào Lǐ Péng.* |

| | | |
|---|---|---|
| 1 | 李友是中国人吗? | *Lǐ Yǒu shì Zhōngguó rén ma?* |
| 2 | 你是王朋吗? | *Nǐ shì Wáng Péng ma?* |
| 3 | 王朋是纽约人吗? | *Wáng Péng shì Niǔyuē rén ma?* |

4 王先生叫王友吗？ *Wáng xiānsheng jiào Wáng Yǒu ma?*

5 你叫李友吗？ *Nǐ jiào Lǐ Yǒu ma?*

## E What about you?

INTERPERSONAL

In pairs, ask and answer the following questions with a partner, using 也 *(yě)* where appropriate.

1 王朋是中国人，你也是中国人吗？

*Wáng Péng shì Zhōngguó rén, nǐ yě shì Zhōngguó rén ma?*

2 李友是纽约人，你也是纽约人吗？

*Lǐ Yǒu shì Niǔyuē rén, nǐ yě shì Niǔyuē rén ma?*

3 王朋不是老师，你呢？

*Wáng Péng bú shì lǎoshī, nǐ ne?*

4 李友不是中国人，你呢？

*Lǐ Yǒu bú shì Zhōngguó rén, nǐ ne?*

5 王朋姓王，你也姓王吗？

*Wáng Péng xìng Wáng, nǐ yě xìng Wáng ma?*

### Characterize it!

What do the characters mean?

What is the common radical?

What does the radical mean?

How does the radical relate to the overall meaning of the characters?

1 呢 2 叫 3 吗 4 名

More characters

## F Where are you from? INTERPERSONAL

Interview your classmates to find out what country, state, or city they're from. Attach the word 人 *(rén)* (person) to the name of the country, state, or city to indicate nationality or place of residence, e.g.:

我是美国 *(Wǒ shì Měiguó)*/California/Boston 人 *(rén)*。

**Student A** 我是美国人，你呢？

*Wǒ shì Měiguó rén, nǐ ne?*

**Student B** ……

. . .

**Student A** 你是 (state) 人吗？

*Nǐ shì* (state) *rén ma?*

**Student B** 我是……人。/

我不是……人，我是……人。

*Wǒ shì . . . rén./Wǒ bú shì . . . rén, wǒ shì . . . rén.*

**Student A** 你是 (city) 人吗？

*Nǐ shì* (city) *rén ma?*

**Student B** 我是 …… 人。你呢？

*Wǒ shì . . . rén, nǐ ne?*

**Student A** 我是 …… 人。

*Wǒ shì . . . rén.*

# Pronunciation

Audio

Practice your pronunciation with the audio exercises below.

## 1 Initials:

| | b | p | d | t |
|---|---|---|---|---|
| 1 | bǎo | pǎo | dā | tā |
| 2 | bān | pān | dí | tí |
| 3 | bù | pù | duì | tuì |
| 4 | bō | pō | dīng | tīng |
| 5 | bēng | pēng | dēng | tēng |

## 2 Initials:

| | j | q | z | c |
|---|---|---|---|---|
| 1 | jiāo | qiāo | zāi | cāi |
| 2 | jǐng | qǐng | zǎo | cǎo |
| 3 | jīn | qīn | zì | cì |
| 4 | jiè | qiè | zè | cè |
| 5 | jiàn | qiàn | zhè | chè |

## 3 Initials:

| | sh | s | x |
|---|---|---|---|
| 1 | shà | sà | xià |
| 2 | shàn | sàn | xiàn |
| 3 | shēn | sēn | xīn |
| 4 | shēng | sēng | xīng |

## 4 Tones:

1 tiāntiān
2 jīnnián
3 jīnglǐ
4 shēngqì
5 xīngqī
6 fādá
7 fāzhǎn
8 shēngdiào

## 5 Tone combinations:

1 nǐ hǎo
2 Lǐ Yǒu
3 lǎohǔ
4 zhǎnlǎn
5 hǎo duō
6 nǐ lái
7 hǎo shū
8 qǐng wèn

## 6 The neutral tone:

1 xiānsheng
2 míngzi
3 xiáojie
4 shénme
5 wǒ de
6 nǐ de
7 tā de
8 shéi de

文化

Continue to explore

# FAMILY names

# 姓氏

Most Chinese family names, 姓 *(xìng)*, are monosyllabic. There are, however, a few disyllabic family names such as 欧阳 *(Ōuyáng)* and 司徒 *(Sītú)*. The number of Chinese family names is fairly limited. According to the most recent census, the most common family names are 王 *(Wáng)*, 李 *(Lǐ)*, 张 *(Zhāng)*, 刘 *(Liú)*, and 陈 *(Chén)*. Family names precede official titles and other forms of address: 王先生 *(Wáng xiānsheng)* (Mister Wang), 李老师 *(Lǐ lǎoshī)* (Teacher Li), etc. When addressing strangers, it is proper to say 先生 *(xiānsheng)* (Mr.) or 小姐 *(xiǎojiě)* (Miss) following their family name.

In China, family names were originally passed down along maternal lines. Indeed, some of the most ancient Chinese family names, such as 姬 *(Jī)*, 妫 *(Guī)*, 姒 *(Sì)*, 姚 *(Yáo)*, and 姜 *(Jiāng)*, as well as the character 姓 *(xìng)*, contain the female radical 女 *(nǚ)*. Aristocratic men and women were born with a 姓 *(xìng)*, which came to indicate paternal lineage in subsequent ages. However, with the expansion of clans, aristocratic men would adopt a 氏 *(shì)* as a secondary family name. By the Western Han period (207 BCE–8 CE), 姓 *(xìng)* and 氏 *(shì)* had become indistinguishable, and even commoners had acquired family names. Thus, family names, 姓 *(xìng)*, are sometimes called 姓氏 *(xìngshì)*.

When talking about family names, many Chinese people will reference the *Hundred Family Names*, 百家姓 *(Bǎi Jiā Xìng)*, which records the known family names of the Northern Song Dynasty in the tenth century. The more than four hundred family names included are arranged in four-character lines, with every other line rhymed. This book was a popular reading primer for schoolchildren.

## COMPARE & CONTRAST

1. Search for the idiom 张三李四 *(Zhāng Sān Lǐ Sì)* using the keywords "张三李四" and "English." Why do you think the family names 张 *(Zhāng)* and 李 *(Lǐ)* are singled out? What is the English equivalent of this idiomatic Chinese expression, and what are some of the most common family names in English?
2. Chinese personal names often carry special meanings. Give examples of personal names with special meanings from other cultures.

# FULL names

In Chinese, family names always precede personal or given names, 名 *(míng)*. Personal names usually carry auspicious meanings. They can be either monosyllabic, written in one character, or disyllabic, written in two characters. A person is seldom referred to by his or her family name alone. For example, Wang Peng, 王朋 *(Wáng Péng)*, should not be referred to as Wang. Additionally, when introducing oneself or someone else, one does not usually mention a monosyllabic personal name alone. For example, Wang Peng would not say ⊗ 我叫朋 *(Wǒ jiào Péng)* or ⊗ 她叫友 *(Tā jiào Yǒu)* when introducing Li You. Instead, he would typically say 我叫王朋 *(Wǒ jiào Wáng Péng)* and 她叫李友 *(Tā jiào Lǐ Yǒu)*.

When meeting someone for the first time, it is polite to first ask for a family name. Then the question 你叫什么名字? *(Nǐ jiào shénme míngzi?)* (What is your name?) can be asked to find out the person's given name or full name.

In Chinese culture, the use of given names often suggests a much higher degree of intimacy than is the case in the West. If one's given name is monosyllabic, its use is even more limited and is usually confined to couples. For example, Wang Peng's girlfriend could address him as Peng, but most people would call him Wang Peng.

# Lesson Wrap-Up

## Make It Flow!

Rearrange the following sentences into a logical sequence. Then combine them into a coherent self-introduction. Remember to omit repetitive elements where appropriate.

_____我是北京人。

_____我叫王朋。

__1__我姓王。

## Role-Play

You are at the first event hosted by your school's Chinese-American Student Association. Be friendly! Meet and greet and introduce yourself.

**Student A** You are an American student from New York City.

**Student B** You are a Chinese student from Beijing.

**Student C** You are an American teacher from Boston.

**Student D** You are a Chinese student from Shanghai.

## Video

Make a short video introducing yourself in Chinese and post it on social media.

**Can-Do Check List**

**Before proceeding to Lesson 2, make sure you can complete the following tasks in Chinese:**

**I can**

- Exchange basic greetings
- Say my family name and full name
- Ask for someone's family name and full name
- Say if I am a student or not
- State my nationality
- Ask where someone's from

# Lesson 2

## 第二课

*Dì èr kè*

# 家庭

*Jiātíng*

# FAMILY

## Learning Objectives

**In this lesson, you will learn to:**

- Use basic kinship terms for family members
- Describe a family photo
- Ask about someone's profession
- Name some common professions

## Relate & Get Ready

**In your own culture/community:**

- What is the typical family structure?
- Do adults consider their parents' house their home?
- Do adults live with their parents?
- When talking about family members, do people mention their father or mother first?
- Is it appropriate to ask about people's professions when you first meet them?

# Looking at a Family Photo

## Dialogue 1

Wang Peng is in Gao Wenzhong's room and points to a picture on the desk.

Audio

Video

高文中，那是你的[1]照片吗？

They walk toward the picture and stand in front of it.

是。这是我爸爸，这是我妈妈。

这[a]个[2]女孩子是谁[3]？

她是我姐姐。

这个男孩子是你弟弟吗？

不是，他是我大哥的儿子[b]。

你大哥有[4]女儿吗？

他没有女儿。

### Pinyin Dialogue

Wang Peng is in Gao Wenzhong's room and points to a picture on the desk.

*Gāo Wénzhōng, nà shì nǐ de[1] zhàopiàn ma?*

They walk toward the picture and stand in front of it.

*Shì. Zhè shì wǒ bàba, zhè shì wǒ māma.*

*Zhè[a] ge[2] nǚ háizi shì shéi[3]?*

*Tā shì wǒ jiějie.*

*Zhè ge nán háizi shì nǐ dìdi ma?*

*Bú shì, tā shì wǒ dàgē de érzi[b].*

*Nǐ dàgē yǒu[4] nǚ'ér ma?*

*Tā méiyǒu nǚ'ér.*

**a 这，那**

In colloquial Chinese, 这 can also be pronounced as ***zhèi*** and 那 as ***nèi*** when they are followed by a measure word or a numeral and a measure word.

**b 儿子 *(érzi)*，女儿 *(nǚ'ér)***

Do not refer to someone's son, 儿子 *(érzi)*, as 男孩子 ***(nán háizi)*** (boy), or someone's daughter, 女儿 ***(nǚ'ér)***, as 女孩子 ***(nǚ háizi)*** (girl).

# Vocabulary

Audio

Flashcards

| No. | Word | Pinyin | Part of Speech | Definition |
|---|---|---|---|---|
| 1 | 那 | *nà* | pr | that |
| 2 | 的 | *de* | p | (a possessive or descriptive particle) [See Grammar 1.] |
| 3 | 照片 | *zhàopiàn* | n | picture, photo |
| 4 | 这 | *zhè* | pr | this |
| 5 | 爸爸 | *bàba* | n | father, dad |
| 6 | 妈妈 | *māma* | n | mother, mom |
| 7 | 个 | *gè/ge* | m | (measure word for many common everyday objects) [See Grammar 2.] |
| 8 | 女 | *nǚ* | adj | female |
| 9 | 孩子 | *háizi* | n | child |
| 10 | 谁 | *shéi* | qpr | who, whom [See Grammar 3.] |

**GET Real WITH CHINESE**

*While on a family trip to Hong Kong, you see this sign. What is the instruction?*

| No. | Word | Pinyin | Part of Speech | Definition |
|---|---|---|---|---|
| 11 | 她 | *tā* | pr | she, her |
| 12 | 姐姐 | *jiějie* | n | older sister |
| 13 | 男 | *nán* | adj | male |
| 14 | 弟弟 | *dìdi* | n | younger brother |
| 15 | 他 | *tā* | pr | he, him |
| 16 | 大哥 | *dàgē* | n | eldest/oldest brother |
| 17 | 儿子 | *érzi* | n | son |
| 18 | 有 | *yǒu* | v | to have, to exist [See Grammar 4 and Grammar 5.] |
| 19 | 女儿 | *nǚ'ér* | n | daughter |
| 20 | 没 | *méi* | adv | not |
| 21 | 高文中 | *Gāo Wénzhōng* | pn | (a personal name) |
| | 高 | *gāo* | pn/adj | (a family name); tall, high |

## 这是谁?

*Zhè shì shéi?*

Who is this?

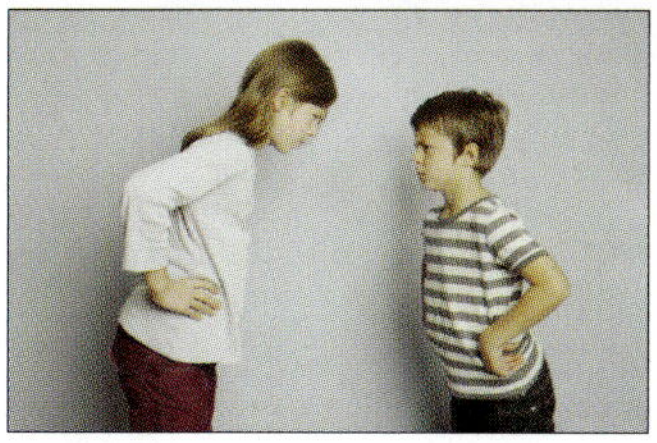

**How About You?**

这是 ________。

*Zhè shì* ________.

Bring a family photo to class, like the ones above, and identify your family members.

# Grammar

## 1 The particle 的 *(de)* (I)

To indicate a possessive relationship, the particle 的 is used between the "possessor" and the "possessed." To that extent, it is equivalent to the "'s" structure in English, as in 老师的名字 *(lǎoshī de míngzi)* (teacher's name). The particle 的 *(de)* is often omitted in colloquial speech after a personal pronoun. Therefore, we say "王朋的妈妈" *(Wáng Péng de māma)* (Wang Peng's mother) but "我妈妈" *(wǒ māma)* (my mother). [See also Grammar 4, Lesson 3.]

More exercises

### EXERCISES

Translate these phrases containing the particle 的.

1 李友的爸爸

2 哥哥的女儿

## 2 Measure words (I)

In Chinese, a numeral is usually not followed immediately by a noun. Instead, a measure word is inserted between the number and the noun, as in (A), (B), and (C). Similarly, a measure word is often inserted between a demonstrative pronoun and a noun, as in (D) and (E). There are over one hundred measure words in Chinese, but you will come across only two or three dozen in everyday speech. Many nouns are associated with specific measure words, which are often related in meaning to the nouns.

个 *(gè/ge)* is the single most common measure word in Chinese. It is also sometimes used as a substitute for other measure words.

**A** 一个人

*yí ge rén*

a person

**B** 一个学生

*yí ge xuésheng*

a student

**C** 一个老师

*yí ge lǎoshī*

a teacher

**D** 这个孩子

*zhè ge háizi*

this child

**E** 那个男学生

*nà ge nán xuésheng*

that male student

**EXERCISES**

Translate these phrases containing the measure word 个.

1 一个中国人

2 三个弟弟

More exercises

## 3 Question pronouns

Question pronouns include 谁 *(shéi)* (who/whom), 什么 *(shénme)* (what), 哪 *(nǎ/něi)* (which) [see Lesson 6], 哪儿 *(nǎr)* (where) [see Lesson 5], and 几 *(jǐ)* (how many). In a question with a question pronoun, the word order is exactly the same as that in a declarative sentence. Therefore, when forming a question with a question pronoun, start with a declarative sentence and then replace the relevant part with the appropriate question pronoun.

**A** 那个女孩子是李友。

*Nà ge nǚ háizi shì Lǐ Yǒu.*

That girl is Li You.

那个女孩子 *(Nà ge nǚ háizi)* can be replaced with 谁 *(shéi)* to form the question below.

谁是李友?

*Shéi shì Lǐ Yǒu?*

Who is Li You?

Here 谁 *(shéi)* functions as the subject of the sentence and occupies the same position as 那个女孩子 *(Nà ge nǚ háizi)* in the corresponding statement. 李友 *(Lǐ Yǒu)* in (A) can also be replaced with 谁 *(shéi)* to form the question below.

那个女孩子是谁?

*Nà ge nǚ háizi shì shéi?*

Who is that girl?

谁 *(shéi)* functions as the object of the sentence and occupies the same position as 李友 *(Lǐ Yǒu)*.

**B**

Q: 谁是老师?

*Shéi shì lǎoshī?*

Who is a teacher?

A: 李先生是老师。

*Lǐ xiānsheng shì lǎoshī.*

Mr. Li is a teacher.

**C**

Q: 那个女孩子姓什么?

*Nà ge nǚ háizi xìng shénme?*

What's that girl's family name?

A: 那个女孩子姓王。

*Nà ge nǚ háizi xìng Wáng.*

That girl's family name is Wang.

**D**

Q: 谁有姐姐?

*Shéi yǒu jiějie?*

Who has older sisters?

A: 高文中有姐姐。

*Gāo Wénzhōng yǒu jiějie.*

Gao Wenzhong has an older sister.

## EXERCISES

Use the question pronoun 谁 to survey your classmates.

1 Q: 谁是_______? A: 我是_______。

2 Q: 谁有_______? A: 我有_______。

**Chinese Chat**

You're about to post this picture of a family member on Instagram. What caption would you write? Use the hashtag #姐姐.

## 4 Indicating possession using 有 *(yǒu)*

有 *(yǒu)* is always negated with 没 *(méi)*, not 不 *(bù)*.

**A** Q: 王先生有弟弟吗?

*Wáng xiānsheng yǒu dìdi ma?*

Does Mr. Wang have a younger brother?

A: 王先生没有弟弟。

*Wáng xiānsheng méiyǒu dìdi.*

Mr. Wang doesn't have any younger brothers.

**B** Q: 我有三个姐姐，你呢?

*Wǒ yǒu sān ge jiějie, nǐ ne?*

I have three older sisters. How about you?

A: 我没有姐姐。

*Wǒ méiyǒu jiějie.*

I don't have any older sisters.

### EXERCISES

In pairs, complete either the question or the answer, inserting 有 where appropriate.

1 Q: 高文中____________________?

A: 高文中有姐姐。

2 Q: 你有哥哥吗?

A: 我____________________。

More exercises

# Language Practice

## A Who's this? INTERPERSONAL

In pairs, identify the IC characters below using 谁 (*shéi*), e.g.:

Q: 这个人/男孩子是谁? *Zhè ge rén/nán háizi shì shéi?*

A: 这个人/男孩子是王朋。 *Zhè ge rén/nán háizi shì Wáng Péng.*

1 

2 

**Chinese Chat**

You've just shared a family photo with a friend on Facebook Messenger and she's asking you about it. How would you reply?

**Characterize it!**

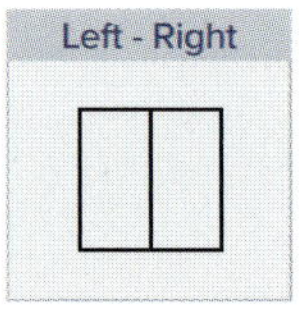


1 那 2 的 3 爸 4 高 5 他

Which of these characters are formed with the pattern on the left?

More characters

## B Family matters

INTERPERSONAL

Form a question-and-answer about family members, inserting 有 *(yǒu)* or 没有 *(méiyǒu)* in the ◇ and 吗 *(ma)* where appropriate, e.g.:

高大哥 ◇ 女儿

*Gāo dàgē ◇ nǚ'ér*

Q: 高大哥有女儿吗?

*Gāo dàgē yǒu nǚ'ér ma?*

A: 他没有女儿。

*Tā méiyǒu nǚ'ér.*

1 高文中 ◇ 姐姐

*Gāo Wénzhōng ◇ jiějie*

2 高大哥 ◇ 儿子

*Gāo dàgē ◇ érzi*

3 你 ◇ 姐姐

*nǐ ◇ jiějie*

4 你 ◇ 弟弟

*nǐ ◇ dìdi*

5 你的老师 ◇ 女儿

*nǐ de lǎoshī ◇ nǚ'ér*

## C Family portrait

INTERPERSONAL PRESENTATIONAL

In pairs, share and discuss family photos.

Q: 这是谁?

*Zhè shì shéi?*

A: 这是我________。

*Zhè shì wǒ ________.*

Now present your family photo to the class and describe the people in the picture.

这是我爸爸，这是我妈妈，……

*Zhè shì wǒ bàba, zhè shì wǒ māma, . . .*

# Discussing Family

## Dialogue 2

Li You and Bai Ying'ai are chatting about their family members and what each of them does.

Audio

Video

白英爱，你家[a]有[5]几口[b]人？

我家有六口人，我爸爸、我妈妈、一[c]个哥哥、两[6]个妹妹和[d]我[e]。李友，你家有几口人？

我家有五口人：爸爸、妈妈、大姐、二姐和我。你爸爸妈妈做什么工作？

我爸爸是律师，妈妈是英文老师，哥哥、妹妹都[7]是大学生。

我妈妈也是老师，我爸爸是医生。

### Pinyin Dialogue

*Bái Yīng'ài, nǐ jiā[a] yǒu[5] jǐ kǒu[b] rén?*

*Wǒ jiā yǒu liù kǒu rén, wǒ bàba, wǒ māma, yí[c] ge gēge, liǎng[6] ge mèimei hé[d] wǒ[e].*

*Lǐ Yǒu, nǐ jiā yǒu jǐ kǒu rén?*

*Wǒ jiā yǒu wǔ kǒu rén: bàba, māma, dàjiě, èrjiě hé wǒ. Nǐ bàba māma zuò shénme gōngzuò?*

*Wǒ bàba shì lǜshī, māma shì Yīngwén lǎoshī, gēge, mèimei dōu[7] shì dàxuéshēng.*

*Wǒ māma yě shì lǎoshī, wǒ bàba shì yīshēng.*

**a** 家 *(jiā)*

This word can refer to one's family or home. 我家有四口人 *(Wǒ jiā yǒu sì kǒu rén)* (There are four people in my family) can be used to describe the number of people in your family and 这是我家 *(Zhè shì wǒ jiā)* (This is my home) can be used to point out your house.

**b** 口 *(kǒu)*

This is the idiomatic measure word used in northern China for number of family members. In the south, people say 个 *(gè/ge)* instead.

**c** 一 *(yī/yí)*

The numeral 一 *(yī)* (one) is pronounced in the first tone *(yī)* in the following cases: when it stands alone; when it implies an ordinal number, e.g., 一楼 *(yī lóu)* (first floor); and when it comes at the end of a phrase. Otherwise, its tone changes according to the following rules:

- Before a fourth-tone word, it becomes second tone: 一个 *(yí gè)*.
- Before a first-, second-, or third-tone word, it is pronounced in the fourth tone, e.g., 一张 *(yì zhāng)* (a sheet), 一盘 *(yì pán)* (one plate), 一本 *(yì běn)* (one volume).

**d** 和 *(hé)*

Unlike "and," 和 *(hé)* cannot link two clauses or two sentences: 我爸爸是老师 *(Wǒ bàba shì lǎoshī)*, ⊗ 和我妈妈是医生.

**e** 、

The pause mark or series comma, 、 , is often used to link two, three, or even more parallel words or phrases, e.g., 爸爸、妈妈、两个妹妹和我 *(bàba, māma, liǎng ge mèimei hé wǒ)* (dad, mom, two younger sisters, and I). [See Language Note A, Dialogue 1, Lesson 4.]

# Vocabulary

Audio

Flashcards

| No. | Word | Pinyin | Part of Speech | Definition |
|---|---|---|---|---|
| 1 | 家 | *jiā* | n | family, home |
| 2 | 几 | *jǐ* | nu | how many, some, a few |
| 3 | 口 | *kǒu* | m | (measure word for number of family members) |
| 4 | 哥哥 | *gēge* | n | older brother |
| 5 | 两 | *liǎng* | nu | two, a couple of [See Grammar 6.] |
| 6 | 妹妹 | *mèimei* | n | younger sister |
| 7 | 和 | *hé* | conj | and |
| 8 | 大姐 | *dàjiě* | n | eldest/oldest sister |
| 9 | 二姐 | *èrjiě* | n | second oldest sister |

**GET Real WITH CHINESE**

*Chinese custom is to present business cards with both hands, ensuring the writing faces the recipient. What type of professional gave out this card?*

| No. | Word | Pinyin | Part of Speech | Definition |
|---|---|---|---|---|
| 10 | 做 | *zuò* | v | to do |
| 11 | 工作 | *gōngzuò* | n/v | job; to work |
| 12 | 律师 | *lǜshī* | n | lawyer |
| 13 | 英文 | *Yīngwén* | n | the English language |
| 14 | 都 | *dōu* | adv | both, all [See Grammar 7.] |
| 15 | 大学生 | *dàxuéshēng* | n | college student |
| | 大学 | *dàxué* | n | university, college |
| 16 | 医生 | *yīshēng* | n | doctor, physician |
| 17 | 白英爱 | *Bái Yīng'ài* | pn | (a personal name) |

## How About You?

他/她做什么工作？你呢？

*Tā zuò shénme gōngzuò? Nǐ ne?*

What does he/she do? How about you?

他/她是______，我是______。

*Tā shì ______ , wǒ shì______.*

See index for corresponding vocabulary or research another term.

# Grammar

## 5 Indicating existence using 有 (*yǒu*)

**A** 我家有五口人。

*Wǒ jiā yǒu wǔ kǒu rén.*

There are five people in my family.

**B** 小高家有两个大学生。

*Xiǎo Gāo jiā yǒu liǎng ge dàxuéshēng.*

There are two college students in Little Gao's family.

More exercises

### EXERCISES

Complete the question or the answer, inserting 有 where appropriate.

1 Q: 你家____________________?

A: 我家有五口人。

2 Q: 白英爱家有几口人?

A: 白英爱家____________________。

## 6 Using 二 (*èr*) and 两 (*liǎng*)

二 (*èr*) and 两 (*liǎng*) both mean "two," but they differ in usage. 两 (*liǎng*) is used in front of common measure words to express a quantity, e.g., 两个人 (*liǎng ge rén*) (two people). When counting numbers, however, 二 (*èr*) is used, e.g., 一, 二, 三, 四 (*yī, èr, sān, sì*) (one, two, three, four). In compound numerals, 二 (*èr*) is always used in the last two digits, e.g., 二十二 (*èrshí'èr*) (22) and 一百二十五 (*yìbǎi èrshí'wǔ*) (125). But 二百二十二 (*èrbǎi èrshí'èr*) (222) can also be expressed as 两百二十二 (*liǎngbǎi èrshí'èr*) (222).

## 7 The adverb 都 (dōu) (both, all)

The word 都 *(dōu)* (both, all) indicates inclusiveness. As it always occurs in front of a verb, it is classified as an adverb. Because it refers to things or people just mentioned, it must be used at the end of an enumeration.

**A** 王朋、李友和高文中都是学生。

*Wáng Péng, Lǐ Yǒu hé Gāo Wénzhōng dōu shì xuésheng.*

Wang Peng, Li You, and Gao Wenzhong are all students.

[都 *(dōu)* refers back to Wang Peng, Li You, and Gao Wenzhong, and therefore appears after them.]

**B** 王朋和李友都不是律师。

*Wáng Péng hé Lǐ Yǒu dōu bú shì lǜshī.*

Neither Wang Peng nor Li You is a lawyer.

**C** 王朋和白英爱都有妹妹。

*Wáng Péng hé Bái Yīng'ài dōu yǒu mèimei.*

Both Wang Peng and Bai Ying'ai have younger sisters.

**D** 高文中和李友都没有弟弟。

*Gāo Wénzhōng hé Lǐ Yǒu dōu méiyǒu dìdi.*

Neither Gao Wenzhong nor Li You has any younger brothers.

没 *(méi)* is always used to negate 有 *(yǒu)*. However, to say "not all of . . . have," we say 不都有 *(bù dōu yǒu)* rather than ✖ 没都有. Whether the negative precedes or follows the word 都 *(dōu)* makes the difference between partial negation and complete negation. Compare the following examples. Note: 他们 *(tāmen)* (they).

**E** 他们不都是中国人。

*Tāmen bù dōu shì Zhōngguó rén.*

Not all of them are Chinese.

**F** 他们都不是中国人。

*Tāmen dōu bú shì Zhōngguó rén.*

None of them are Chinese.

**G** 他们不都有弟弟。

*Tāmen bù dōu yǒu dìdi.*

Not all of them have younger brothers.

**H** 他们都没有弟弟。

*Tāmen dōu méiyǒu dìdi.*

None of them have any younger brothers.

More exercises

## EXERCISES

Join these sentences to indicate inclusiveness, inserting 都 where appropriate. Use exercise 1 as an example.

1 白英爱的妈妈是老师。
李友的妈妈是老师。
→ 白英爱的妈妈和李友的妈妈都是老师。

2 白英爱没有弟弟。
李友没有弟弟。

3 我姐姐有两个女儿。
小李的姐姐有两个女儿。

# Language Practice

## E INTERPERSONAL One big family? PRESENTATIONAL

Interview your classmates to find out how many family members they have and report back to the class. Use 有 (*yǒu*), e.g.:

Q: 请问，你家有几口人？

*Qǐng wèn, nǐ jiā yǒu jǐ kǒu rén?*

A: 我家有四口人。

*Wǒ jiā yǒu sì kǒu rén.*

## F All about the cast

Complete the following questions-and-answers by inserting 谁 (*shéi*) or another appropriate question pronoun, e.g.:

Q: 这是谁？

*Zhè shì shéi?*

A: 这是王朋。

*Zhè shì Wáng Péng.*

1 Q: ______有儿子？

______ *yǒu érzi?*

A: 高文中的大哥有儿子。

*Gāo Wénzhōng de dàgē yǒu érzi.*

2 Q: 李友家有______口人？

*Lǐ Yǒu jiā yǒu* ______ *kǒu rén?*

A: 李友家有五口人。

*Lǐ Yǒu jiā yǒu wǔ kǒu rén.*

**3** Q: 白英爱有______个妹妹？

*Bái Yīng'ài yǒu ______ ge mèimei?*

A: 白英爱有两个妹妹。

*Bái Yīng'ài yǒu liǎng ge mèimei.*

**4** Q: 李友的爸爸做______工作？

*Lǐ Yǒu de bàba zuò ______ gōngzuò?*

A: 李友的爸爸是医生。

*Lǐ Yǒu de bàba shì yīshēng.*

**5** Q: 白英爱的妈妈做______工作？

*Bái Yīng'ài de māma zuò ______ gōngzuò?*

A: 白英爱的妈妈是英文老师。

*Bái Yīng'ài de māma shì Yīngwén lǎoshī.*

## G World traveler

INTERPERSONAL

You're staying at a hostel in China. Using the images below, ask your international roommates where they're from and what they do.

你是______人吗？

*Nǐ shì ______ rén ma?*

or

你做什么工作？你是______吗？

*Nǐ zuò shénme gōngzuò? Nǐ shì______ ma?*

1 

2 

3 

4 

5 

## H Common denominator

Based on the information given, rephrase the sentences using 都 (*dōu*), e.g.:

王朋是学生，李友也是学生。

*Wáng Péng shì xuésheng, Lǐ Yǒu yě shì xuésheng.*

王朋和李友都是学生。

*Wáng Péng hé Lǐ Yǒu dōu shì xuésheng.*

1 白英爱的妈妈是老师，李友的妈妈也是老师。

*Bái Yīng'ài de māma shì lǎoshī, Lǐ Yǒu de māma yě shì lǎoshī.*

________________________________________

2 李友有姐姐，高文中也有姐姐。

*Lǐ Yǒu yǒu jiějie, Gāo Wénzhōng yě yǒu jiějie.*

________________________________________

3 王朋不是纽约人，高文中也不是纽约人。

*Wáng Péng bú shì Niǔyuē rén, Gāo Wénzhōng yě bú shì Niǔyuē rén.*

________________________________________

4 王朋没有哥哥，李友也没有哥哥。

*Wáng Péng méiyǒu gēge, Lǐ Yǒu yě méiyǒu gēge.*

________________________________________

## I To have or have not

PRESENTATIONAL

The following chart shows the similarities and differences among Wang Peng, Li You, Gao Wenzhong, and Bai Ying'ai. Based on the information given, make negative sentences using 都 *(dōu)* with 不 *(bù)* or 没有 *(méiyǒu)* appropriately. Note: 他们 *(tāmen)* (they).

| | 律师 *lǜshī* | 弟弟 *dìdi* | 照片 *zhàopiàn* | 姐姐 *jiějie* |
|---|---|---|---|---|
|  | ✗ | ✗ | ✓ | ✗ |
|  | ✗ | ✗ | ✓ | ✗ |
|  | ✗ | ✗ | ✓ | ✓ |
|  | ✗ | ✗ | ✗ | ✗ |

## J #1 fan

PRESENTATIONAL

Who is your favorite celebrity? As a true fan *(fěnsī)*, introduce him or her to your friends through a post on social media. Include biographical information such as name, nationality, and family details.

### Characterize it!

More characters

- What do the characters mean?
- What is the common radical?
- What does the radical mean?
- How does the radical relate to the overall meaning of the characters?

1 妈 2 姐 3 妹 4 她 5 姓

# Pronunciation

Audio

Practice your pronunciation with the audio exercises below.

**1 Initials:**

1 *zhè chè shè rè*
2 *zhǎo chǎo shǎo rǎo*
3 *zhèn chèn shèn rèn*
4 *zhāng chāng shāng rāng*

**2 The final "e":**

1 *gē dé zhè hē*
2 *kē tè chē shé*
3 *zé cè sè rè*

**3 Compound finals:**

1 *dōu duō tóu tuó*
2 *duī diū shuǐ xuě*
3 *shùn xùn jiū zhuī*
4 *lüè nüè juè què*

**4 Tones:**

1 *chénggōng*
2 *chángcháng*
3 *rénkǒu*
4 *xuéxiào*
5 *Chángjiāng*
6 *Chángchéng*
7 *míngxiǎn*
8 *chídào*

**5 The neutral tone:**

1 *māma*
2 *dìdi*
3 *jiějie*
4 *mèimei*
5 *bàba*
6 *gēge*
7 *jǐ ge*
8 *zhè ge*

## Chinese Chat

Your friend just posted a photo of her family with a short description on Instagram. What comment would you leave?

Instagram

andreacameron_86 20min

♥ 75 likes

andreacameron_86 这是我家人的照片。我家有三口人：妈妈、姐姐和我。我妈妈是医生，姐姐是律师。我是学生。你家有几口人？有照片吗？

20 MINUTES AGO

Comment

文化
Continue to explore

# Kinship terms

When expressing kinship terms, the Chinese customarily put male before female: 爸爸妈妈 *(bàba māma)* (dad and mom), 哥哥姐姐 *(gēge jiějie)* (older brothers and sisters), and 弟弟妹妹 *(dìdi mèimei)* (younger brothers and sisters). When pairing up kinship terms for the same gender, the one with seniority is mentioned first: 哥哥弟弟 *(gēge dìdi)* (older and younger brothers), 姐姐妹妹 *(jiějie mèimei)* (older and younger sisters).

Siblings are 兄弟姐妹 *(xiōng dì jiě mèi)*. To ask whether someone has any siblings, say 你有兄弟姐妹吗? *(Nǐ yǒu xiōng dì jiě mèi ma?)* (Do you have any brothers or sisters?). Oldest siblings are called 大哥 *(dàgē)* (oldest brother) and 大姐 *(dàjiě)* (oldest sister); the youngest are 小弟 *(xiǎodì)* (youngest brother) and 小妹 *(xiǎomèi)* (youngest sister). The rest are ranked by numerals according to their birth order, e.g., 二姐 *(èrjiě)* (second oldest sister), 三弟 *(sāndì)* (third youngest brother). Younger siblings generally do not refer to their older brothers and sisters by name but use the appropriate kinship terms instead. Because of the one-child policy, however, many Chinese people have only cousins but no siblings.

# Family structure

In traditional Chinese society, multiple generations often lived in the same house, thus the term 四代同堂 *(sì dài tóng táng)* (four generations under the same roof). It was common for the head of the household to live with his sons and daughters-in-law, grandchildren, and even his great-grandchildren. Nowadays, while some couples still live with the husband's parents, nuclear families living independently are more and more common. Due to family planning policies in China since the late 1970s, many Chinese people do not have any brothers or sisters. In 2015, the government abandoned the one-child policy and allowed every couple to have two children. The new policy came into effect on January 1, 2016.

## COMPARE & CONTRAST

1 How does the family structure of traditional and modern China compare and contrast with that of your society or culture?

2 Below is a Chinese government poster. Look up 一样 *(yíyàng)* in the Vocabulary Index. What does the headline 男孩女孩一样好 *(Nánhái nǚhái yíyàng hǎo)* mean? What orientation is the government trying to change? Does the same orientation exist in your culture?

# Lesson Wrap-Up

## Make It Flow!

Rearrange the following sentences into a logical sequence. Then combine them into a coherent narrative. Remember to omit repetitive elements and substitute subjects with personal pronouns where appropriate. Don't forget to incorporate the adverb 都 *(dōu)*.

____白英爱的妹妹是大学生。

____白英爱的哥哥是大学生。

__1__白英爱的爸爸是律师。

____白英爱的妈妈是英文老师。

## Role-Play

In groups, create your own "family," assigning roles to each person. Then, as a group, introduce yourselves to the class by stating your new names and family roles.

## Family Photo

After you have introduced your new "family" to the class, take a family photo. Then, label the picture with everyone's Chinese name and family role and post it on social media.

## Can-Do Check List

Before proceeding to Lesson 3, make sure you can complete the following tasks in Chinese:

I can

- Say and write basic kinship terms
- Identify different family members in a photo
- Ask someone about family size
- Ask someone if he or she has any siblings
- Mention my family's professions and my own
- Ask someone what he or she does professionally
- Say and write some common professions

# Lesson 3

第三课

*Dì sān kè*

# 时间

*Shíjiān*

## TIME AND DATE

### Learning Objectives

**In this lesson, you will learn to:**

- Discuss times and dates
- Talk about ages and birthdays
- Arrange a dinner date with someone

### Relate & Get Ready

**In your own culture/community:**

- Do people write the month before the day or vice versa?
- Is it appropriate to ask someone's age and birthday?
- What do people typically do to celebrate their birthday?

# Out for a Birthday Dinner

## Dialogue 1

Gao Wenzhong is talking to Bai Ying'ai about a special day coming up.

Audio

Video

白英爱，九月十二[1][a]号[2]是星期几[2]？

是星期四。

那天[b]是我的[3]生日。

是吗？你今年多大[c]？

十八岁[d]。

我星期四请你吃饭[4]，怎么样？

太好了[e]！谢谢，谢谢[f]。

你喜欢吃中国菜还是[5]美国菜？

我是英国人，可是我喜欢吃中国菜。

好，我们吃中国菜。

星期四几点？

七点半怎么样？

好，星期四晚上见。

再见！

*Bái Yīng'ài, jiǔyuè shí'èr* [1a] *hào* [2] *shì xīngqījǐ* [2] *?*

*Shì xīngqīsì.*

*Nà tiān* [b] *shì wǒ de* [3] *shēngrì.*

*Shì ma? Nǐ jīnnián duō dà* [c] *?*

*Shíbā suì* [d] *.*

*Wǒ xīngqīsì qǐng nǐ chī fàn* [4] *, zěnmeyàng?*

*Tài hǎo le* [e] *! Xièxie, xièxie* [f] *.*

*Nǐ xǐhuan chī Zhōngguó cài háishi* [5] *Měiguó cài?*

*Wǒ shì Yīngguó rén, kěshì wǒ xǐhuan chī Zhōngguó cài.*

*Hǎo, wǒmen chī Zhōngguó cài.*

*Xīngqīsì jǐ diǎn?*

*Qī diǎn bàn zěnmeyàng?*

*Hǎo, xīngqīsì wǎnshang jiàn.*

*Zàijiàn!*

## Language Notes

**a** 时间 *(Shíjiān)*

Chinese time expressions proceed from the largest to the smallest unit, e.g., 二〇一九年八月十二日晚上七点 *(èr líng yī jiǔ nián bāyuè shí'èr rì wǎnshang qī diǎn)* (2019, August 12, 7:00 p.m.).

**b** 天 *(tiān)* and 年 *(nián)*

These nouns do not require a measure word because they function as measure words on their own.

**c** 你今年多大? *(Nǐ jīnnián duō dà?)*

Say this to find out someone's age. If you're asking a child, use 你今年几岁? *(Nǐ jīnnián jǐ suì?)*. To ask an older person, use the polite forms 您多大年纪了? *(Nín duō dà niánjì le?)* or 您多大岁数了? *(Nín duō dà suìshù le?)*.

**d** 十八岁 *(shíbā suì)*

State your age by saying 我十八岁 *(wǒ shíbā suì)* (I'm eighteen years old). The verb 是 *(shì)* is usually not needed, and the word 岁 *(suì)* (years of age) can often be dropped. However, if the age is ten or under, the word 岁 *(suì)* cannot be omitted: ✖ 我十 or ✖ 我八. Note that it is incorrect to say, ✖ 我十八年.

**e** 太…了 *(tài . . . le)*

When 太…了 *(tài . . . le)* is used in an exclamation (as in the case here), the stress usually falls on 太 *(tài)*, and it can typically be translated as "so" or "really."

**f** 谢谢 *(xièxie)*

To express gratitude, say 谢谢 *(xièxie)*, or 谢谢，谢谢 *(xièxie, xièxie)*, which is more polite and exuberant.

# Vocabulary

Audio

Flashcards

| No. | Word | Pinyin | Part of Speech | Definition |
|---|---|---|---|---|
| 1 | 九月 | *jiǔyuè* | n | September |
| 2 | 月 | *yuè* | n | month |
| 3 | 十二 | *shí'èr* | nu | twelve |
| 4 | 号 | *hào* | m | (measure word for position in a numerical series, day of the month) |
| 5 | 星期 | *xīngqī* | n | week |
| 6 | 星期四 | *xīngqīsì* | n | Thursday |
| 7 | 天 | *tiān* | n | day |
| 8 | 生日 | *shēngrì* | n | birthday |
| | 生 | *shēng* | v | to give birth to, to be born |
| | 日 | *rì* | n | day, sun |
| 9 | 今年 | *jīnnián* | t | this year |
| | 年 | *nián* | n | year |
| 10 | 多 | *duō* | adv | how many/much, to what extent |
| 11 | 大 | *dà* | adj | big, old |
| 12 | 十八 | *shíbā* | nu | eighteen |
| 13 | 岁 | *suì* | n | year (of age) |
| 14 | 吃 | *chī* | v | to eat |
| 15 | 饭 | *fàn* | n | meal, (cooked) rice |
| 16 | 怎么样 | *zěnmeyàng* | qpr | Is it OK? How is that? How does that sound? |
| 17 | 太…了 | *tài . . . le* | | too, extremely |
| 18 | 谢谢 | *xièxie* | v | to thank |

| No. | Word | Pinyin | Part of Speech | Definition |
|---|---|---|---|---|
| 19 | 喜欢 | *xǐhuan* | v | to like |
| 20 | 菜 | *cài* | n | dish, cuisine |
| 21 | 还是 | *háishi* | conj | or [See Grammar 6.] |
| 22 | 可是 | *kěshì* | conj | but |
| 23 | 我们 | *wǒmen* | pr | we, us |
| 24 | 点 | *diǎn* | m | o'clock (lit. dot, point, thus "points on the clock") |
| 25 | 半 | *bàn* | nu | half, half an hour |
| 26 | 晚上 | *wǎnshang* | t | evening, night |
| 27 | 见 | *jiàn* | v | to see |
| 28 | 再见 | *zàijiàn* | v | goodbye, see you again |
| | 再 | *zài* | adv | again |
| 29 | 英国 | *Yīngguó* | pn | Britain |

## How About You?

你喜欢吃什么菜?

*Nǐ xǐhuan chī shénme cài?*

What do you like to eat?

我喜欢吃 ________。

*Wǒ xǐhuan chī ________.*

See index for vocabulary corresponding to national cuisine or research another term.

# Grammar

## 1 Numbers up to 100

The characters below serve as the basis for the Chinese numeration system.

| | | | | | |
|---|---|---|---|---|---|
| 〇 (*líng*) zero | 一 (*yī*) one | 二 (*èr*) two | 三 (*sān*) three | 四 (*sì*) four | 五 (*wǔ*) five |
| 六 (*liù*) six | 七 (*qī*) seven | 八 (*bā*) eight | 九 (*jiǔ*) nine | 十 (*shí*) ten | |

All other double-digit numbers can be formed using numbers from 一 (*yī*) to 十 (*shí*), following the patterns below.

| Pattern | Application | Example |
|---|---|---|
| 十 (*shí*) + Single Digit | 11, 12–18, 19 | 十五 (*shíwǔ*) (15) |
| Single Digit + 十 (*shí*) | 20, 30–80, 90 | 四十 (*sìshí*) (40) |
| Single Digit + 十 (*shí*) + Single Digit | 21, 22–98, 99 | 八十三 (*bāshísān*) (83) |

When counting by hundreds, the pattern is single digit + 百 (*bǎi*) (hundred), e.g.: 一百 (*yìbǎi*) (one hundred), 二百/两百 (*èrbǎi/liǎngbǎi*) (two hundred).

More exercises

### EXERCISES

Say the following numbers in Chinese.

9 18 27 36 90 100

## 2 Dates

### *Days of the week*

星期几 (*xīngqījǐ*) is the standard way to ask the day of the week. To answer the question, simply replace the word 几 (*jǐ*) (how many) with the number indicating the day of the week. The following table shows varying degrees of formality. Note that 周 (*zhōu*) (week) is formal, 星期 (*xīngqī*) (week) is standard, and 礼拜 (*lǐbài*) (week) is informal.

| ENGLISH | CHINESE | | |
|---|---|---|---|
| | Standard | Informal[a] | Formal |
| Monday | 星期一 (xīngqīyī) | 礼拜一 (lǐbàiyī) | 周一 (zhōuyī) |
| Tuesday | 星期二 (xīngqī'èr) | 礼拜二 (lǐbài'èr) | 周二 (zhōu'èr) |
| Wednesday | 星期三 (xīngqīsān) | 礼拜三 (lǐbàisān) | 周三 (zhōusān) |
| Thursday | 星期四 (xīngqīsì) | 礼拜四 (lǐbàisì) | 周四 (zhōusì) |
| Friday | 星期五 (xīngqīwǔ) | 礼拜五 (lǐbàiwǔ) | 周五 (zhōuwǔ) |
| Saturday | 星期六 (xīngqīliù) | 礼拜六 (lǐbàiliù) | 周六 (zhōuliù) |
| Sunday | 星期日 (xīngqīrì) or 星期天[b] (xīngqītiān) | 礼拜日 (lǐbàirì) or 礼拜天 (lǐbàitiān) | 周日 (zhōurì) |
| Weekend | | | 周末[c] (zhōumò) |

[a] The expression 礼拜 (lǐbài) is generally used in spoken Chinese and is more colloquial than 星期 (xīngqī).
[b] 星期日 (xīngqīrì) is used more in written Chinese, whereas 星期天 (xīngqītiān) is used more in spoken Chinese.
[c] 周末 (zhōumò) is used in standard, informal, and formal Chinese. [See Lesson 4.]

### *Months*

| English | Chinese | Pinyin |
|---|---|---|
| January | 一月 | *yīyuè* |
| February | 二月 | *èryuè* |
| March | 三月 | *sānyuè* |
| April | 四月 | *sìyuè* |
| May | 五月 | *wǔyuè* |
| June | 六月 | *liùyuè* |
| July | 七月 | *qīyuè* |
| August | 八月 | *bāyuè* |
| September | 九月 | *jiǔyuè* |
| October | 十月 | *shíyuè* |
| November | 十一月 | *shíyīyuè* |
| December | 十二月 | *shí'èryuè* |

### *Dates*

In spoken Chinese, 号 *(hào)* (number) is used to refer to dates. However, in written Chinese, 日 *(rì)* (day) is used instead.

**A**

二月五号 (spoken)

*èryuè wǔ hào*

February 5

二月五日 (written)

*èryuè wǔ rì*

February 5

### *Year*

The word 年 *(nián)* (year) always follows the number referring to a specific year. Years are read one digit at a time.

**B**

一七八六年

*yī qī bā liù nián*

1786

二〇三九年

*èr líng sān jiǔ nián*

2039

### *Word order for dates*

To specify a date in Chinese, observe the following order.

| X年 *(X nián)* | X月 *(X yuè)* | X号/日 *(X hào/rì)* | 星期X *(xīngqī X)* |
|---|---|---|---|
| Year | Month | Day | Day of the Week |

**C**

二〇一九年七月二十六号/日星期五

*èr líng yī jiǔ nián qīyuè èrshíliù hào/rì, xīngqīwǔ*

Friday, July 26, 2019

More exercises

## EXERCISES

Say the following dates in Chinese.

1 Saturday, October 1, 1949

2 Friday, September 9, 1988

3 Tuesday, May 12, 2020

3

# Time

The terms used to tell the time are: 点 *(diǎn)*/点钟 *(diǎnzhōng)* (o'clock), 半 *(bàn)* (half hour), 刻 *(kè)* (quarter hour), and 分 *(fēn)* (minute).

### Hour

**A**

两点（钟）
*liǎng diǎn (zhōng)*
2:00

十一点（钟）
*shíyī diǎn (zhōng)*
11:00

钟 *(zhōng)* can be omitted from 点钟 *(diǎnzhōng)*. ✗ 二点（钟） is not used.

### Minute

**B**

十二点四十（分）
*shí'èr diǎn sìshí (fēn)*
12:40

五点二十（分）
*wǔ diǎn èrshí (fēn)*
5:20

两点〇五（分）
*liǎng diǎn líng wǔ (fēn)*
2:05

八点十分
*bā diǎn shí fēn*
8:10

When telling the time, 〇 *(líng)* (zero) is usually added before a single-digit number and 分 *(fēn)* (minute), e.g., 两点〇五分 *(liǎng diǎn líng wǔ fēn)* (2:05). 分 *(fēn)* can be omitted from the end of the expression if the number for the minutes appears in two syllables. Another way of looking at this is that 分 *(fēn)* has to be added if the number for the minutes appears in one syllable.

**C**

一点四十
*yī diǎn sìshí*
1:40

一点十分
*yī diǎn shí fēn*
1:10

[✗ 一点十]

两点〇五
*liǎng diǎn líng wǔ*
2:05

两点五分
*liǎng diǎn wǔ fēn*
2:05

[✗ 两点五]

*Quarter hour*

**D**

两点一刻
*liǎng diǎn yí kè*
2:15

十一点三刻
*shíyī diǎn sān kè*
11:45

[✖ 两刻 (two quarters) is not used]

*Half hour*

**E**

两点半
*liǎng diǎn bàn*
2:30

十二点半
*shí'èr diǎn bàn*
12:30

*Evening*

**F**

晚上七点（钟）
*wǎnshang qī diǎn (zhōng)*
7:00 p.m.

晚上八点〇五（分）
*wǎnshang bā diǎn líng wǔ (fēn)*
8:05 p.m.

晚上九点一刻
*wǎnshang jiǔ diǎn yí kè*
9:15 p.m.

晚上十点半
*wǎnshang shí diǎn bàn*
10:30 p.m.

Observe the temporal progression from general to specific and from largest to smallest unit.

More exercises

## EXERCISES

Say the following times in Chinese.

1 3:45
2 4:00
3 9:09 p.m.

## 4 Pronouns as modifiers and the particle 的 (*de*) (II)

When personal pronouns such as 我 (*wǒ*) (I), 我们 (*wǒmen*) (we), 你 (*nǐ*) (you), 他 (*tā*) (he), and 她 (*tā*) (she) are followed by a term indicating a close personal relationship, the particle 的 (*de*) can be omitted, e.g., 我妈妈 (*wǒ māma*) (my mother), 你弟弟 (*nǐ dìdi*) (your younger brother), 我们家 (*wǒmen jiā*) (our family). Otherwise 的 (*de*) is generally required, e.g., 他的医生 (*tā de yīshēng*) (his doctor), 我的照片 (*wǒ de zhàopiàn*) (my photo).

## 5 The sentence structure of 我请你吃饭 (*wǒ qǐng nǐ chī fàn*)

In the sentence 我请你吃饭 (*wǒ qǐng nǐ chī fàn*) (I will treat you to dinner), 你 (*nǐ*) (you) is the object of the verb 请 (*qǐng*) (to treat) as well as the subject of the second verb, 吃 (*chī*) (to eat).

**A** 明天李先生请你吃中国菜。

*Míngtiān Lǐ xiānsheng qǐng nǐ chī Zhōngguó cài.*

Mr. Li is inviting you to have Chinese food tomorrow.

**B** 今天晚上我请你和你妹妹吃美国菜，怎么样？

*Jīntiān wǎnshang wǒ qǐng nǐ hé nǐ mèimei chī Měiguó cài, zěnmeyàng?*

I'll treat you and your younger sister to American food tonight. How about it?

### EXERCISES

Rearrange the words to form a question, and then answer it.

1 谁 七点半 白英爱 吃饭 请 星期四

2 怎么样 吃饭 星期五 请 你 我

More exercises

## 6 Alternative questions

The structure (是)…还是… *([shì] . . . háishi . . .)* ( . . . or . . . ) is used to form an alternative question. If there is another verb used in the predicate, the first 是 *(shì)* (to be) can often be omitted.

**A** 你哥哥是老师还是学生?

*Nǐ gēge shì lǎoshī háishi xuésheng?*

Is your older brother a teacher or a student?

**B** Q: 他（是）喜欢吃中国菜还是喜欢吃美国菜?

*Tā (shì) xǐhuan chī Zhōngguó cài háishi xǐhuan chī Měiguó cài?*

Does he like to eat Chinese or American food?

A: 中国菜、美国菜他都喜欢（吃）。

*Zhōngguó cài, Měiguó cài tā dōu xǐhuan (chī).*

He likes both Chinese food and American food.

**C** 你是中国人还是美国人?

*Nǐ shì Zhōngguó rén háishi Měiguó rén?*

Are you Chinese or American?

**D** Q: 他（是）姓高还是姓王?

*Tā (shì) xìng Gāo háishi xìng Wáng?*

Is his family name Gao or Wang?

A: 他不姓高，也不姓王。他姓李。

*Tā bú xìng Gāo, yě bú xìng Wáng. Tā xìng Lǐ.*

His family name is not Gao or Wang. His family name is Li.

### EXERCISES

More exercises

In pairs, ask and answer these alternative questions.

1 你是中国人还是美国人?

2 李友有姐姐还是有妹妹?

# Language Practice

## A March madness INTERPERSONAL

**三月**

| 日 | 一 | 二 | 三 | 四 | 五 | 六 |
|---|---|---|---|---|---|---|
| | | | | 1 十二 | 2 十三 | 3 十四 |
| 4 十五 | 5 十六 | 6 惊蛰 | 7 十八 | 8 十九 | 9 二十 | 10 廿一 |
| 11 廿二 | 12 廿三 | 13 廿四 | 14 廿五 | 15 廿六 | 16 廿七 | 17 廿八 |
| 18 廿九 | 19 二月 | 20 初二 | 21 春分 | 22 初四 | 23 初五 | 24 初六 |
| 25 初七 | 26 初八 | 27 初九 | 28 初十 | 29 十一 | 30 十二 | 31 十三 |

In pairs, form a question-and-answer about dates based on the calendar above, e.g.:

三月二十一号

*sānyuè èrshíyī hào*

Q: 三月二十一号（是）星期几？

*Sānyuè èrshíyī hào (shì) xīngqījǐ?*

A: 三月二十一号（是）星期三。

*Sānyuè èrshíyī hào (shì) xīngqīsān.*

1 三月十八号 *sānyuè shíbā hào*

2 三月二十号 *sānyuè èrshí hào*

3 三月二十三号 *sānyuè èrshísān hào*

4 三月二十四号 *sānyuè èrshísì hào*

## B See you then

INTERPERSONAL

Based on the visual clues given, ask your partner what time you will meet, e.g.:

7:30 Q: 我们几点见?
*Wǒmen jǐ diǎn jiàn?*

A: 我们七点半见。
*Wǒmen qī diǎn bàn jiàn.*

1 

2 

3 

4 

## C When's your birthday?

INTERPERSONAL

Find out when people's birthdays are, e.g.:

Q: 高文中的生日（是）几月几号?
*Gāo Wénzhōng de shēngrì (shì) jǐ yuè jǐ hào?*

A: 高文中的生日（是）九月十二号。
*Gāo Wénzhōng de shēngrì (shì) jiǔyuè shí'èr hào.*

1 你
*nǐ*

2 你爸爸
*nǐ bàba*

3 你妈妈
*nǐ māma*

4 你哥哥/姐姐/弟弟/妹妹
*nǐ gēge/jiějie/dìdi/mèimei*

5 你们（的）老师
*nǐmen (de) lǎoshī*

## D Which is it? INTERPERSONAL

In pairs, form a question-and-answer by inserting 还是 *(háishi)* in the ◇, e.g.:

高大哥有儿子◇女儿

*Gāo dàgē yǒu érzi ◇ nǚ'ér*

Q: 高大哥有儿子还是有女儿? *Gāo dàgē yǒu érzi háishi yǒu nǚ'ér?*

A: 高大哥有儿子。 *Gāo dàgē yǒu érzi.*

1 王朋是学生◇老师 *Wáng Péng shì xuésheng ◇ lǎoshī*

2 高文中今年十八岁◇十九岁 *Gāo Wénzhōng jīnnián shíbā suì ◇ shíjiǔ suì*

3 白英爱的爸爸是医生◇律师 *Bái Yīng'ài de bàba shì yīshēng ◇ lǜshī*

4 李友是美国人◇英国人 *Lǐ Yǒu shì Měiguó rén ◇ Yīngguó rén*

5 你喜欢星期五◇星期六 *Nǐ xǐhuan xīngqīwǔ ◇ xīngqīliù*

6 你喜欢吃美国菜◇中国菜 *Nǐ xǐhuan chī Měiguó cài ◇ Zhōngguó cài*

## E Form a birthday dragon INTERPERSONAL

Mobilize the class to ask each other's birthday and form a line. Students whose birthdays are earlier in the year will line up before people whose birthdays are later. After the line is formed, the teacher will ask the first student: 你的生日（是）几月几号? *(Nǐ de shēngrì [shì] jǐ yuè jǐ hào?)*. After answering the question, the first student will ask the second student the same question, the second student will answer and ask the third, and so on. Then sing the "Happy Birthday" song in Chinese to the student with the most recent birthday:

祝你生日快乐 *zhù nǐ shēngrì kuàilè*

祝你生日快乐 *zhù nǐ shēngrì kuàilè*

祝你生日快乐 *zhù nǐ shēngrì kuàilè*

祝你生日快乐 *zhù nǐ shēngrì kuàilè*

## F INTERPERSONAL D.O.B. PRESENTATIONAL

Share your and your family's birthdays with a partner or the class. Your teacher will then ask questions about the information reported.

**Chris** 我的生日（是）______月______号，
我爸爸的生日（是）______月______号，
……

*Wǒ de shēngrì (shì)______yuè______hào,*

*wǒ bàba de shēngrì (shì)______yuè______hào,*

...

**Teacher** Chris 的生日（是）几月几号？
Chris 爸爸的生日（是）几月几号？

Chris *de shēngrì (shì) jǐ yuè jǐ hào?* Chris *bàba de shēngrì (shì) jǐ yuè jǐ hào?*

## G Let's eat! INTERPERSONAL

In pairs, ask and answer the following questions about food preferences.

Q: 你喜欢吃什么菜？
英国菜还是美国菜？
*Nǐ xǐhuan chī shénme cài?*
*Yīngguó cài háishi Měiguó cài?*

A: 我喜欢吃______菜。
*Wǒ xǐhuan chī ______cài.*

Q: 你喜欢吃______菜吗？
*Nǐ xǐhuan chī ______cài ma?*

A: 我也喜欢吃/我不喜欢吃______菜。
*Wǒ yě xǐhuan chī/Wǒ bù xǐhuan chī ______cài.*

*On festive occasions, Chinese give out red envelopes (红包) (hóngbāo) containing money for good fortune. What celebration is this envelope for?*

**GET Real WITH CHINESE**

## Characterize it!

1. 九
2. 星
3. 多
4. 日
5. 岁

Which of these characters are formed with the pattern on the right?

Top - Bottom

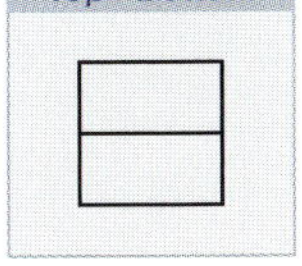

More characters

## Chinese Chat

You're discussing your upcoming birthday on WeChat with a friend. How would you reply to her question?

# Dinner Invitation

## Dialogue 2

Bai Ying'ai asks Wang Peng about his plans for tomorrow.

Audio

Video

白英爱，现在几点？

五点三刻。

我六点一刻有事儿。

你今天很忙[a]，明天忙不忙[6]？

我今天很忙，可是明天不忙。
有事儿吗？

明天我请你吃晚饭，怎么样？

你为什么请我吃饭？

因为明天是高文中的生日。

是吗？好。还[7]请谁？

还请我的同学李友。

那太好了，我认识李友，
她也是我的朋友。明天几点？

明天晚上七点半。

好，明天七点半见。

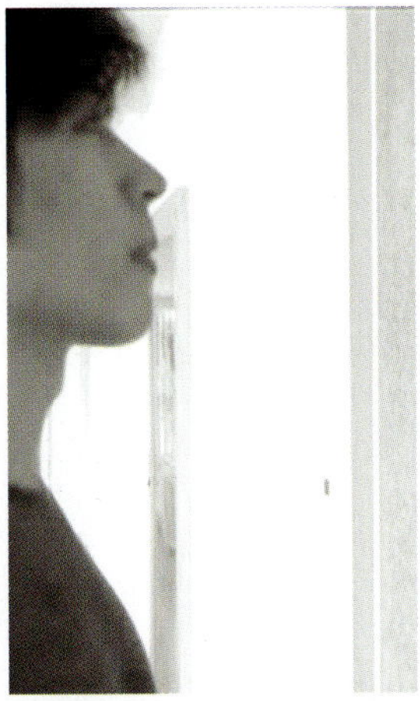

*Bái Yīng'ài, xiànzài jǐ diǎn?*

*Wǔ diǎn sān kè.*

*Wǒ liù diǎn yí kè yǒu shìr.*

*Nǐ jīntiān hěn máng* [a]*, míngtiān máng bu máng* [6]*?*

*Wǒ jīntiān hěn máng, kěshì míngtiān bù máng.*

*Yǒu shìr ma?*

*Míngtian wǒ qǐng nǐ chī wǎnfàn, zěnmeyàng?*

*Nǐ wèishénme qǐng wǒ chī fàn?*

*Yīnwèi míngtiān shì Gāo Wénzhōng de shēngrì.*

*Shì ma? Hǎo, hái* [7] *qǐng shéi?*

*Hái qǐng wǒ de tóngxué Lǐ Yǒu.*

*Nà tài hǎo le! Wǒ rènshi Lǐ Yǒu, tā yě shì*

*wǒ de péngyou. Míngtiān jǐ diǎn?*

*Míngtiān wǎnshang qī diǎn bàn.*

*Hǎo, míngtiān qī diǎn bàn jiàn.*

## Language Note

**a** 很 *(hěn)*

When an adjective functions as a predicate, it is usually preceded by adverbial modifiers such as 很 *(hěn)* (very). [See Grammar 2, Lesson 5.]

# Vocabulary

Audio

Flashcards

| No. | Word | Pinyin | Part of Speech | Definition |
|---|---|---|---|---|
| 1 | 现在 | *xiànzài* | t | now |
| 2 | 刻 | *kè* | m | quarter (of an hour) |
| 3 | 事（儿） | *shì(r)* | n | matter, affair, event |
| 4 | 今天 | *jīntiān* | t | today |
| 5 | 很 | *hěn* | adv | very |
| 6 | 忙 | *máng* | adj | busy |
| 7 | 明天 | *míngtiān* | t | tomorrow |
| 8 | 晚饭 | *wǎnfàn* | n | dinner, supper |
| 9 | 为什么 | *wèishénme* | qpr | why |
| | 为 | *wèi* | prep | for |
| 10 | 因为 | *yīnwèi* | conj | because |
| 11 | 还 | *hái* | adv | also, too, as well [See Grammar 8.] |
| 12 | 同学 | *tóngxué* | n | classmate |
| 13 | 认识 | *rènshi* | v | to be acquainted with, to recognize |
| 14 | 朋友 | *péngyou* | n | friend |

## How About You?

你的生日是几月几号？

*Nǐ de shēngrì shì jǐ yuè jǐ hào?*

When is your birthday?

我的生日是______月______号。

*Wǒ de shēngrì shì______yuè______hào.*

See Grammar 1 and 2 for vocabulary corresponding to dates.

# Grammar

## 7 Affirmative + negative (A-not-A) questions (I)

Besides adding the question particle 吗 (*ma*) to a declarative sentence, another common way of forming a question is to repeat the verb or adjective in its affirmative and negative form.

**A**

Q: 你今天忙不忙？

*Nǐ jīntiān máng bu máng?*

Are you busy today?

A: 我今天很忙。

*Wǒ jīntiān hěn máng.*

I am very busy today.

**B**

Q: 你妈妈喜欢不喜欢吃中国菜？

*Nǐ māma xǐhuan bu xǐhuan chī Zhōngguó cài?*

Does your mother like to eat Chinese food or not?

A: 我妈妈不喜欢吃中国菜。

*Wǒ māma bù xǐhuan chī Zhōngguó cài.*

My mother doesn't like to eat Chinese food.

**C**

Q: 请问，王律师今天有没有事儿？

*Qǐng wèn, Wáng lǜshī jīntiān yǒu méi yǒu shìr?*

Excuse me, is Lawyer Wang free today or not?

A: 王律师今天没有事儿。

*Wáng lǜshī jīntiān méi yǒu shìr.*

Lawyer Wang is free today.

### EXERCISES

Change the …吗 questions below into A-not-A questions. Use exercise 1 as an example.

More exercises

1 王朋是北京人吗？ → 王朋是不是北京人？

2 高文中的哥哥有儿子吗？

3 白英爱的爸爸是律师吗？

## 8 The adverb 还 (*hái*) (also, too, as well)

As an adverb, 还 (*hái*) (also, too, as well) indicates that the action or situation denoted by the verb involves someone or something else.

**A** 白英爱请高文中和王朋，还请李友。

*Bái Yīng'ài qǐng Gāo Wénzhōng hé Wáng Péng, hái qǐng Lǐ Yǒu.*

Bai Ying'ai is inviting Gao Wenzhong and Wang Peng, and Li You, too.

**B** 王朋喜欢吃中国菜，还喜欢吃美国菜。

*Wáng Péng xǐhuan chī Zhōngguó cài, hái xǐhuan chī Měiguó cài.*

Wang Peng likes to eat Chinese food, and American food, too.

More exercises

### EXERCISES

Add more information to the sentences by inserting 还 where appropriate. Use exercise 1 as an example.

1 高文中有姐姐。 哥哥

→ 高文中有姐姐，还有哥哥。

2 白英爱明天请高文中吃饭。 王朋

3 王朋认识白英爱。 李友

< Messages Ying Wang Contact

明天晚上忙吗？我请你吃饭。

...

明天星期六，也是我二十岁的生日。

...

你，还有我的同学小王。

...

晚上六点半，怎么样？

...

iMessage Send

**Chinese Chat**

You and a friend are using iMessage to set up a dinner date. How would you respond to finalize your plans?

# Language Practice

## H Just double-checking

INTERPERSONAL

In pairs, take turns rearranging the declarative sentence into an A-not-A question for your partner to answer, e.g.:

王朋是◇北京人 *Wáng Péng shì ◇ Běijīng rén*

Q: 王朋是不是北京人? *Wáng Péng shì bu shì Běijīng rén?*

A: 王朋是北京人。 *Wáng Péng shì Běijīng rén.*

1 今天是◇星期五 *jīntiān shì ◇ xīngqīwǔ*

______________________________

2 高大哥有◇女儿 *Gāo dàgē yǒu ◇ nǚ'ér*

______________________________

3 你喜欢◇高文中 *nǐ xǐhuan ◇ Gāo Wénzhōng*

______________________________

4 王朋认识◇白英爱 *Wáng Péng rènshi ◇ Bái Yīng'ài*

______________________________

5 我们的老师忙◇ *wǒmen de lǎoshī máng ◇*

______________________________

6 美国大◇ *Měiguó dà ◇*

______________________________

## I This and that

INTERPERSONAL

In pairs, ask and answer the following questions. Use 还 (*hái*), e.g.:

Q: 白英爱喜欢吃什么菜?

*Bái Yīng'ài xǐhuan chī shénme cài?*

A: 白英爱喜欢吃美国菜，还喜欢吃中国菜。

*Bái Yīng'ài xǐhuan chī Měiguó cài, hái xǐhuan chī Zhōngguó cài.*

1 Q: 白英爱请谁吃饭?

*Bái Yīng'ài qǐng shéi chī fàn?*

A: ____________________

2 Q: 李友认识谁?

*Lǐ Yǒu rènshi shéi?*

A: ____________________

## J When are you free?

INTERPERSONAL PRESENTATIONAL

Find out when your partner is free this week, e.g.:

Q: 你星期一忙不忙? *Nǐ xīngqīyī máng bu máng?*

A: 我星期一很忙/不忙。 *Wǒ xīngqīyī hěn máng/bù máng.*

How about Tuesday?

Q: 星期二呢? 你忙不忙? *Xīngqī'èr ne? Nǐ máng bu máng?*

A: …… . . .

Go through the days of the week. Then report to the class when your partner is free.

Emma 星期一、________、________……很忙，星期二、________、________……不忙。

Emma *xīngqīyī, ________, ________ . . . hěn máng, xīngqī'èr, ________, ________ . . . bù máng.*

## K Making dinner plans

INTERPERSONAL

Ask your friend out to dinner.

我星期____请你吃晚饭，怎么样？

*Wǒ xīngqī____qǐng nǐ chī wǎnfàn, zěnmeyàng?*

Your friend is busy that day, and suggests an alternative time:

星期____，我很忙。

*Xīngqī____, wǒ hěn máng.*

星期____，怎么样？

*Xīngqī____, zěnmeyàng?*

Your response:

________________________________________

Your friend wants to find out who else will be there, and asks:

你还请谁？

*Nǐ hái qǐng shéi?*

Your answer:

我还请________________________________________。

*Wǒ hái qǐng* ________________________________________.

**Chinese Chat**

Li You just posted this on Twitter during an evening out with friends. How do you think she is feeling?

Li You @liyou_88 • Aug 10

Follow

今天是我的生日，朋友请我吃饭！

25 28

# Pronunciation

Audio

Practice your pronunciation with the audio exercises below.

## 1 The initial r:

1 *shēngrì*
2 *rìjì*
3 *rèqíng*
4 *rénmín*
5 *réngrán*
6 *ránhòu*
7 *ruìlì*
8 *ràngbù*

## 2 Finals:

| | | | | | |
|---|---|---|---|---|---|
| 1 | *ie* | *jiè* | *xiě* | *qié* | *tiě* |
| 2 | *ue* | *jué* | *xué* | *quē* | *qiē* |
| 3 | *uo* | *duō* | *tuō* | *zuò* | *cuò* |
| 4 | *ou* | *dōu* | *tóu* | *zǒu* | *còu* |
| 5 | *u* | *zhū* | *chū* | *zū* | *cū* |

## 3 Two-syllable words:

1 *dāndāng*
2 *shōuhuò*
3 *qūchú*
4 *yúnwù*
5 *jiǎozhà*
6 *chūnqiū*
7 *juébié*
8 *kuìjiù*

## 4 The neutral tone:

1 *zhè ge*
2 *nà ge*
3 *wǒmen*
4 *nǐmen*
5 *wǎnshang*
6 *xièxie*
7 *xǐhuan*
8 *rènshi*

## 5 Tone sandhi:

[See D.2, Basics]

1 *zhǎnlǎn*
2 *lǚguǎn*
3 *yǔsǎn*
4 *qǔshě*
5 *shǒufǎ*
6 *yǔnxǔ*
7 *xuǎnjǔ*
8 *guǎngchǎng*

**GET Real WITH CHINESE**

*In addition to widely circulated papers like China's official People's Daily, vibrant local media serve Chinese communities worldwide. When was this issue of The China Press Weekly published?*

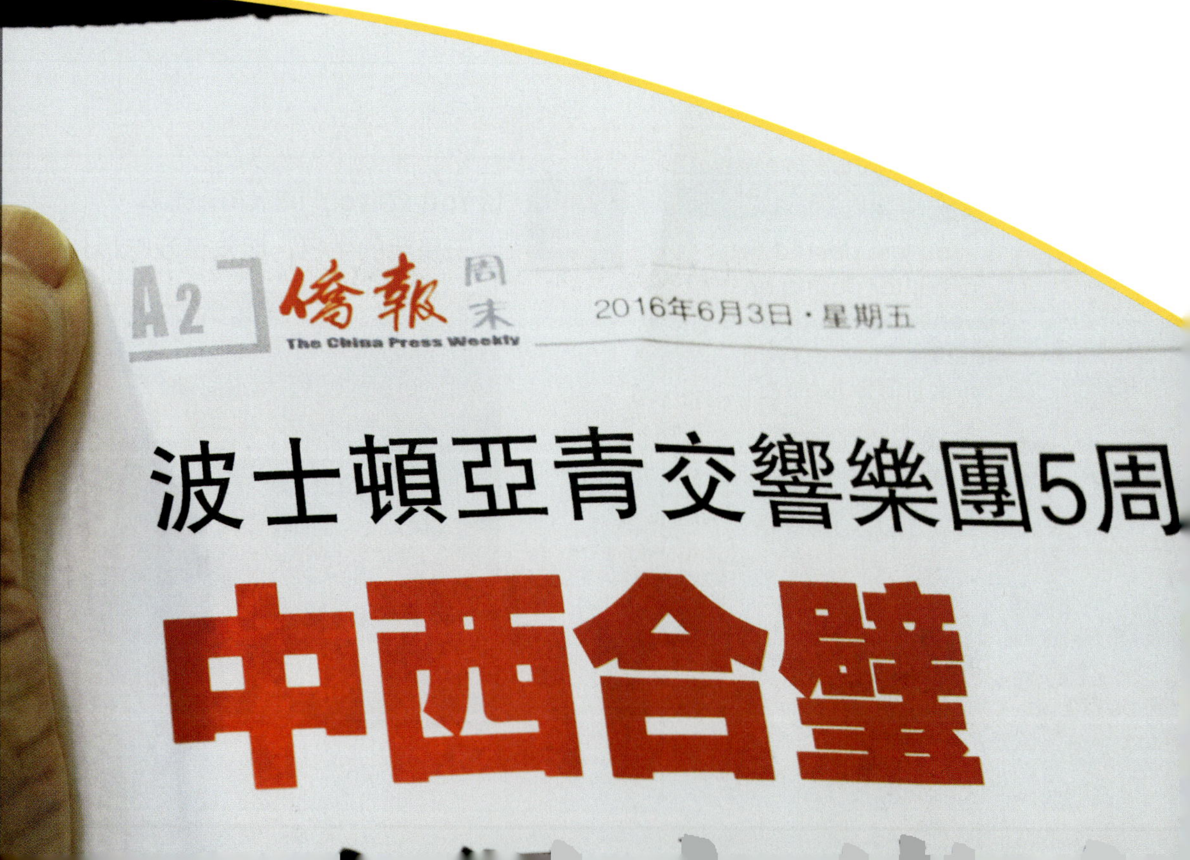

## Characterize it!

| What do the characters mean? |
| --- |
| What is the common radical? |
| What does the radical mean? |
| How does the radical relate to the overall meaning of the characters? |

1 星　2 晚　3 明

More characters

## Chinese Chat

You receive a group message from Bai Ying'ai about dinner plans on WeChat（微信）(*Wēixìn*), one of the most popular messaging apps in China. What would you need to ask in order to add the event to your calendar?

文化
Continue to explore

# Calendars

When you open a Chinese calendar, you will most likely see two different dates for any given day of the year, one according to the traditional lunar calendar and the other according to the international solar calendar. Typically, the lunar calendar date lags about one month behind its corresponding date in the solar calendar. In most years, the Lunar New Year falls in late January or early February.

## Age

The traditional Chinese manner of counting age, which is still in use among many (mainly older) people on non-official occasions, is based on the number of calendar years one has lived in, rather than the length of time in actual years that one has lived. For example, a child born in January 2016 is said to have turned two in January 2017, since the child has by then lived during two calendar years, 2016 and 2017. But for official purposes, for instance in the census, the child would still be considered one year old. The former is called the child's nominal age, 虚岁 *(xūsuì)*, and the latter his/her actual age, 实岁 *(shísuì)*.

## COMPARE & CONTRAST

1 Research holidays and festivals observed in Chinese-speaking countries. Are similar holidays and festivals observed in your own country or culture?

2 Certain numbers in Chinese are considered auspicious because they sound similar to words with lucky meanings. Look up the word 久 *(jiǔ)* in a dictionary. What number is it a homophone of, and why do you think this number is popular at weddings? Can you think of another culture in which numbers carry auspicious meaning?

## Birthday traditions

Noodles are the traditional Chinese equivalent of the birthday cake. Because of their length, they are considered a symbol of longevity. They are thus called longevity noodles, 长寿面 *(chángshòu miàn)*. Birthday cakes, however, are also increasingly popular in China.

# Lesson Wrap-Up

## Make It Flow!

Rearrange the following sentences into a logical sequence. Then combine them into a coherent narrative. Try to replace a proper noun with a personal pronoun and **星期四** *(xīngqīsì)* with **那天** *(nà tiān)* wherever appropriate.

_____星期四是高文中的生日。

__1__高文中今年十八岁。

_____白英爱星期四请高文中吃饭。

_____白英爱和高文中吃中国菜。

## Birthday Party

Share your date of birth with your classmates. If anyone is celebrating his or her birthday this or next month, organize a party to celebrate! Find out when everyone is free and what type of food they like. When everyone has agreed on the time, confirm it: **好** *(hǎo)*, _______**见** *(jiàn)*!

## Birthday Card

Write your friend's Chinese or English name and age, combined with **祝你生日快乐!** *(Zhù nǐ shēngrì kuài lè!)* (Happy Birthday), on a birthday card. Don't forget to date and sign it before delivery.

## Can-Do Check List

**Before proceeding to Lesson 4, make sure you can complete the following tasks in Chinese:**

**I can**

- Say and write times and dates
- Ask someone's age and birthday
- Give my age and birthday
- Name my favorite cuisine
- Ask about someone's availability and set up a dinner appointment

# Lesson 4

## 第四课

*Dì sì kè*

# 爱好

*Àihào*

# HOBBIES

## Learning Objectives

**In this lesson, you will learn to:**

- Name common hobbies
- Ask about someone's hobbies
- Make plans for the weekend with friends

## Relate & Get Ready

**In your own culture/community:**

- What are people's favorite pastimes?
- What do people usually do on weekends?

# Discussing Hobbies

## Dialogue 1

Gao Wenzhong asks Bai Ying'ai about her weekend plans and wants to invite her to a movie; however . . .

Audio

Video

白英爱，你周末喜欢做什么[1]？

我喜欢打球、看电视[a]。你呢？

我喜欢唱歌、跳舞，还喜欢听音乐。你也喜欢看书，对不对？

对，有的时候也喜欢看书。

你喜欢不喜欢[2]看电影？

喜欢。我周末常常看电影。

那[3]我们今天晚上去看[4]一个外国电影，怎么样？我请客。

为什么你请客？

因为昨天你请我吃饭，所以今天我请你看电影。

那你也请王朋、李友，好吗[5]？

……好。

## Pinyin Dialogue

*Bái Yīng'ài, nǐ zhōumò xǐhuan zuò shénme*[1]*?*

*Wǒ xǐhuan dǎ qiú, kàn diànshì*[a]*. Nǐ ne?*

*Wǒ xǐhuan chàng gē, tiào wǔ, hái xǐhuan tīng yīnyuè. Nǐ yě xǐhuan kàn shū, duì bu duì?*

*Duì, yǒude shíhou yě xǐhuan kàn shū.*

*Nǐ xǐhuan bu xǐhuan*[2] *kàn diànyǐng?*

*Xǐhuan. Wǒ zhōumò chángcháng kàn diànyǐng.*

*Nà*[3] *wǒmen jīntiān wǎnshang qù kàn*[4] *yí ge wàiguó diànyǐng, zěnmeyàng? Wǒ qǐng kè.*

*Wèishénme nǐ qǐng kè?*

*Yīnwèi zuótiān nǐ qǐng wǒ chī fàn, suǒyǐ jīntiān wǒ qǐng nǐ kàn diànyǐng.*

*Nà nǐ yě qǐng Wáng Péng, Lǐ Yǒu, hǎo ma*[5]*?*

*. . . Hǎo.*

## Language Note

**a** 、

When nouns or pronouns occur in a series, "、 " is used to separate them. The conjunction 和 (*hé*) connects the last two items in the series, e.g., 我、你和她 (*wǒ, nǐ hé tā*) (me, you, and her); 中国、美国、英国和法国 (*Zhōngguó, Měiguó, Yīngguó hé Fǎguó*) (China, United States, Britain, and France). The series comma can also be used between two or more verbs or adjectives, as in 我常常打球、跳舞、看电视 (*Wǒ chángcháng dǎ qiú, tiào wǔ, kàn diànshì*) (I often play ball, dance, and watch TV).

# Vocabulary

Audio

Flashcards

| No. | Word | Pinyin | Part of Speech | Definition |
|---|---|---|---|---|
| 1 | 周末 | *zhōumò* | n | weekend |
| 2 | 打球 | *dă qiú* | vo | to play ball |
| | 打 | *dă* | v | to hit |
| | 球 | *qiú* | n | ball |
| 3 | 看 | *kàn* | v | to watch, to look, to read |
| 4 | 电视 | *diànshì* | n | television |
| | 电 | *diàn* | n | electricity |
| | 视 | *shì* | n | vision |
| 5 | 唱歌（儿） | *chàng gē(r)* | vo | to sing (a song) |
| | 唱 | *chàng* | v | to sing |
| | 歌 | *gē* | n | song |
| 6 | 跳舞 | *tiào wŭ* | vo | to dance |
| | 跳 | *tiào* | v | to jump |
| | 舞 | *wŭ* | n | dance |
| 7 | 听 | *tīng* | v | to listen |
| 8 | 音乐 | *yīnyuè* | n | music |
| 9 | 书 | *shū* | n | book |
| 10 | 对 | *duì* | adj | right, correct |
| 11 | 有的 | *yŏude* | pr | some |
| 12 | 时候 | *shíhou* | n | (a point in) time, moment, (a duration of) time |
| 13 | 电影 | *diànyĭng* | n | movie |
| | 影 | *yĭng* | n | shadow |
| 14 | 常常 | *chángcháng* | adv | often |

*Your friend in Shanghai is taking you out for the night and gives you this ticket. Where will you be going?*

**GET Real WITH CHINESE**

| No. | Word | Pinyin | Part of Speech | Definition |
|---|---|---|---|---|
| 15 | 那 | *nà* | conj | in that case, then |
| 16 | 去 | *qù* | v | to go |
| 17 | 外国 | *wàiguó* | n | foreign country |
| 18 | 请客 | *qǐng kè* | vo | to invite someone (to dinner, coffee, etc.), to play the host |
| 19 | 昨天 | *zuótiān* | t | yesterday |
| 20 | 所以 | *suǒyǐ* | conj | so |

## 你周末喜欢做什么？

*Nǐ zhōumò xǐhuan zuò shénme?*

What do you like to do on weekends?

**How About You?**

我喜欢 ________。

*Wǒ xǐhuan ________.*

See index for corresponding vocabulary or research another term.

# Grammar

## 1 Word order

The basic word order in a Chinese sentence is as follows.

| **Subject** (agent of the action) | **Adverbial** (time, place, manner, etc.) | **Verb** | **(Object)** (receiver of the action) |
|---|---|---|---|
| 白医生 *Bái yīshēng* | 星期六、星期天 *xīngqīliù, xīngqītiān* | 工作 *gōngzuò* | |
| Dr. Bai works on Saturdays and Sundays. | | | |
| 王朋 *Wáng Péng* | 周末/常常 *zhōumò/chángcháng* | 听 *tīng* | 音乐 *yīnyuè* |
| Wang Peng often listens to music on weekends. | | | |
| 李友 *Lǐ Yǒu* | 明天 *míngtiān* | 吃 *chī* | 中国菜 *Zhōngguó cài* |
| Li You will have Chinese food tomorrow. | | | |
| 高文中 *Gāo Wénzhōng* | 今天下午五点半 *jīntiān xiàwǔ wǔ diǎn bàn* | 去看 *qù kàn* | 外国电影 *wàiguó diànyǐng* |
| Gao Wenzhong will go to see a foreign movie at 5:30 this afternoon. | | | |

While this is the most common word order in a Chinese sentence, the norm varies depending on context.

## 2 Affirmative + negative (A-not-A) questions (II)

In this type of question, there can be no adverbials before the verb other than time words, as in (A) and (B). If there is an adverbial—such as 都 *(dōu)* (both, all) or 常常 *(chángcháng)* (often)—before the verb, the 吗 *(ma)* type question must be used instead, as in (C) and (D). If there is more than one verb, the question form applies to the first verb, as seen in (E) and (F).

**A** 你明天去不去？

*Nǐ míngtiān qù bu qù?*

Are you going tomorrow?

**B** 她今天晚上看不看电视？

*Tā jīntiān wǎnshang kàn bu kàn diànshì?*

Is she going to watch TV tonight?

**C** 他们都是学生吗？ [✗ 他们都是不是学生？]

*Tāmen dōu shì xuésheng ma?*

Are they all students?

**D** 你常常看电影吗？ [✗ 你常常看不看电影？]

*Nǐ chángcháng kàn diànyǐng ma?*

Do you often go to the movies?

**E** 你喜欢不喜欢跳舞？ [✗ 你喜欢跳不跳舞？]

*Nǐ xǐhuan bu xǐhuan tiào wǔ?*

Do you like dancing?

**F** 你的同学去不去打球？

*Nǐ de tóngxué qù bu qù dǎ qiú?*

Are your classmates going to play ball?

[✗ 你的同学去打不打球？]

### EXERCISES

In pairs, form an A-not-A question-and-answer based on the information below. Use exercise 1 as an example.

More exercises

1 白英爱 明天 去跳舞

→ Q: 白英爱明天去不去跳舞？

A: 白英爱明天去/不去跳舞。

2 李友 今天晚上 听中国音乐

3 白英爱 明天晚上 请李友吃饭

## 3 The conjunction 那（么）(*nà [me]*) (then, in that case)

In conversation, immediately following a statement by speaker A, speaker B can often start with 那（么）(*nà [me]*) (then, in that case), which links up the sentences by the two speakers.

**A**

**Student A** 今天晚上没事儿。

*Jīntiān wǎnshang méi shìr.*

We have nothing to do tonight.

**Student B** 那么我们去看电影，怎么样？

*Nàme wǒmen qù kàn diànyǐng, zěnmeyàng?*

In that case, let's go to see a movie. How about that?

**Student A** 好，我请客。

*Hǎo, wǒ qǐng kè.*

OK, my treat.

**Student B** 是吗？太好了！

*Shì ma? Tài hǎo le.*

Really? Great!

**B**

**Student A** 我今天很忙，晚上不去吃晚饭。

*Wǒ jīntiān hěn máng, wǎnshang bú qù chī wǎnfàn.*

I'm very busy today, and will not go to dinner tonight.

**Student B** 那明天呢？

*Nà míngtiān ne?*

Then how about tomorrow?

**C** **Student A** 你喜欢不喜欢吃美国菜?

*Nǐ xǐhuan bu xǐhuan chī Měiguó cài?*

Do you like to eat American food or not?

**Student B** 不喜欢。

*Bù xǐhuan.*

No, I don't.

**Student A** 那我们吃中国菜，怎么样?

*Nà wǒmen chī Zhōngguó cài, zěnmeyàng?*

Then let's eat Chinese food. How about that?

**Student B** 我也不喜欢。

*Wǒ yě bù xǐhuan.*

I don't like that either.

## EXERCISES

Form questions based on the context, inserting 那（么） where appropriate. Use exercise 1 as an example.

More exercises

1 **Student A** 我今天不忙。

**Student B** 那我们去看电影，怎么样?

2 **Student A** 我不喜欢跳舞。

**Student B** ______________________________?

3 **Student A** 王朋星期六很忙。

**Student B** ______________________________?

## 4 去 (*qù*) (to go) + action

If the performance of an action involves a change of location, then use the construction below.

**A** 我们明天去看电影。

*Wǒmen míngtiān qù kàn diànyǐng.*

We are going to see a movie tomorrow.

**B** 周末我去跳舞，你去不去？

*Zhōumò wǒ qù tiào wǔ, nǐ qù bu qù?*

I'll go dancing this weekend. Are you going?

**C** 晚上我不去跳舞。

*Wǎnshang wǒ bú qù tiào wǔ.*

I will not go dancing tonight.

More exercises

### EXERCISES

Answer these questions, inserting the given verb phrases and 去 where appropriate. Use exercise 1 as an example.

1 Q: 李友明天晚上做什么？ 看中国电影

→ A: 李友明天晚上去看中国电影。

2 Q: 白英爱星期天晚上做什么？ 打球

3 Q: 王朋和李友今天晚上做什么？ 吃美国菜

## 5 Questions with 好吗 (*hǎo ma*) (OK?)

To solicit someone's opinion, we can ask 好吗 (*hǎo ma*) (OK?) after stating an idea or suggestion. As an alternative, we can also say 好不好 (*hǎo bu hǎo*) (all right?).

**A** 我们去看电影，好吗？

*Wǒmen qù kàn diànyǐng, hǎo ma?*

We'll go see a movie, OK?

**B** 我们今天晚上吃中国菜，好吗？

*Wǒmen jīntiān wǎnshang chī Zhōngguó cài, hǎo ma?*

We'll eat Chinese food tonight, OK?

# Language Practice

## A What a week! PRESENTATIONAL

Using the images below, take turns describing Little Wang's schedule this week, e.g.:

小王星期一看书。

*Xiǎo Wáng xīngqīyī kàn shū.*

1 星期一 *(xīngqīyī)* 

2 星期二 *(xīngqī'èr)* 

3 星期三 *(xīngqīsān)* 

4 星期四 *(xīngqīsì)* 

5 星期五 *(xīngqīwǔ)* 

6 星期六 *(xīngqīliù)* 

7 星期天 *(xīngqītiān)* 

What does your calendar look like? Share your schedule with the class, e.g.:

我星期一去跳舞。 *Wǒ xīngqīyī qù tiào wǔ.*

## B Shall we? INTERPERSONAL

In pairs, use the images to find out what your partner likes to do and invite him/her out tomorrow night by using 去 *(qù)* and 好吗 *(hǎo ma)*, e.g.:

Q: 你喜欢看电影吗？
我们明天晚上去看电影，好吗？
*Nǐ xǐhuan kàn diànyǐng ma?*
*Wǒmen míngtiān wǎnshang qù kàn diànyǐng, hǎo ma?*

A: 好！ (agreeing, confirming, accepting)
*Hǎo!*

A: 我明天很忙，也不喜欢看电影。 (declining)
*Wǒ míngtiān hěn máng, yě bù xǐhuan kàn diànyǐng.*

1  2  3  4 

## C That's why!

INTERPERSONAL

In pairs, form a question-and-answer about why you will or won't do something by using 因为…所以… (*yīnwèi . . . suǒyǐ . . .*), e.g.:

Q: 你为什么不去看电影？ （很忙）
*Nǐ weìshénme bú qù kàn diànyǐng?* (*hěn máng*)

A: 因为我很忙，所以不去看电影。
*Yīnwèi wǒ hěn máng, suǒyǐ bú qù kàn diànyǐng.*

1 你为什么不去打球？ （有事儿）
*Nǐ wèishénme bú qù dǎ qiú?* (*yǒu shìr*)

2 你为什么不去看外国电影？ （不喜欢）
*Nǐ wèishénme bú qù kàn wàiguó diànyǐng?* (*bù xǐhuan*)

3 你为什么星期五请我吃晚饭？ （你的生日）
*Nǐ wèishénme xīngqīwǔ qǐng wǒ chī wǎnfàn?* (*nǐ de shēngrì*)

4 你为什么不去跳舞？ （不喜欢）
*Nǐ wèishénme bú qù tiào wǔ?* (*bù xǐhuan*)

5 你为什么不听音乐？ （很忙）
*Nǐ wèishénme bù tīng yīnyuè?* (*hěn máng*)

### Characterize it!

Semi - Enclosing

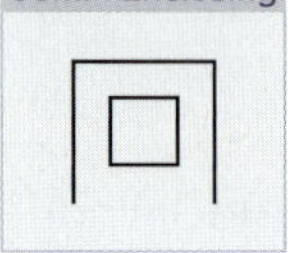

1 歌 2 问 3 去 4 电 5 同

Which of these characters are formed with the pattern on the left?

More characters

## D  Weekend warrior

INTERPERSONAL  PRESENTATIONAL

In pairs, find out what your partner likes to do on weekends, e.g.:

Q: 你周末喜欢做什么？

*Nǐ zhōumò xǐhuan zuò shénme?*

A: 我周末喜欢________________。

*Wǒ zhōumò xǐhuan* ________________.

Report to the class and be prepared to answer the teacher's questions.

Juan 周末喜欢做什么？

Juan *zhōumò xǐhuan zuò shénme?*

Kristen 呢？ Kristen 周末喜欢不喜欢看书？……

Kristen *ne?* Kristen *xǐhuan bù xǐhuan kàn shū?* . . .

## E  Trending now

INTERPERSONAL

Survey your classmates about their favorite singers, movie stars, athletes, and dancers using the questions below.

你喜欢听谁的歌？

你喜欢看谁的电影？

你喜欢看谁打球？

你喜欢看谁跳舞？

**Chinese Chat**

Wang Peng just shared a new status on WeChat and Li You left a comment. What is Li You proposing?

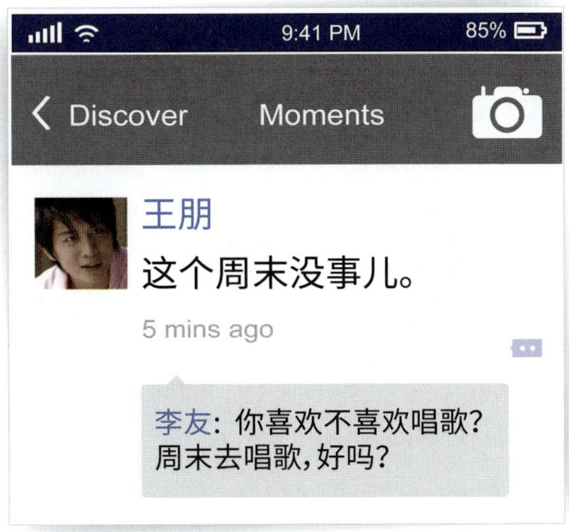

# Let's Play Ball

## Dialogue 2

Wang Peng visits Gao Wenzhong and invites him to play ball over the weekend.

Audio

Video

小高[a]，好久不见[b]，你好吗[c]？

我很好。你怎么样？

我也不错。这个周末你想[6]做什么？想不想去打球？

打球？我不喜欢打球。

那我们去看球，怎么样？

看球？我觉得看球也没有意思[d]。

那你这个周末想做什么？

我只想吃饭、睡觉[7][e]。

算了，我去找别人。

### Pinyin Dialogue

*Xiǎo Gāo*[a], *hǎo jiǔ bú jiàn*[b], *nǐ hǎo ma*[c]?

*Wǒ hěn hǎo. Nǐ zěnmeyàng?*

*Wǒ yě búcuò. Zhè ge zhōumò nǐ xiǎng*[6] *zuò shénme? Xiǎng bu xiǎng qù dǎ qiú?*

*Dǎ qiú? Wǒ bù xǐhuan dǎ qiú.*

*Nà wǒmen qù kàn qiú, zěnmeyàng?*

*Kàn qiú? Wǒ juéde kàn qiú yě méiyǒu yìsi*[d].

*Nà nǐ zhè ge zhōumò xiǎng zuò shénme?*

*Wǒ zhǐ xiǎng chī fàn, shuì jiào*[7][e].

*Suàn le, wǒ qù zhǎo biérén.*

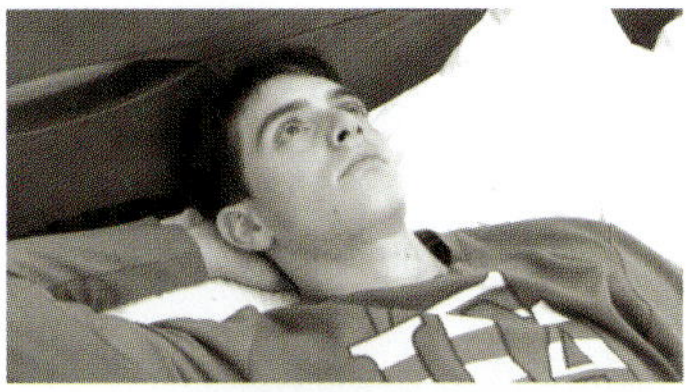

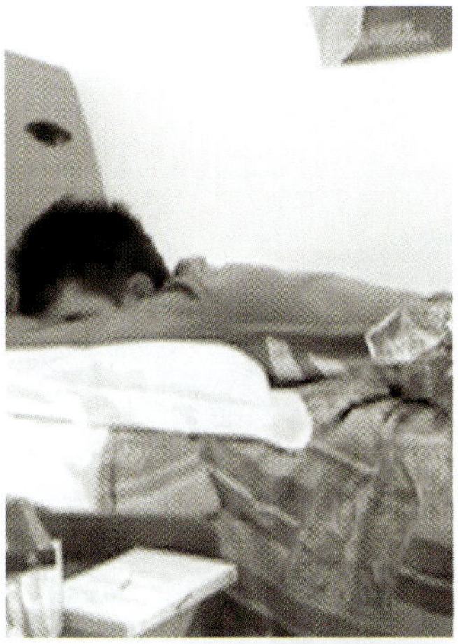

## Language Notes

**a** 小 *(xiǎo)*

A familiar and affectionate way of addressing a young person is to add 小 *(xiǎo)* (little, small) to the family name, e.g., 小王 *(Xiǎo Wáng)* (Little Wang). Similarly, to address an older acquaintance, 老 *(lǎo)* (old) can be used with the family name, e.g., 老王 *(Lǎo Wáng)* (Old Wang). However, such terms are rarely used to address a relative or a superior.

**b** 好久不见 *(hǎo jiǔ bú jiàn)*

Now you know where the expression "Long time no see" comes from.

**c** 你好吗？ *(Nǐ hǎo ma?)*

This question (meaning "How are you?") is typically asked of people you already know. The answer is usually 我很好 *(Wǒ hěn hǎo)* (I am fine).

**d** 觉得没有意思 *(juéde méiyǒu yìsi)*

The position of negatives in Chinese is not always the same as it is in English. An English speaker would say: "I don't think going to the movies is much fun," but a Chinese speaker would say 我觉得看电影没有意思 *(Wǒ juéde kàn diànyǐng méiyǒu yìsi)*, which literally means, "I think going to the movies is not much fun."

**e** 觉 *(jué/jiào)*

The character 觉 is pronounced in two different ways and has two different meanings: *jué* as in 觉得 *(juéde)* (to feel) and *jiào* as in 睡觉 *(shuì jiào)* (to sleep).

# Vocabulary

Audio

Flashcards

| No. | Word | Pinyin | Part of Speech | Definition |
|---|---|---|---|---|
| 1 | 小 | *xiǎo* | adj | small, little |
| 2 | 好久 | *hǎo jiǔ* | | a long time |
| | 好 | *hǎo* | adv | very |
| | 久 | *jiǔ* | adj | long (of time) |
| 3 | 不错 | *búcuò* | adj | pretty good |
| | 错 | *cuò* | adj | wrong |
| 4 | 想 | *xiǎng* | mv | to want to, would like to [See Grammar 6.] |
| 5 | 觉得 | *juéde* | v | to feel, to think [See Grammar 6.] |

**GET Real WITH CHINESE**

*Your roommate puts this on before lying down on the couch. What is she trying to tell you?*

| No. | Word | Pinyin | Part of Speech | Definition |
|---|---|---|---|---|
| 6 | 有意思 | *yǒu yìsi* | adj | interesting |
| | 意思 | *yìsi* | n | meaning |
| 7 | 只 | *zhǐ* | adv | only |
| 8 | 睡觉 | *shuì jiào* | vo | to sleep |
| | 睡 | *shuì* | v | to sleep |
| | 觉 | *jiào* | n | sleep |
| 9 | 算了 | *suàn le* | | forget it, never mind |
| 10 | 找 | *zhǎo* | v | to look for |
| 11 | 别人 | *biérén* | n | other people, another person |
| | 别（的） | *bié (de)* | adj | other |

## 这个周末你想做什么？

*Zhè ge zhōumò nǐ xiǎng zuò shénme?*

What would you like to do this weekend?

### How About You?

我想____________________。

*Wǒ xiǎng* ____________________.

See index for corresponding vocabulary or research another term.

# Grammar

## 6 The modal verb 想 *(xiǎng)* (want to, would like to)

想 *(xiǎng)* has several meanings. In this lesson, it is a modal verb indicating a desire to do something. It must be followed by a verb or a clause.

**A** 你想听音乐吗？

*Nǐ xiǎng tīng yīnyuè ma?*

Would you like to listen to some music?

**B** 白老师想打球，可是王老师不想打。

*Bái lǎoshī xiǎng dǎ qiú, kěshì Wáng lǎoshī bù xiǎng dǎ.*

Teacher Bai felt like playing ball, but Teacher Wang didn't.

**C** 你想不想看中国电影？

*Nǐ xiǎng bu xiǎng kàn Zhōngguó diànyǐng?*

Do you feel like going to see a Chinese movie?

**D** 你想不想听外国音乐？

*Nǐ xiǎng bu xiǎng tīng wàiguó yīnyuè?*

Do you feel like listening to some foreign music?

**想 *(xiǎng)* vs. 喜欢 *(xǐhuan)***

想 *(xiǎng)* can be translated as "would like to" or "to have a desire to." 喜欢 *(xǐhuan)* is "to like," meaning "to be fond of." 想 *(xiǎng)* and 喜欢 *(xǐhuan)* are different, and are not interchangeable.

**想 *(xiǎng)* vs. 觉得 *(juéde)***

Both 想 *(xiǎng)* and 觉得 *(juéde)* can be translated as "to think," but the former is used to express a desire, whereas the latter is to express an opinion or comment on something.

**EXERCISES**

In pairs, form a question-and-answer about your partner's intent, inserting 想 where appropriate. Use exercise 1 as an example.

More exercises

1 吃中国菜

→ Q: 你晚上想吃中国菜吗？

A: 我想吃中国菜。 (affirmative)

A: 我不想吃中国菜。 (negative)

2 请同学去看电影

3 去听中国音乐

## 7 Verb + object as a detachable compound

Even though 睡觉 *(shuì jiào)* (to sleep), 唱歌 *(chàng gē)* (to sing), and 跳舞 *(tiào wǔ)* (to dance) are each treated as a word, grammatically speaking, they are all verb-object compounds. When an attributive element modifies the object, such as an adjective or a number-measure word combination, it must be inserted between the verb and the noun. Such a compound does not take an object, and is called a "detachable compound."

| | | |
|---|---|---|
| A | 睡觉<br>*shuì jiào*<br>to sleep | 睡一个好觉<br>*shuì yí ge hǎo jiào*<br>have a good sleep |
| B | 唱歌<br>*chàng gē*<br>to sing | 唱英文歌<br>*chàng Yīngwén gē*<br>sing an English song |
| C | 跳舞<br>*tiào wǔ*<br>to dance | 跳中国舞<br>*tiào Zhōngguó wǔ*<br>do a Chinese dance |

In later lessons, you will see examples of other elements, like aspect markers, being inserted between the verb and the object in a detachable compound.

# Language Practice

## F Let the weekend begin!

INTERPERSONAL

In pairs, discuss what you'd like to do over the weekend by using 想 *(xiǎng)*, e.g.:

Q: 你周末想不想打球?

*Nǐ zhōumò xiǎng bu xiǎng dǎ qiú?*

A: 我（周末）想打球。(affirmative)

*Wǒ zhōumò xiǎng dǎ qiú.*

A: 我（周末）不想打球。(negative)

*Wǒ zhōumò bu xiǎng dǎ qiú.*

1 

2 

3 

4 

5 

## G How interesting

INTERPERSONAL PRESENTATIONAL

In pairs, determine your partner's interest level in these activities and report to the class by using 很有意思 *(hěn yǒu yìsi)* or 没有意思 *(méiyǒu yìsi)*, e.g.:

| | |
|---|---|
| 打球（小高） | 小高觉得打球很有意思。 |
| *dǎ qiú (Xiǎo Gāo)* | *Xiǎo Gāo juéde dǎ qiú hěn yǒu yìsi.* |

1 跳舞
*tiào wǔ*

2 听中国音乐
*tīng Zhōngguó yīnyuè*

3 看外国电影
*kàn wàiguó diànyǐng*

4 看英文书
*kàn Yīngwén shū*

5 看电视
*kàn diànshì*

## H Weekend ahead

INTERPERSONAL

In pairs, complete these sentences and role-play the discussion about the weekend ahead.

Q: 你这个周末想做什么？

*Nǐ zhè ge zhōumò xiǎng zuò shénme?*

A: 我这个周末想____________________。

*Wǒ zhè ge zhōumò xiǎng* ____________________.

Then find out if your partner feels like doing something else this weekend.

Q: 你想____________________吗？

*Nǐ xiǎng* ____________________ *ma?*

A: 我想____________________。 (affirmative)

*Wǒ xiǎng* ____________________.

A: 我不想____________________。 (negative)

*Wǒ bù xiǎng* ____________________.

What types of activities does your partner think are interesting?

Q: 你觉得（看电影、打球，etc.）有意思吗？

*Nǐ juéde (kàn diànyǐng, dǎ qiú,* etc.*) yǒu yìsi ma?*

A: 我觉得____________________很有意思。 (affirmative)

*Wǒ juéde* ____________________*hěn yǒu yìsi.*

A: 我觉得____________________没有意思。 (negative)

*Wǒ juéde* ____________________*méi yǒu yìsi.*

### Characterize it!

**What do the characters mean?**

**What is the common radical?**

**What does the radical mean?**

**How does the radical relate to the overall meaning of the characters?**

1 想

2 思

More characters

文化
Continue to explore

# MAHJONG

Mahjong, 麻将 (*májiàng*), is one of the most popular Chinese pastimes, involving four players. To win, one has to draw various tiles to form different combinations, which have all been assigned scores based on pre-set rules. The more difficult the combination, the higher the score. There are usually four games in each round, and the players can decide how many rounds they wish to play. Normally, people play either eight or twelve rounds.

The two teams of Chinese chess pieces are identified by colors, typically black and red. They are set up as shown. Since you have learned the character/radical meaning "horse," can you find where the "horse" is on the board?

Chinese chess, 象棋 (*xiàngqí*), is another popular pastime, especially among senior citizens. While international chess has such pieces as king, queen, rook, knight, and pawn, Chinese chess has commander-in-chief, general, chariot, horse, and soldier. Both mahjong and Chinese chess go back centuries. Community centers and clubhouses in China often have a 棋牌室 (*qípáishì*), or chess-and-poker room, where residents, especially retirees, meet for chess and mahjong marathons. In neighborhood parks, it is also common to find onlookers gathering around chess players.

# CHINESE CHESS

## COMPARE & CONTRAST

1 Organize a lunch or dinner with two or three friends. Use the end of Dialogue 1 as a model. Decide if you want to treat or to split the bill with your friends by using 今天我请客 (*Jīntiān wǒ qǐngkè*) or 我们今天AA制 (*Wǒmen jīntiān AA zhì*), explained below. How often do people treat in your culture?

2 Nowadays, binge-watching is a hobby for many people. Dramas produced in Mainland China and Taiwan have been gaining popularity in many Chinese-speaking countries, and even among viewers who do not speak Chinese. Research some of the most popular Chinese dramas. How do they compare with popular dramas in your own country?

## Go

Arguably less popular but more prestigious is the game of Encirclement, 围棋 (*wéiqí*), better known in the West by its Japanese name, Go. It is a deceptively simple game played with counters or stones on a board. The objective of the game is to surround and capture the opponent's counters. Every year, major corporations sponsor tournaments with master players from China, Japan, and South Korea participating and TV stations providing live coverage of important matches.

## FEASTING

When Chinese people go out to eat with friends, they rarely split the check. Usually, someone will insist on picking up the tab by saying 今天我请客 (*Jīntiān wǒ qǐngkè*) (It's my treat today). The unspoken expectation is that someone else will offer to pay the next time. Often, more than one person will reach for the bill and there might be a little struggle over who gets to pay. Among young urban white-collar professionals and college students, it is increasingly common to separate the check or adopt the AA制 (*AA zhì*) except on celebratory or festive occasions.

# Lesson Wrap-Up

## Make It Flow!

Rearrange the following sentences into a logical sequence according to Gao Wenzhong and Bai Ying'ai's likes and dislikes. Then combine them into a coherent narrative. If the subject is the same, remember not to repeat it in subsequent clauses. Replace the proper noun in the previous clause with a personal pronoun if beginning a new sentence.

____高文中不喜欢打球。

____白英爱还喜欢看电影。

____高文中觉得看球没有意思。

__1__高文中喜欢唱歌、跳舞。

____白英爱喜欢打球、看电视。

____白英爱有的时候也喜欢看书。

____高文中还喜欢听音乐。

____白英爱周末常常去看电影。

____高文中也不喜欢看球。

## Interview

Interview your classmates about what their families like to do.

你爸爸、妈妈喜欢做什么？

你哥哥、姐姐、弟弟、妹妹喜欢做什么？

## Hang Out

Do your classmates share your interests? Survey them about their hobbies on social media: 你喜欢……？ (*Nǐ xǐhuan . . . ?*). Arrange a time to hang out with classmates who share your interests.

## Can-Do Check List

Before proceeding to Lesson 5, be sure you can complete the following tasks in Chinese:

I can

- Talk about my favorite pastimes and ask about someone else's
- Comment on whether certain activities appeal to me
- Invite someone to do something over the weekend
- Accept or decline an invitation to do something over the weekend

# Lesson 5

## 第五课

*Dì wǔ kè*

# 看朋友

*Kàn péngyou*

# VISITING FRIENDS

## Learning Objectives

**In this lesson, you will learn to:**

- Welcome a visitor
- Introduce one person to another
- Be a gracious guest
- Ask for beverages as a guest
- Offer beverages to a visitor
- Briefly describe a visit to a friend's place

## Relate & Get Ready

**In your own culture/community:**

- Is it common to visit a friend's place without advance notice?
- Do people bring anything when visiting a friend's home?
- What food and drinks do hosts commonly offer guests?

# Visiting a Friend's Place

## Dialogue

Audio

Video

Wang Peng and Li You visit Gao Wenzhong and meet his sister, Gao Xiaoyin.
(The doorbell rings.)

谁呀？

是我，王朋，还有李友。

请进，请进，快进来！来，我介绍一下[1]，这是我姐姐，高小音。

小音，你好。认识你很高兴。

认识你们我也很高兴。

你们家很大[2]，也很漂亮。

是吗？[a] 请坐，请坐。

小音，你在[3]哪儿[b]工作？

我在学校工作。你们想喝点儿[1]什么？喝茶还是喝咖啡？

我喝茶吧[4]。

我要一瓶可乐，可以吗？

对不起，我们家没有可乐。

那给我一杯水吧。

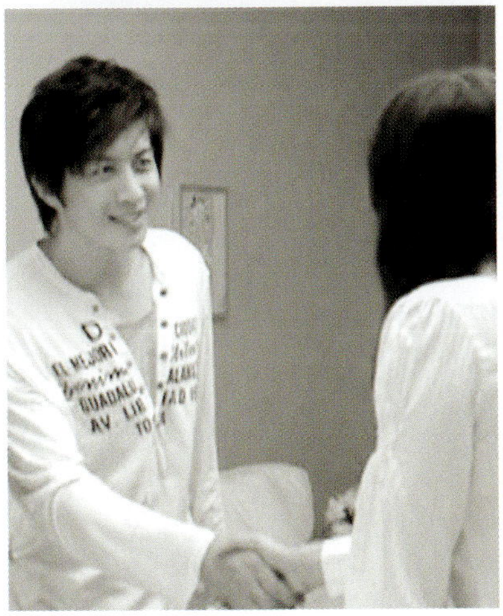

(The doorbell rings.)

*Shéi ya?*

*Shì wǒ, Wáng Péng, hái yǒu Lǐ Yǒu.*

*Qǐng jìn, qǐng jìn, kuài jìn lai! Lái, wǒ jièshào yí xià*[1]*, zhè shì wǒ jiějie, Gāo Xiǎoyīn.*

*Xiǎoyīn, nǐ hǎo. Rènshi nǐ hěn gāoxìng.*

*Rènshi nǐmen wǒ yě hěn gāoxìng.*

*Nǐmen jiā hěn dà*[2]*, yě hěn piàoliang.*

*Shì ma?*[a] *Qǐng zuò, qǐng zuò.*

*Xiǎoyīn, nǐ zài*[3] *nǎr*[b] *gōngzuò?*

*Wǒ zài xuéxiào gōngzuò. Nǐmen xiǎng hē diǎnr*[1] *shénme? Hē chá háishi hē kāfēi?*

*Wǒ hē chá ba*[4]*.*

*Wǒ yào yì píng kělè, kěyǐ ma?*

*Duìbuqǐ, wǒmen jiā méi yǒu kělè.*

*Nà gěi wǒ yì bēi shuǐ ba.*

## Language Notes

**a** 是吗? *(Shì ma?)*

"Is that so?" or "Really?" It is a rhetorical question here. This is a modest way to respond to a compliment.

**b** 哪儿 *(nǎr)*

A question word meaning "where." Do not confuse it with 那儿 *(nàr)* (there). "Here" is 这儿 *(zhèr)*.

# Vocabulary

Audio

Flashcards

| No. | Word | Pinyin | Part of Speech | Definition |
|---|---|---|---|---|
| 1 | 呀 | *ya* | p | (interjectory particle used to soften a question) |
| 2 | 进 | *jìn* | v | to enter |
| 3 | 快 | *kuài* | adv/adj | fast, quick; quickly |
| 4 | 进来 | *jìn lai* | vc | to come in |
| 5 | 来 | *lái* | v | to come |
| 6 | 介绍 | *jièshào* | v | to introduce |
| 7 | 一下 | *yí xià* | n+m | once, a bit [See Grammar 1.] |
| 8 | 高兴 | *gāoxìng* | adj | happy, pleased |
| 9 | 漂亮 | *piàoliang* | adj | pretty |
| 10 | 坐 | *zuò* | v | to sit |
| 11 | 在 | *zài* | prep | at, in, on [See Grammar 3.] |
| 12 | 哪儿 | *nǎr* | qpr | where |
| 13 | 学校 | *xuéxiào* | n | school |
| 14 | 喝 | *hē* | v | to drink |
| 15 | 点（儿） | *diǎn(r)* | m | a little, a bit, some [See Grammar 1.] |
| 16 | 茶 | *chá* | n | tea |
| 17 | 咖啡 | *kāfēi* | n | coffee |
| 18 | 吧 | *ba* | p | (a sentence-final particle) [See Grammar 4.] |
| 19 | 要 | *yào* | v | to want |
| 20 | 瓶 | *píng* | m | (measure word for bottled liquid, etc.) |
| 21 | 可乐 | *kělè* | n | cola |

*China's booming soft drinks market offers consumers a variety of choices. Can you identify these flavors?*

**GET Real WITH CHINESE**

| No. | Word | Pinyin | Part of Speech | Definition |
|---|---|---|---|---|
| 22 | 可以 | *kěyǐ* | mv | can, may |
| 23 | 对不起 | *duìbuqǐ* | v | sorry |
| 24 | 给 | *gěi* | v | to give |
| 25 | 杯 | *bēi* | m | (measure word for things contained in a cup or glass) |
| 26 | 水 | *shuǐ* | n | water |
| 27 | 高小音 | *Gāo Xiǎoyīn* | pn | (a personal name) |

## How About You?

**你喜欢喝什么？**

*Nǐ xǐhuan hē shénme?*

What do you like to drink?

我喜欢喝 ________。

*Wǒ xǐhuan hē* ________.

See index for corresponding vocabulary or research another term.

# Grammar

## 1 Moderating tone of voice: 一下 *(yí xià)* and （一）点儿 *(\[yì\] diǎnr)*

Following a verb, both 一下 *(yí xià)* (lit. "once") and （一）点儿 *([yì] diǎnr)* ("a bit") can soften the tone of a question or an imperative sentence, making it more polite. When used in this way, 一下 *(yí xià)* modifies the verb, while （一）点儿 *([yì] diǎnr)* modifies the object.

**A** 你看一下，这是谁的照片？

*Nǐ kàn yí xià, zhè shì shéi de zhàopiàn?*

Take a look. Whose photo is this?

**B** 你想吃点儿什么？

*Nǐ xiǎng chī diǎnr shénme?*

What would you like to eat?

**C** 你进来一下。

*Nǐ jìn lai yí xià.*

Come in for a minute.

**D** 你喝一点儿茶吧。

*Nǐ hē yì diǎnr chá ba.*

Have some tea.

More exercises

### EXERCISES

Moderate the tone of these sentences by inserting 一下 or （一）点儿.

Use exercise 1 as an example.

1 我看________你的照片 → 我看一下你的照片。

2 我看________你的书。

3 你喝________咖啡。

## 2 Adjectives as predicates using 很 *(hěn)* (very)

When an adjective functions as a predicate, it is not preceded by the verb 是 *(shì)* (to be). It is usually modified by 很 *(hěn)* (very)—as in (A), (B), (C), and (D)—or some other adverbial modifier. Although usually translated as "very," 很 *(hěn)* is not quite as strong as its English equivalent when not stressed. It acts as an affirmative indicator. When forming a question with an adjective as the predicate, 很 *(hěn)* is not used, as in (E) and (F).

**A** 我今天很高兴。

*Wǒ jīntiān hěn gāoxìng.*

I'm very happy today.

**B** 他妹妹很漂亮。

*Tā mèimei hěn piàoliang.*

His younger sister is very pretty.

**C** 那个电影很好。

*Nà ge diànyǐng hěn hǎo.*

That movie is very good.

**D** 你们大学很大。

*Nǐmen dàxué hěn dà.*

Your university is very large.

**E** Q: 你弟弟高吗?

*Nǐ dìdi gāo ma?*

Is your younger brother tall?

A: 他很高。

*Tā hěn gāo.*

He is very tall.

**F** Q: 你家大吗?

*Nǐ jiā dà ma?*

Is your house big?

A: 我家不大，很小。

*Wǒ jiā bú dà, hěn xiǎo.*

My house is not big; it's very small.

Chinese adjectives without 很 (*hěn*) or any sort of modifier before them can often imply comparison or contrast, as in (G) and (H).

**G** Q: 姐姐忙还是妹妹忙?

*Jiějie máng háishi mèimei máng?*

Who's busier, the older sister or the younger sister?

A: 妹妹忙。

*Mèimei máng.*

The younger sister is busier.

**H** 哥哥的中文好，我的中文不好。

*Gēge de Zhōngwén hǎo, wǒ de Zhōngwén bù hǎo.*

My older brother's Chinese is good. My Chinese is not good.

More exercises

### EXERCISES

Use adjectives as predicates by inserting 很. Use exercise 1 as an example.

1 我弟弟______高。→ 我弟弟很高。

2 我妹妹今天______高兴。

3 王律师的中文______好。

## 3 The preposition 在 (*zài*) (at, in, on)

在 (*zài*) is a verb in (A).

**A** Q: 我的书在哪儿?

*Wǒ de shū zài nǎr?*

Where is my book?

A: 在那儿。

*Zài nàr.*

It's over there.

It is a preposition when a "在 (*zài*) + location" appears before a verb, as in (B), (C), and (D).

**B** Q: 你在哪儿工作?

*Nǐ zài nǎr gōngzuò?*

Where do you work?

A: 我在这儿工作。

*Wǒ zài zhèr gōngzuò.*

I work here.

# At a Friend's Place

## Narrative

Wang Peng and Li You visited Gao Wenzhong and Gao Xiayon.

Audio

Video

昨天晚上，王朋和李友去高文中家玩儿。在高文中家，他们认识了[5]高文中的姐姐。她叫高小音，在学校的图书馆工作。她请王朋喝[a]茶，王朋喝了[5]两杯。李友不喝茶，只喝了一杯水。他们一起聊天儿、看电视。王朋和李友晚上十二点才[6]回家。

### Pinyin Narrative

*Zuótiān wǎnshang, Wáng Péng hé Lǐ Yǒu qù Gāo Wénzhōng jiā wánr. Zài Gāo Wénzhōng jiā, tāmen rènshi le*[5] *Gāo Wénzhōng de jiějie. Tā jiào Gāo Xiǎoyīn, zài xuéxiào de túshūguǎn gōngzuò. Tā qǐng Wáng Péng hē*[a] *chá, Wáng Péng hē le*[5] *liǎng bēi. Lǐ Yǒu bù hē chá, zhǐ hē le yì bēi shuǐ. Tāmen yìqǐ liáo tiānr, kàn diànshì. Wáng Péng hé Lǐ Yǒu wǎnshang shí'èr diǎn cái*[6] *huí jiā.*

### Language Note

**a** 喝 *(hē)*

Unlike its English counterpart, 喝 *(hē)* always functions as a transitive verb, i.e., unless it's clear from the context, the beverage has to be specified. Therefore, 他常常喝 *(Tā chángcháng hē)* is not a complete sentence unless the beverage is understood; e.g., when it occurs as an affirmative answer to a question:

| | |
|---|---|
| **Q:** 他常常喝咖啡吗？ | **A:** 他常常喝。 |
| *Tā chángcháng hē kāfēi ma?* | *Tā chángcháng hē.* |
| Does he often drink coffee? | He often does. |

# Vocabulary

Audio

Flashcards

| No. | Word | Pinyin | Part of Speech | Definition |
|---|---|---|---|---|
| 1 | 玩（儿） | *wán(r)* | v | to have fun, to play |
| 2 | 了 | *le* | p | (a dynamic particle) [See Grammar 5.] |
| 3 | 图书馆 | *túshūguǎn* | n | library |
| 4 | 一起 | *yìqǐ* | adv | together |
| 5 | 聊天（儿） | *liáo tiān(r)* | vo | to chat |
| | 聊 | *liáo* | v | to chat |
| | 天 | *tiān* | n | sky |
| 6 | 才 | *cái* | adv | not until, only then [See Grammar 6.] |
| 7 | 回家 | *huí jiā* | vo | to go home |
| | 回 | *huí* | v | to return |

## How About You?

你在哪儿看书？

*Nǐ zài nǎr kàn shū?*

Where do you read books?

我在 ______________ 看书。

*Wǒ zài ______________ kàn shū.*

See index for corresponding vocabulary or research another term.

## Characterize it!

Enclosing

□

1 图　2 了　3 回　4 玩　5 馆

Which of these characters are formed with the pattern on the left?

More characters

# Grammar

## 5 The particle 了 *(le)* (I)

The dynamic particle 了 *(le)* signifies : 1) the occurrence or completion of an action or event, or 2) the emergence of a situation. The action, event, or situation usually pertains to the past, but sometimes it can refer to the future. Therefore 了 *(le)* is not a "past tense" marker and should not be taken as the equivalent of the past tense in English. In this lesson, it indicates the occurrence or completion of an action or event. It is usually used directly after a verb. In interrogative and declarative sentences, it sometimes appears after a verb and the object of the verb.

**A** 今天妈妈喝了三杯水。

*Jīntiān Māma hē le sān bēi shuǐ.*

Mom drank three glasses of water today.

OCCURRENCE OR COMPLETION OF AN ACTION, IN THE PAST.

**B** 星期一小高请我喝了一瓶可乐。

*Xīngqīyī Xiǎo Gāo qǐng wǒ hē le yì píng kělè.*

On Monday, Little Gao bought me a bottle of cola.

OCCURRENCE OR COMPLETION OF AN EVENT, IN THE PAST.

**C** Q: 昨天晚上你去打球了吗？

*Zuótiān wǎnshang nǐ qù dǎ qiú le ma?*

Did you play ball last night?

OCCURRENCE OR COMPLETION OF AN EVENT, IN THE PAST, INTERROGATIVE

A: 昨天晚上我去打球了。

*Zuótiān wǎnshang wǒ qù dǎ qiú le.*

I went to play ball last night.

OCCURRENCE OR COMPLETION OF AN EVENT, IN THE PAST.

**D** 明天我吃了晚饭去看电影。

*Míngtiān wǒ chī le wǎnfàn qù kàn diànyǐng.*

Tomorrow I'll go see a movie after I eat dinner.

OCCURRENCE OR COMPLETION OF AN ACTION IN THE FIRST PART OF THE SENTENCE, IN THE FUTURE

There is often a specific time phrase in a sentence with the dynamic particle 了 *(le)*, such as:

- 今天 *(jīntiān)* (today) in (A)
- 昨天晚上 *(zuótiān wǎnshang)* (last night) in (C)
- 星期一 *(xīngqīyī)* (Monday) in (B)

When 了 *(le)* is used between the verb and the object, the object is usually preceded by a modifier. The following "numeral + measure word" is the most common type of modifier for the object:

- 三杯 *(sān bēi)* (three cups/glasses) in (A)
- 一瓶 *(yì píng)* (one bottle) in (B)

If there are other phrases or sentences following the object of the first clause, then the object does not need a modifier. See (D) above. This v 了 o+v (o) structure can be used to depict a sequence of actions regardless of the time of their occurrence.

If the object following 了 *(le)* is a proper noun, it doesn't need a modifier either. See (E).

**E** 我昨天看了《星球大战》，那个电影很好。

*Wǒ zuótiān kàn le «Xīngqiú Dàzhàn», nà ge diànyǐng hěn hǎo.*

I saw *Star Wars* yesterday. The movie was very good.

To say that an action did not take place in the past, use 没（有）*(méi [yǒu])* instead of 不…了 *(bù . . . le)* or 没有…了 *(méiyǒu . . . le)*, as in the example below.

**F** 昨天我没有听音乐。[✗ 昨天我不听音乐了。] [✗ 昨天我没有听音乐了。]

*Zuótiān wǒ bù tīng yīnyuè le.*

I didn't listen to music yesterday.

The following are examples of interrogative forms:

**G** Q: 你吃饭了吗？ or 你吃饭了没有？ A: 我没吃。

*Nǐ chī fàn le ma? or Nǐ chī fàn le méiyǒu?* *Wǒ méi chī.*

Have you eaten? No, I haven't.

**H** Q: 你喝了几杯水？ A: 我喝了一杯水。

*Nǐ hē le jǐ bēi shuǐ?* *Wǒ hē le yì bēi shuǐ.*

How many glasses of water did you drink? I drank one glass of water.

## EXERCISES

Rearrange the words to form a sentence by inserting 了 after the verb and before the numeral and measure word. Use exercise 1 as an example.

More exercises

1 我 喝 可乐 一 → 我喝了一瓶可乐。

2 他昨天 看 中国电影 一

3 李友今天 认识 人 四

## 6 The adverb 才 (*cái*) (not until)

The adverb 才 (*cái*) (not until) indicates the occurrence of an action or situation later than the speaker expects. That lateness is perceived by the speaker, and is not necessarily objective, as in (B) and (C). 才 (*cái*) never takes the particle 了 (*le*), even if it pertains to a past action or situation.

**A** 我请他六点吃晚饭，他六点半才来。

*Wǒ qǐng tā liù diǎn chī wǎnfàn, tā liù diǎn bàn cái lái.*

I invited him out to dinner at six o'clock. He didn't arrive until six-thirty.

**B** 小高常常晚上十二点才回家。

*Xiǎo Gāo chángcháng wǎnshang shí'èr diǎn cái huí jiā.*

Little Gao often doesn't come home until midnight.

**C** 她晚上很晚才睡觉。

*Tā wǎnshang hěn wǎn cái shuì jiào.*

She goes to bed very late at night.

## EXERCISES

Indicate perceived lateness by joining these sentences. Insert 才 where appropriate. Use exercise 1 as an example.

More exercises

1 我们六点吃饭。她六点一刻来。
→ 我们六点吃饭，她六点一刻才来。

2 我们十点钟回家。王朋十一点回家。

3 我们两点去打球。我弟弟四点去打球。

# Language Practice

## H You did what?

Little Gao has so much energy! He can do a lot in one day. Based on the images, recap what he did yesterday by using 了 *(le)*, e.g.:

x4

小高昨天喝了四杯咖啡。

*Xiǎo Gāo zuótiān hē le sì bēi kāfēi.*

1  x1

2  x3

3  x5

4  x4

## I Fashionably late!

PRESENTATIONAL

Your roommate is a procrastinator and does everything later than you. Present your different schedules to the class using 才 *(cái)*, e.g.:

7:00 vs. 8:00

我七点喝咖啡，她八点才喝（咖啡）。

*Wǒ qī diǎn hē kāfēi, tā bā diǎn cái hē (kāfēi).*

1  9:00 vs. 9:30

2  2:15 vs. 2:45

3  6:00 vs. 7:15

4  8:00 vs. 8:30

5  9:30 vs. 12:00

## J What did you do last night?

INTERPERSONAL | PRESENTATIONAL

Interview your classmates about what they did last night, e.g.:

你昨天晚上去朋友家玩儿了吗？

*Nǐ zuótiān wǎnshang qù péngyou jiā wánr le ma?*

If the answer is negative, then ask:

你昨天晚上去哪儿了？ 你喝什么了？
你喝了几杯/几瓶？

*Nǐ zuótiān wǎnshang qù nǎr le? Nǐ hē shénme le? Nǐ hē le jǐ bēi/jǐ píng?*

Then report to the class what your partner did last night, e.g.:

Mark 昨天晚上去朋友家玩儿了/没有去朋友家玩儿……

Mark *zuótiān wǎnshang qù péngyou jiā wánr le/méiyǒu qù péngyou jiā wánr . . .*

## K Birthday itinerary

PRESENTATIONAL

Describe what Little Wang did on his birthday, and when, according to these images.

1

2

3

**Chinese Chat**

A friend is texting you about taking a coffee break. How would you reply?

Continue to explore

## COMPARE & CONTRAST

1 "Host" and "guest" are 主 *(zhǔ)* and 客 *(kè)*. The Chinese often say 客随主便 *(kè suí zhǔ biàn)*, "A good guest goes along with whatever is convenient for the host." A related expression is 入乡随俗 *(rù xiāng suí sú)*, "Wherever you find yourself, follow local customs." The phrase 反客为主 *(fǎn kè wéi zhǔ)*, meanwhile, describes a presumptive guest who usurps the place of the host. Are there similar sayings in your culture?

2 When you visit a friend in China, you should bring a gift. You might be asked to change into slippers and be offered something to drink. Normally, food is served family style to indicate abundance and respect for the guests. Dishes are brought out one course at a time, so the host will not join the meal until all the dishes are served. It is polite to wait for the host to urge you to start eating. If a Chinese friend asks you about visiting etiquette in your culture, what would you say?

3 The tea plant is native to China. The beverage made from its leaves is often called some derivative of the Mandarin or Southern Min dialect pronunciation of the Chinese word for tea. The Russian *chai* comes from Mandarin, whereas tea in English comes from the Southern Min dialect. Do you know what tea is called in any other language?

# Tea

茶 *(chá)* can probably be called the national drink of China. Indeed, the practice of drinking tea originated there. According to legend, tea was discovered by the ancient Chinese emperor 神农 *(Shénnóng)* when leaves from a nearby shrub fell into the water he was boiling. It depends on whom you ask, but in general, Chinese tea may be classified into the following categories according to the different methods by which tea leaves are processed: green tea, black tea, Wulong tea, compressed tea, and scented tea.

Chrysanthemum tea, 菊花茶 *(júhuā chá)*, is a type of scented tea, whereas Longjing tea, 龙井茶 *(lóngjǐng chá)*, belongs to the green tea family. Nowadays, bubble tea, 珍珠奶茶 *(zhēnzhū nǎichá)*, is gaining popularity in the West.

Although tea remains the most popular beverage in China, the number of coffee drinkers has been on the rise in recent years. Coffee is now widely available in supermarkets. Coffee shops, including international chains such as Starbucks, 星巴克 *(Xīngbākè)*, and Coffee Bean & Tea Leaf, are familiar sights in many Chinese cities.

Do you know where bubble tea originated? 奶茶 *(nǎichá)* literally means milk tea. How about 珍珠 *(zhēnzhū)*? What are they really?

认识你很高兴 *(rènshi nǐ hěn gāoxìng)* or 很高兴认识你 *(hěn gāoxìng rènshi nǐ)* is basically a translation of **"I'm very happy to meet you."** This form of greeting is becoming more common, even though to some Chinese it sounds a bit formal.

# Greetings

## *Etiquette*

Traditionally, privacy is a somewhat less sacrosanct concept in Chinese culture than it is in the West: you would not necessarily be considered intrusive if you dropped by a friend's place without warning; nor would topics such as age, marital status, and salary necessarily be off limits in a polite conversation. For those who believe in the traditional Chinese notion of friendship or personal loyalty, sharing such personal information is an important gesture of trust. But there is a more prosaic explanation. Until relatively recently, most people lived in close proximity to one another and everyone followed more or less the same prescribed track in life. The income gap was limited. Therefore, there were few secrets. Everyone knew what their neighbors did and how much money they made.

This is changing, however; particularly due to disparity in incomes and urbanization of communities. Chinese citizens have become more conscious of their "right to privacy," or 隐私权 *(yǐnsī quán)*. Nowadays, Chinese people consider it more and more important to give notice before visiting friends and to avoid asking about personal information.

# Lesson Wrap-Up

## Make It Flow!

Rearrange the following sentences into a logical sequence. Then combine them into a coherent narrative. Remember to omit repetitive elements and substitute subjects with personal pronouns where appropriate. Time expressions and place words can also serve as useful connective devices.

____高文中的姐姐叫高小音。

____他们一起聊天儿、看电视。

__1__昨天晚上，王朋和李友去高文中家玩儿。

____晚上十二点王朋和李友才回家。

____在高文中家王朋和李友认识了高文中的姐姐。

____高小音在图书馆工作。

## Role-Play

**Student A** You are the host. Introduce your guests and ask what they would like to drink.

**Student B** Meet and greet the other guest. Compliment the host's home. Ask where the other guest works. Tell the host that you don't drink tea, coffee, or cola. Ask for a glass of water instead.

**Student C** Meet and greet the other guest. Tell the other guest that you are delighted to meet him/her. Tell the other guest that you don't work; you are a student. Let the host know that you would like a cup of tea.

## Email

Email your Chinese-speaking friend about your visit to a friend's place last night. Include the following information:

- Where you went
- Whom you met there, what they did, and whether you found them interesting
- What your friend's home was like, e.g., big, nicely decorated
- What you did
- When you returned home

## Can-Do Check List

Before proceeding to Lesson 6, make sure you can complete the following tasks in Chinese:

I can

- ☐ Introduce one person to another
- ☐ Greet guests when they visit my home
- ☐ Offer drinks to my guests
- ☐ As a guest, ask the host/hostess for a beverage
- ☐ Briefly describe a visit to a friend's place

# Keeping It Casual (L1–L5)

**Before you progress to the next half of the text, we'll review how some of the functional expressions from Lessons 1–5 are used in casual Chinese. After you complete the review, note any other casual expressions you would like to learn, then share the list with your teacher.**

## 1 算了 *(suàn le)* (forget it, never mind)

Say this when you've put someone in an awkward position, or when someone's made a mistake that you're willing to let go. You can also say this when you're dissatisfied with what someone is doing and want him/her to stop. [See Lesson 4.]

**A**

**Student A** 明天我们去打球，怎么样？
*Míngtiān wǒmen qù dǎ qiú, zěnmeyàng?*
Let's go play ball tomorrow, all right?

**Student B** 明天我很忙。
*Míngtiān wǒ hěn máng.*
I'm very busy tomorrow.

**Student A** 那算了。
*Nà suàn le.*
Never mind then.

**B**

**Student A** 你今年多大？
*Nǐ jīnnián duō dà?*
How old are you this year?

**Student B** 你为什么问我多大？
*Nǐ wèishénme wèn wǒ duō dà?*
Why are you asking me how old I am?

**Student A** 算了，我不问了。
*Suàn le, wǒ bú wèn le.*
Never mind. I won't ask then.

## 2 谁呀 *(shéi ya)* **(who is it?)**

Say this when someone knocks on your door. [See Lesson 5.]

**A**

*(Knocking on the door.)*

**Wang Peng** 谁呀？
*Shéi ya?*
Who is it?

**Li You** 是我，李友。
*Shì wǒ, Lǐ Yǒu.*
It's me, Li You.

**Wang Peng** 请进。
*Qǐng jìn.*
Please come in.

**B**

*(Knocking on the door.)*

**Gao Wenzhong** 谁呀？
*Shéi ya?*
Who is it?

**Little Wang** 我，小王。
*Wǒ, Xiǎo Wáng.*
It's me, Little Wang.

**Gao Wenzhong** 进来。
*Jìn lai.*
Come in.

## 3 是吗 *(shì ma)* **(really, is that so?)**

Say this when you hear something unexpected. [See Lesson 5.]

**A**

**Student A** 我昨天晚上三点半才睡觉。
*Wǒ zuótiān wǎnshang sān diǎn bàn cái shuì jiào.*
Last night, I didn't go to sleep until 3:30.

**Student B** 是吗？为什么？
*Shì ma? Wèishénme?*
Really? Why?

**Student A** 因为昨天我很忙。
*Yīnwèi zuótiān wǒ hěn máng.*
Because I was so busy yesterday.

**B**

**Student A** 周末我去跳舞。
*Zhōumò wǒ qù tiào wǔ.*
I'm going dancing this weekend.

**Student B** 是吗？我也去。
*Shì ma? Wǒ yě qù.*
Really? I'm going as well.

# Lesson 6

## 第六课

*Dì liù kè*

# 约时间

*Yuē shíjiān*

# MAKING APPOINTMENTS

## Learning Objectives

**In this lesson, you will learn to:**

- Answer a phone call and initiate a phone conversation
- Set up an appointment with a teacher on the phone
- Ask a favor
- Ask someone to return your call

## Relate & Get Ready

**In your own culture/community:**

- How do you answer the phone?
- How do students address their teachers?
- How do you ask for a favor?

# Calling Your Teacher

## Dialogue 1

李友给[1]常老师打电话……

Audio

Video

喂？

喂，请问，常老师在吗？

我就是。**您**[a]是哪位？

老师，您好。我是李友。

李友，有事儿吗？

老师，今天下午您**有时间**[b]吗？我想**问**[c]您几个问题。

对不起，今天下午我要[2]开会。

明天呢？

明天上午我有两**节**[d]课，下午三点要给二年级考试。

您**什么时候**[e]有空儿？

明天四点**以后**[f]才有空儿。

**要是**[g]您方便，四点半我到您的办公室去，行吗？

四点半，**没问题**[h]。我在办公室等你。

谢谢您。

别[3]客气。

## Pinyin Dialogue

*Lǐ Yǒu gěi*[1] *Cháng lǎoshī dǎ diànhuà . . .*

*Wéi?*

*Wéi, qǐng wèn, Cháng lǎoshī zài ma?*

*Wǒ jiù shì. Nín*[a] *shì nǎ wèi?*

*Lǎoshī, nín hǎo. Wǒ shì Lǐ Yǒu.*

*Lǐ Yǒu, yǒu shìr ma?*

*Lǎoshī, jīntiān xiàwǔ nín yǒu shíjiān*[b] *ma? Wǒ xiǎng wèn*[c] *nín jǐ ge wèntí.*

*Duìbuqǐ, jīntiān xiàwǔ wǒ yào*[2] *kāi huì.*

*Míngtiān ne?*

*Míngtiān shàngwǔ wǒ yǒu liǎng jié*[d] *kè, xiàwǔ sān diǎn yào gěi èr niánjí kǎo shì.*

*Nín shénme shíhou*[e] *yǒu kòngr?*

*Míngtiān sì diǎn yǐhòu*[f] *cái yǒu kòngr.*

*Yàoshi*[g] *nín fāngbiàn, sì diǎn bàn wǒ dào nín de bàngōngshì qù, xíng ma?*

*Sì diǎn bàn, méi wèntí*[h]*. Wǒ zài bàngōngshì děng nǐ.*

*Xièxie nín.*

*Bié*[3] *kèqi.*

## Language Notes

### a 您 *(nín)*

This personal pronoun is often used to address an older person or someone of higher social rank. It is common for strangers to address each other with 您 *(nín)* and then switch to 你 *(nǐ)* as they get acquainted.

### b 有时间 *(yǒu shíjiān)*

"To have free time" is 有时间 *(yǒu shíjiān)* or 有空儿 *(yǒu kòngr)*, never 有时候 *(yǒu shíhou)*.

### c 问 *(wèn)*

Both 问 *(wèn)* and 请 *(qǐng)* are often translated as "to ask" in English. However, the verb 问 *(wèn)* means "to inquire," e.g., 我问她一个问题 *(Wǒ wèn tā yí ge wèntí)* (I ask her a question), whereas 请 *(qǐng)* means "to invite" or "to request," e.g., 我请她跳舞 *(Wǒ qǐng tā tiào wǔ)* (I invite her to dance).

### d 节 *(jié)*

The measure word for academic courses is 门 *(mén)*. Compare: 三门课 *(sān mén kè)* (three courses), 三节课 *(sān jié kè)* (three class periods), and 三课 *(sān kè)* (three lessons).

### e 什么时候 *(shénme shíhou)*

几点 *(jǐ diǎn)* is used to ask for a specific time of day. To ask about time in general, use the expression 什么时候 *(shénme shíhou)* (when).

### f 以后 *(yǐhòu)*

The Chinese equivalent of "after four o'clock" is 四点以后 *(sìdiǎn yǐhòu)*. Note the difference in word order. Likewise, "before Monday" is 星期一以前 *(xīngqīyī yǐqián)*.

### g 要是 *(yàoshi)*

要是 *(yàoshi)* (if) is a conjunction used to introduce a contingent or hypothetical action or situation. Unlike "if," it cannot introduce a subordinate clause: ⊗ 我不知道要是他明天来.

### h 没问题 *(méi wèntí)*

This phrase, meaning "no problem," is a reassuring reply to a tentative inquiry. It suggests that the speaker does not foresee any problems. When people thank you and say 谢谢 *(xièxie)*, the appropriate answer is 不谢 *(bú xiè)* or 别客气 *(bié kèqi)* rather than 没问题 *(méi wèntí)*.

# Vocabulary

Audio

Flashcards

| No. | Word | Pinyin | Part of Speech | Definition |
|---|---|---|---|---|
| 1 | 给 | *gěi* | prep | to, for [See Grammar 1.] |
| 2 | 打电话 | *dǎ diànhuà* | vo | to make a phone call |
| | 电话 | *diànhuà* | n | telephone |
| 3 | 喂 | *wéi/wèi* | interj | (on the phone) Hello!, Hey! |
| 4 | 在 | *zài* | v | to be present, to be at (a place) |
| 5 | 就 | *jiù* | adv | precisely, exactly |
| 6 | 您 | *nín* | pr | you (honorific for 你) |
| 7 | 哪 | *nǎ/něi* | qpr | which |
| 8 | 位 | *wèi* | m | (polite measure word for people) |
| 9 | 下午 | *xiàwǔ* | t | afternoon |
| 10 | 时间 | *shíjiān* | n | time |
| 11 | 问题 | *wèntí* | n | question, problem |
| 12 | 要 | *yào* | mv | will, to be going to, to want to, to have a desire to [See Grammar 2.] |
| 13 | 开会 | *kāi huì* | vo | to have a meeting |
| | 开 | *kāi* | v | to open, to hold (a meeting, party, etc.) |
| | 会 | *huì* | n | meeting |
| 14 | 上午 | *shàngwǔ* | t | morning |
| 15 | 节 | *jié* | m | (measure word for class periods) |
| 16 | 课 | *kè* | n | class, course, lesson |
| 17 | 年级 | *niánjí* | n | grade in school |
| 18 | 考试 | *kǎo shì* | vo/n | to give or take a test; test |
| | 考 | *kǎo* | v | to give or take a test |
| | 试 | *shì* | n/v | test; to try, to experiment |
| 19 | 以后 | *yǐhòu* | t | after, from now on, later on |
| 20 | 空（儿） | *kòng(r)* | n | free time |
| 21 | 要是 | *yàoshi* | conj | if |
| 22 | 方便 | *fāngbiàn* | adj | convenient |
| 23 | 到 | *dào* | v | to go to, to arrive |

Confucius （孔子）(Kǒng Zǐ), considered China's "First Teacher" （先师）(Xiānshī), is associated with wisdom. Why do you think Confucius is referenced on this packaging? How does this pen refill claim to help students?

**GET Real WITH CHINESE**

| No. | Word | Pinyin | Part of Speech | Definition |
|---|---|---|---|---|
| 24 | 办公室 | *bàngōngshì* | n | office |
| 25 | 行 | *xíng* | v | all right, OK |
| 26 | 等 | *děng* | v | to wait, to wait for |
| 27 | 别 | *bié* | adv | don't [See Grammar 3.] |
| 28 | 客气 | *kèqi* | adj | polite |
| 29 | 常老师 | *Cháng lǎoshī* | pn | Teacher Chang |

## How About You?

我们在哪儿见面？

*Wǒmen zài nǎr jiànmiàn?*

Where will we meet?

我在 ________________ 等你。

*Wǒ zài ________________ děng nǐ.*

See index for corresponding vocabulary or research another term.

# Grammar

## 1 The preposition 给 *(gěi)* (to, for)

给 *(gěi)* (to, for) can be a verb or a preposition. As a preposition, 给 *(gěi)* is generally combined with nouns or pronouns to form prepositional phrases, which appear before verbs as adverbials.

**A** 他给我打了一个电话。

*Tā gěi wǒ dǎ le yí ge diànhuà.*

He gave me a call.

**B** 他是谁？请你给我们介绍一下。

*Tā shì shéi? Qǐng nǐ gěi wǒmen jièshào yí xià.*

Who is he? Please introduce us.

**C** 你有你姐姐的照片吗？给我看一下，行吗？

*Nǐ yǒu nǐ jiějie de zhàopiàn ma? Gěi wǒ kàn yí xià, xíng ma?*

Do you have a picture of your older sister? Can I have a look?

**D** 我昨天很忙，没给妈妈打电话。

*Wǒ zuótiān hěn máng, méi gěi māma dǎ diànhuà.*

I was very busy yesterday. I didn't call my mother.

More exercises

### EXERCISES

Rearrange the words to form a sentence by inserting 给 where appropriate. Use exercise 1 as an example.

1 高文中　介绍他姐姐　我们
→ 高文中给我们介绍他姐姐。

2 李老师　介绍中国音乐　他的学生

3 我妈妈　看她的照片　我们

## 2 The modal verb 要 *(yào)* (will, be going to) (I)

The modal verb 要 *(yào)* (will, be going to) has several meanings. In this lesson, 要 *(yào)* indicates a future action, particularly a scheduled event or an activity that one is committed to. The negative form of 要 *(yào)* is 不 *(bù)* (no, not) rather than 不要 *(bú yào)*.

**A** 明天下午三点我要给二年级考试。

*Míngtiān xiàwǔ sān diǎn wǒ yào gěi èr niánjí kǎo shì.*

I'm going to give the second-year class a test at 3:00 p.m. tomorrow.

**B** 今天晚上妹妹要去看电影。

*Jīntiān wǎnshang mèimei yào qù kàn diànyǐng.*

My younger sister is going to see a movie tonight.

**C** Q: 明天我要去小白家玩儿。你呢？

*Míngtiān wǒ yào qù Xiǎo Bái jiā wánr. Nǐ ne?*

I'm going to visit Little Bai tomorrow. How about you?

A: 明天我不去小白家玩儿，我要开会。

*Míngtiān wǒ bú qù Xiǎo Bái jiā wánr, wǒ yào kāi huì.*

I'm not going to visit Little Bai tomorrow. I am going to a meeting.

### EXERCISES

In pairs, form a question-and-answer about people's scheduled activities by using 要. Use exercise 1 as an example.

More exercises

1 小李今天晚上　　去听音乐

→ Q: 小李今天晚上要做什么？

A: 他今天晚上要去听音乐。

2 王朋星期三　　去高文中家玩儿

3 王律师的弟弟明天晚上　　去学校看电影

## 3 The adverb 别 *(bié)* (don't)

别 *(bié)* (don't) is used to advise someone to refrain from doing something. Depending on the context, it can be used to express a polite request, a gentle reminder, or a serious admonition.

**A** 别客气。

*Bié kèqi.*

You're welcome.

**B** 你别说。

*Nǐ bié shuō.*

Don't say anything.

**C** 别进来!

*Bié jìn lai!*

Don't come in!

**D** 那个电影没有意思,你别看了。

*Nà ge diànyǐng méi yǒu yìsi, nǐ bié kàn le.*

That movie is boring. Don't go see it.

**E** 别给小王打电话!

*Bié gěi Xiǎo Wáng dǎ diànhuà!*

Don't call Little Wang!

More exercises

### EXERCISES

In pairs, suggest your partner refrain from doing something by using the bracketed phrase and inserting 别 where appropriate. Use exercise 1 as an example.

1 **Student A** 我今天晚上想去看电影。 (没意思)

**Student B** 那个电影没意思,别去看了。

2 **Student A** 我想请小高吃美国菜。 (不喜欢)

**Student B** 小高 ______________________。

3 **Student A** 我想给小英打电话。 (很忙)

**Student B** 小英 ______________________。

# Language Practice

## A BFF

PRESENTATIONAL

Recap what Little Gao often does for his friends. Use 给 *(gěi)* where appropriate, e.g.:

| | |
|---|---|
| 打电话 | *dǎ diànhuà* |
| 小高常常给他们打电话。 | *Xiǎo Gāo chángcháng gěi tāmen dǎ diànhuà.* |
| 1 看他爸爸妈妈的照片 | *kàn tā bàba māma de zhàopiàn* |
| 2 听中国音乐 | *tīng Zhōngguó yīnyuè* |
| 3 喝英国茶 | *hē Yīngguó chá* |
| 4 介绍新电影 | *jièshào xīn diànyǐng* |

你呢？ Now share what you do for your friends with the class.

## B To-do list

INTERPERSONAL

Li You has the next few days all planned out. In pairs, form a question-and-answer about what she will be doing by inserting 要 *(yào)* in the ◇, e.g.:

| | |
|---|---|
| 明天◇去跳舞 | *míngtiān ◇ qù tiào wǔ* |
| Q: 李友明天做什么？ | *Lǐ Yǒu míngtiān zuò shénme?* |
| A: 李友明天要去跳舞。 | *Lǐ Yǒu míngtiān yào qù tiào wǔ.* |
| 1 今天晚上◇请朋友喝咖啡 | *jīntiān wǎnshang ◇ qǐng péngyou hē kāfēi* |
| 2 明天上午◇<br>去同学家练习中文 | *míngtiān shàngwǔ ◇*<br>*qù tóngxué jiā liànxí Zhōngwén* |
| 3 明天下午◇<br>去老师的办公室问问题 | *míngtiān xiàwǔ ◇*<br>*qù lǎoshī de bàngōngshì wèn wèntí* |
| 4 这个星期五◇<br>去学校看电影 | *zhè ge xīngqīwǔ ◇*<br>*qù xuéxiào kàn diànyǐng* |
| 5 这个周末◇<br>给小高介绍一个朋友 | *zhè ge zhōumò ◇*<br>*gěi Xiǎo Gāo jièshào yí ge péngyou* |

Then ask about your partner's plans for the next few days.

## C I have another suggestion

PRESENTATIONAL

Using the images, practice how to be accommodating. Insert 要是 *(yàoshi)* where appropriate, e.g.:

不喜欢 *(bù xǐhuan)*  喜欢 *(xǐhuan)* 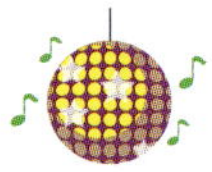

要是你不喜欢唱歌，我们跳舞，怎么样？

*Yàoshi nǐ bù xǐhuan chàng gē, wǒmen tiào wǔ, zěnmeyàng?*

1 不想 *(bù xiǎng)*  想 *(xiǎng)* 

2 觉得……没有意思 *(juéde . . . méiyǒu yìsi)* 
觉得……有意思 *(juéde . . . yǒu yìsi)* 

3 不喜欢 *(bù xǐhuan)*  喜欢 *(xǐhuan)* 

4 没有空儿 *(méi yǒu kòngr)* today 有空儿 *(yǒu kòngr)* tomorrow

## D What if?

INTERPERSONAL

In pairs, take turns asking and answering the following questions.

1 要是你有时间，你想去哪儿玩儿？

*Yàoshi nǐ yǒu shíjiān, nǐ xiǎng qù nǎr wánr?*

2 要是朋友请你吃饭，你想吃什么菜？

*Yàoshi péngyou qǐng nǐ chī fàn, nǐ xiǎng chī shénme cài?*

3 要是同学请你看电影，你想看什么电影？

*Yàoshi tóngxué qǐng nǐ kàn diànyǐng, nǐ xiǎng kàn shénme diànyǐng?*

4 要是朋友请你去跳舞，你想去哪儿跳舞？

*Yàoshi péngyou qǐng nǐ qù tiào wǔ, nǐ xiǎng qù nǎr tiào wǔ?*

5 要是朋友找你打球，你什么时候有时间？

*Yàoshi péngyou zhǎo nǐ dǎ qiú, nǐ shénme shíhou yǒu shíjiān?*

## E Calling up

INTERPERSONAL

You are calling your friend to arrange a time to hang out. In pairs, role-play the conversation between the caller and the person (either your friend or your friend's sibling) who answers.

| | | |
|---|---|---|
| **Caller** | 喂，请问，________在吗？ | *Wéi, qǐngwèn, ______zài ma?* |
| **Friend** | 我就是。/ | *Wǒ jiù shì. /* |
| **Friend's Sibling** | ________不在。 | *______bú zài.* |
| **Friend/Friend's Sibling** | 您是哪位？ | *Nín shì nǎ wèi?* |
| **Caller** | 我是________。 | *Wǒ shì ______.* |
| **Friend/Friend's Sibling** | ________，你好！有事儿吗？ | *______, nǐ hǎo! Yǒu shìr ma?* |

**Caller** ······ (You ask if you can come over this evening to watch TV.)

**Friend/Friend's Sibling** ······ (They have a ball game, but are free tomorrow night.)

**Caller** ······ (Tomorrow night works for you, so you set a time before saying goodbye.)

### Characterize it!

- What do the characters mean?
- What is the common radical?
- What does the radical mean?
- How does the radical relate to the overall meaning of the characters?

1 打　2 找

More characters

### Chinese Chat

Teacher Chang just posted a tweet. When do you think her students can make an appointment with her?

Teacher Chang
@Teacher_Chang66

Follow

明天上午有两节课，还要开会……十一点半以后才有空儿。

10:07 PM - 14 Nov 2016

25　28

# Calling a Friend for Help

## Dialogue 2 李友给王朋打电话……

Audio

Video

喂，请问，王朋在吗？

我就是。你是李友**吧**[a]？

王朋，我**下个星期**[4]要考中文，你帮我准备一下，跟我练习说中文，好吗？

好啊，但是你**得**[5]请我喝咖啡。

喝咖啡，没问题。那我什么时候跟你**见面**[b]？你今天晚上有空儿吗？

今天晚上白英爱请我吃饭。

是吗？白英爱请你吃饭？

对。我**回来**[6]以后给你打电话。

好，我等你的电话。

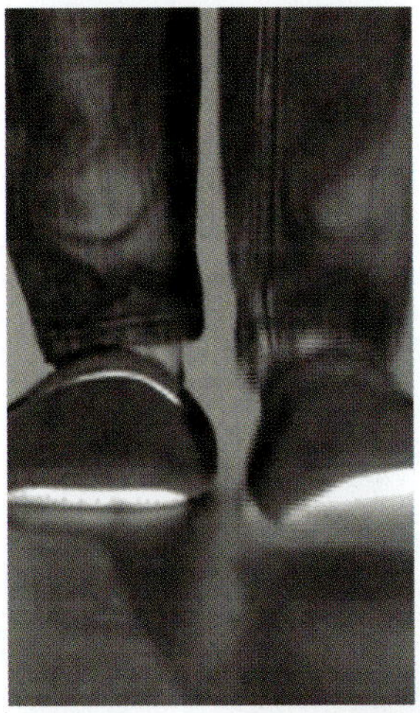

## Pinyin Dialogue

*Lǐ Yǒu gěi Wáng Péng dǎ diànhuà . . .*

*Wéi, qǐng wèn, Wáng Péng zài ma?*

*Wǒ jiù shì. Nǐ shì Lǐ Yǒu ba*[a] *?*

*Wáng Péng, wǒ xià ge xīngqī*[4] *yào kǎo Zhōngwén, nǐ bāng wǒ zhǔnbèi yí xià, gēn wǒ liànxí shuō Zhōngwén, hǎo ma?*

*Hǎo a, dànshì nǐ děi*[5] *qǐng wǒ hē kāfēi.*

*Hē kāfēi, méi wèntí. Nà wǒ shénme shíhou gēn nǐ jiàn miàn*[b] *? Nǐ jīntiān wǎnshang yǒu kòngr ma?*

*Jīntiān wǎnshang Bái Yīng'ài qǐng wǒ chī fàn.*

*Shì ma? Bái Yīng'ài qǐng nǐ chī fàn?*

*Duì. Wǒ huí lai*[6] *yǐhòu gěi nǐ dǎ diànhuà.*

*Hǎo, wǒ děng nǐ de diànhuà.*

## Language Notes

**a** 吧 *(ba)*

Compare the two particles 吧 *(ba)* and 吗 *(ma)*:

你是李友吧?

*Nǐ shì Lǐ Yǒu ba?*

You are Li You, aren't you?

(I think you're Li You. Am I right?)

你是李友吗?

*Nǐ shì Lǐ Yǒu ma?*

Are you Li You?

(I am not quite sure.)

**b** 见面 *(jiàn miàn)*

"A meets B" is "A 跟 *(gēn)* B 见面 *(jiàn miàn)*," not "✗ A 见面 B."

# Vocabulary

Audio

Flashcards

| No. | Word | Pinyin | Part of Speech | Definition |
|---|---|---|---|---|
| 1 | 下个 | *xià ge* | | next |
| | 下 | *xià* | | below, next |
| 2 | 中文 | *Zhōngwén* | n | Chinese language |
| | 文 | *wén* | n | language, script, written language |
| 3 | 帮 | *bāng* | v | to help |
| 4 | 准备 | *zhǔnbèi* | v | to prepare |
| 5 | 练习 | *liànxí* | v | to practice |
| 6 | 说 | *shuō* | v | to say, to speak |
| 7 | 啊 | *a* | p | (a sentence-final particle of exclamation, interrogation, etc.) |
| 8 | 但是 | *dànshì* | conj | but |
| 9 | 得 | *děi* | av | must, to have to |
| 10 | 跟 | *gēn* | prep | with |
| 11 | 见面 | *jiàn miàn* | vo | to meet up, to meet with |
| | 面 | *miàn* | n | face |
| 12 | 回来 | *huí lai* | vc | to come back |

## How About You?

我学中文，你呢？

*Wǒ xué Zhōngwén, nǐ ne?*

I study Chinese. How about you?

我（也）学 ＿＿＿＿＿＿＿＿。

*Wǒ (yě) xué* ＿＿＿＿＿＿＿＿.

See index for corresponding vocabulary or research another term.

# Grammar

## 4 Time expressions

年 *(nián)* (year), 月 *(yuè)* (month), 星期 *(xīngqī)* (week), and 天 *(tiān)* (day) are all nouns, but 年 *(nián)* (year) and 天 *(tiān)* (day) are also measure words. Therefore, they are used differently, following the patterns below.

| Pattern | Examples |
|---|---|
| Numeral + 年/天 | 一年 *(yì nián)* (one year), 五天 *(wǔ tiān)* (five days) |
| Numeral + Measure Word + 月/星期 | 一个月 *(yí ge yuè)* (one month),<br>三个星期 *(sān ge xīngqī)* (three weeks) |

"One week" is 一个星期 *(yí ge xīngqī)*, therefore "one week later" is 一个星期以后 *(yí ge xīngqī yǐhòu)*. "One month" is 一个月 *(yí ge yuè)*, therefore "one month later" is 一个月以后 *(yí ge yuè yǐhòu)*. Please note that "one month" is not 一月 *(yīyuè)* (January). The time expressions 月 *(yuè)* and 星期 *(xīngqī)* can be formed by using 下 *(xià)* (below) and 上 *(shàng)* (above), following the patterns below. "Below" （下） *(xià)* is used to refer to weeks and months in the future, and "above" （上） *(shàng)* to refer to weeks and months in the past.

| 月[a] *(yuè)* **(month)** | 星期[b] *(xīngqī)* **(week)** |
|---|---|
| 上上个月 *(shàng shàng ge yuè)*<br>(the month before last) | 上上（个）星期 *(shàng shàng [ge] xīngqī)*<br>(the week before last) |
| 上个月 *(shàng ge yuè)*<br>(last month) | 上（个）星期 *(shàng [ge] xīngqī)*<br>(last week) |
| 这个月 *(zhè ge yuè)*<br>(this month) | 这（个）星期 *(zhè [ge] xīngqī)*<br>(this week) |
| 下个月 *(xià ge yuè)*<br>(next month) | 下（个）星期 *(xià [ge] xīngqī)*<br>(next week) |
| 下下个月 *(xià xià ge yuè)*<br>(the month after next) | 下下（个）星期 *(xià xià [ge] xīngqī)*<br>(the week after next) |

[a] We don't say ✖ 上月/下月.

[b] The measure word 个 can be omitted for 星期: 下个星期=下星期; 上个星期=上星期.

The below expressions using 天 *(tiān)* (day) and 年 *(nián)* (year) form two parallel series except for 昨天 *(zuótiān)* (yesterday) and 去年 *(qùnián)* (last year).

| 天 *(tiān)* **(day)** | 年 *(nián)* **(year)** |
|---|---|
| 大前天 *(dàqiántiān)* (three days ago) | 大前年 *(dàqiánnián)* (three years ago) |
| 前天 *(qiántiān)* (the day before yesterday) | 前年 *(qiánnián)* (the year before last) |
| 昨天 *(zuótiān)* (yesterday) | 去年 *(qùnián)* (last year) |
| 今天 *(jīntiān)* (today) | 今年 *(jīnnián)* (this year) |
| 明天 *(míngtiān)* (tomorrow) | 明年 *(míngnián)* (next year) |
| 后天 *(hòutiān)* (the day after tomorrow) | 后年 *(hòunián)* (the year after next) |
| 大后天 *(dàhòutiān)* (three days from today) | 大后年 *(dàhòunián)* (three years from now) |

More exercises

## EXERCISES

Based on the information given, fill in the blanks with the appropriate time expressions. Exercise 1 includes an example.

1 这个月是五月：上个月是四月，_______是三月，_______是六月，_______是七月。

2 今天是星期三：昨天是_______，前天是_______，明天是_______，后天是_______。

## 5 The modal verb 得 *(děi)* (must, have to)

The modal verb 得 *(děi)* means "have to" or "must."

**A** 我现在得去开会，没空儿跟你聊天儿。

*Wǒ xiànzài děi qù kāi huì, méi kòngr gēn nǐ liáo tiānr.*

I have to go to a meeting right now, and don't have time to chat with you.

**B** 我有事儿，得去学校。

*Wǒ yǒu shìr, děi qù xuéxiào.*

I have some business to attend to. I have to go to school.

The negative form of 得 *(děi)* is 不用 *(bú yòng)* (need not) or 不必 *(bú bì)* (need not), ✗ 不得.

Therefore, the correct way to say "You don't have to go to the library" is (C).

**C** 你不用去图书馆。 or 你不必去图书馆。

*Nǐ bú yòng qù túshūguǎn.* *Nǐ bú bì qù túshūguǎn.*

[✗ 你不得去图书馆 。]

### EXERCISES

In pairs, role-play the completed question-and-answers below by inserting 得 where appropriate. Use exercise 1 as an example.

More exercises

1 Q: 今天晚上我们去看电影，好吗?

A: 对不起/不行，今天晚上我得看书。

2 Q: 老师，下午三点我去您的办公室问问题，行吗?

A: ________，________________上课。

3 Q: 白律师，明年二月你可以来我们这儿工作吗?

A: ________，________________去英国开会。

## 6 Directional complements (I)

来 *(lái)* (to come) and 去 *(qù)* (to go) can serve as directional complements after such verbs as 进 *(jìn)* (to enter) and 回 *(huí)* (to return). 来 *(lái)* signifies movement toward the speaker, as in (A) and (B). 去 *(qù)* (to go) signifies movement away from the speaker, as in (C), or the speaker's own movement away from a current location, as in (D).

(You're bored in your dorm, so you ask your roommate when she's returning.)

**A** 你什么时候回来?

*Nǐ shénme shíhou huí lai?*

When are you coming back?

(After you knock on the door, your teacher invites you into her office.)

**B** 进来。

*Jìn lai.*

Come in.

(Upon arrival at the airport, your friend drops you off and reminds you to hurry up.)

**C** 快进去吧!

*Kuài jìn qu ba!*

Just go in, quickly!

(While shopping at the mall, you text your mom to tell her when you'll be home.)

**D** 我六点回去。

*Wǒ liù diǎn huí qu.*

I'll be back at six.

More exercises

### EXERCISES

Complete the sentences below by inserting the appropriate directional complements.

1 白英爱：老师，我可以进____吗？

2 常老师：快进____。

# Language Practice

## F It takes two

INTERPERSONAL

Based on the information below, practice saying who does what with whom by using 跟 *(gēn)* where appropriate, e.g.:

 说中文 *(shuō Zhōngwén)*

常老师跟李友说中文。

*Cháng lǎoshī gēn Lǐ Yǒu shuō Zhōngwén.*

1  聊天儿 *(liáo tiānr)*

2  跳舞 *(tiào wǔ)*

3  说英文 *(shuō Yīngwén)*

4  见面吃晚饭 *(jiàn miàn chī wǎnfàn)*

Then ask your partner whom they often speak Chinese with.

## G Do's and don't's

PRESENTATIONAL

Practice persuading someone to do one thing instead of another. Insert 别 *(bié)* and 得 *(děi)* where appropriate, e.g.:

✗ 聊天儿 *liáo tiānr*

✓ 看书 *kàn shū*

你别聊天儿，你得看书。

*Nǐ bié liáo tiānr, nǐ děi kàn shū.*

1 ✗ 喝茶 *hē chá* ✓ 睡觉 *shuì jiào*

2 ✗ 看电视 *kàn diànshì* ✓ 给老师打电话 *gěi lǎoshī dǎ diànhuà*

3 ✗ 睡觉 *shuì jiào* ✓ 去考试 *qù kǎo shì*

4 ✗ 打球 *dǎ qiú* ✓ 练习说中文 *liànxí shuō Zhōngwén*

5 ✗ 去朋友家玩儿 *qù péngyou jiā wánr* ✓ 去学校工作 *qù xuéxiào gōngzuò*

Then present a list of study habits to improve your Chinese language skills to your classmates.

## H Meeting up

PRESENTATIONAL

Indicate which IC characters you would or would not like to meet, using 跟 *(gēn)* and 见面 *(jiàn miàn)* where appropriate, e.g.:

我（不）想跟王朋见面。

*Wǒ (bù) xiǎng gēn Wáng Péng jiàn miàn.*

1 

2 

3 

4 

5 

## L Day planner

INTERPERSONAL

In pairs, ask questions about your partner's schedule.

你这个星期天上午（要）做什么？

*Nǐ zhè ge xīngqītiān shàngwǔ (yào) zuò shénme?*

你下个星期三下午（要）做什么？

*Nǐ xià ge xīngqīsān xiàwǔ (yào) zuò shénme?*

你下个星期五晚上（要）做什么？

*Nǐ xià ge xīngqīwǔ wǎnshang (yào) zuò shénme?*

## J One good turn deserves another

INTERPERSONAL

Use the information and the pattern to reply to requests for help.

1. Study Chinese
2. Practice playing ball
3. Practice singing
4. Practice dancing

"If I help you . . . , you have to . . . "

要是我帮你 ____________，你得____________。

*Yàoshi wǒ bāng nǐ ____________, nǐ děi ____________.*

Suppose you have an oral exam tomorrow. Convince your classmate to help you study by modifying the pattern above.

### Characterize it!

What do the characters mean?

What is the common radical?

What does the radical mean?

How does the radical relate to the overall meaning of the characters?

1 话　2 课　3 试

More characters

## K Call me back

INTERPERSONAL

You are calling your Chinese friend to arrange a date. In pairs, role-play the conversation between the caller and the parent who answers the phone.

**Caller** 您好！请问李音在吗？

*Nín hǎo! Qǐng wèn Lǐ Yīn zài ma?*

**Parent** 不在。你是哪位？

*Bú zài. Nǐ shì nǎ wèi?*

**Caller** 我是_______。

*Wǒ shì _______.*

**Parent** 你找_______有事儿吗？

*Nǐ zhǎo _______yǒu shìr ma?*

**Caller** 我明天晚上想请她_______。

*Wǒ míngtiān wǎnshang xiǎng qǐng tā _______.*

**Parent** 她明天晚上要_______，没空儿。

*Tā míngtiān wǎnshang yào _______, méi kòngr.*

**Caller** 那她_______有时间吗？

*Nà tā _______yǒu shíjiān ma?*

**Parent** 她_______要_______，没时间。

*Tā _______ yào _______, méi shíjiān.*

**Caller** 那请她回来以后_______，我等她的电话。

*Nà qǐng tā huí lai yǐhòu _______, wǒ děng tā de diànhuà.*

**Parent** 好，再见。

*Hǎo, zàijiàn.*

**Caller** 谢谢您！再见。

*Xièxie nín! Zàijiàn.*

*You have a date tonight in Beijing's hip Gulou neighborhood and want to look your best. What would you use this product for?*

**GET Real WITH CHINESE**

## Chinese Chat

Your classmate is chatting with you on HipChat to set up a study session. How would you reply?

文化
Continue to explore

## Phone etiquette

The receiver of the call usually does not self-identify immediately on answering, as is common in some other cultures. Instead, the receiver typically only says 喂 *(wéi/wèi)* and lets the caller initiate the conversation.

## Cell phones

To call a cell phone, or 手机 *(shǒujī)*, neither 0 nor an area code is needed before dialing the eleven-digit cell phone number. China is now the largest cell phone market in the world. Since the early 2010s, a messaging app called WeChat, or 微信 *(Wēixìn)* (lit. micro message), has quickly become a major social media platform on cell phones and other mobile devices. Because users can call each other through the app as well as send voice messages, it is now a very popular communication tool among people in China and overseas Chinese. In English-language materials in China, the term "mobile phone" rather than "cell phone" is preferred, as in the name of the country's largest cell phone service provider, China Mobile.

# Chinese

Both 中文 *(Zhōngwén)* and 汉语 *(Hànyǔ)* mean "the Chinese language." Derived from the name of one of the longest dynasties of unified China, Han 汉 *(Hàn)* refers to the predominant ethnic group in China, and 汉语 *(Hànyǔ)* literally means "the language of the Han people." Thus, many Chinese citizens of non-Han ethnic backgrounds usually refer to the Chinese language as 汉语 *(Hànyǔ)* rather than 中文 *(Zhōngwén)*, which can be understood as the language of China. Additionally, there is a subtle difference between 语 *(yǔ)* (speech) and 文 *(wén)* (writing), but for most purposes 汉语 *(Hànyǔ)* and 中文 *(Zhōngwén)* are generally considered synonymous.

The Chinese language has the most number of speakers out of any language, and is spoken in at least thirty-three countries. It is important to note that what you are currently studying is Standard Chinese, also known as Modern Standard Mandarin, or simply Mandarin. Mandarin is the standard form of the language. It is referred to as 普通话 *(Pǔtōnghuà)* ("common language") in Mainland China, 国语 *(Guóyǔ)* ("national language") in Taiwan, and 华语 *(Huáyǔ)* ("language spoken by ethnic Chinese people") in Southeast Asia.

## COMPARE & CONTRAST

**1** China is comparable in size to the United States, and yet there is only one time zone in the entire country: 北京时间 *(Běijīng shíjiān)* (Beijing Time). Consequently, people in the western part of the country have to make adjustments to their daily schedules. When most people in Beijing go to work at 8:00 a.m., it is hardly daybreak yet in the western city of Urumqi (乌鲁木齐) *(Wūlǔmùqí)*. Based on the time zone differences, what do you think people in China are doing right now as you read this question?

**2** How many time zones are there in your country? Are there other large countries that have only one time zone? Discuss the pros and cons of having one versus multiple time zones within a country.

# Lesson Wrap-Up

## Make It Flow!

Turn the following eight short sentences into a coherent narrative. Remember to omit repetitive elements and substitute subjects with personal pronouns where appropriate. Use the connective devices 因为 *(yīnwèi)*, 所以 *(suǒyǐ)*, and 可是 *(kěshì)* where appropriate.

今天是星期三。李友星期五要考试。李友想星期四下午去问常老师问题。常老师说她很忙。常老师星期三下午要开会。常老师星期四上午有课。常老师星期四下午四点以后才有空。李友说星期四下午四点半到老师的办公室去。

## Make an Appointment

Make an appointment with your teacher by email or text. Begin your message with a greeting and introduce yourself. Pick a time and find out if your teacher is free. Explain why you would like to see him/her. After you hear back from your teacher, confirm your appointment and express your thanks.

## Make a Call

Call a friend who speaks Chinese. Make sure you remember how to begin a phone conversation. Ask if your friend can help you study for an upcoming Chinese exam, or would like to study together. Pick a time and find out if your friend is free. Ask if he/she would like to have Chinese food afterwards.

**Can-Do Check List**

**Before proceeding to Lesson 7, be sure you can complete the following tasks in Chinese:**

I can

- Answer a phone call and initiate a phone conversation
- Politely ask for a favor
- Set up an appointment on the phone
- Negotiate a time to meet
- Request that my call be returned

# Lesson 7

## 第七课

*Dì qī kè*

# 学中文

*Xué Zhōngwén*

# STUDYING CHINESE

## Learning Objectives

**In this lesson, you will learn to:**

- Discuss your exam performance
- Comment on your character writing
- Discuss your experience learning Chinese
- Talk about your study habits
- Describe typical classroom situations

## Relate & Get Ready

**In your own culture/community:**

- How do people talk about academic achievements?
- What are considered good study habits for learning a foreign language?

# How Did You Do on the Exam?

## Dialogue 1

王朋跟李友说话……

Audio

Video

李友，你上个星期考试考得[1]怎么样？

因为你帮我复习，所以考得不错。
但是我写中国字写得太[2]慢了！

是吗？以后我跟你一起练习写字，好不好[a]？

那太好了！我们现在就[3]写，怎么样？

好，给我一枝笔[4]、一张纸。写什么字？

你教我怎么写“懂”字吧。

好吧。

你写字写得真[2]好，真快。

哪里，哪里[b]。你明天有中文课吗？
我帮你预习。

明天我们学第七[5]课。第七课的语法
很容易，我都懂，可是生词太多，
汉字也有一点儿[6]难。

没问题，我帮你。

## Pinyin Dialogue

*Wáng Péng gēn Lǐ Yǒu shuō huà . . .*

*Lǐ Yǒu, nǐ shàng ge xīngqī kǎo shì kǎo de[1] zěnmeyàng?*

*Yīnwèi nǐ bāng wǒ fùxí, suǒyǐ kǎo de búcuò. Dànshì wǒ xiě Zhōngguó zì xiě de tài[2] màn le!*

*Shì ma? Yǐhòu wǒ gēn nǐ yìqǐ liànxí xiě zì, hǎo bu hǎo[a]?*

*Nà tài hǎo le! Wǒmen xiànzài jiù[3] xiě, zěnmeyàng?*

*Hǎo, gěi wǒ yì zhī bǐ[4], yì zhāng zhǐ. Xiě shénme zì?*

*Nǐ jiāo wǒ zěnme xiě "dǒng" zì ba.*

*Hǎo ba.*

*Nǐ xiě zì xiě de zhēn[2] hǎo, zhēn kuài.*

*Nǎli, nǎli[b]. Nǐ míngtiān yǒu Zhōngwén kè ma? Wǒ bāng nǐ yùxí.*

*Míngtiān wǒmen xué dì qī[5] kè. Dì qī kè de yǔfǎ hěn róngyì, wǒ dōu dǒng, kěshì shēngcí tài duō, Hànzì yě yǒuyìdiǎnr[6] nán.*

*Méi wèntí, wǒ bāng nǐ.*

## Language Notes

**a** 好不好 *(hǎo bu hǎo)*

Like 行吗 *(xíng ma)* and 好吗 *(hǎo ma)*, this expression can be used to seek someone's approval of a proposal.

**b** 哪里 *(nǎli)*

This literally means "where," and is a polite reply to a compliment. In recent times, however, the phrase has become a bit old-fashioned. Many people will respond to a compliment by saying 是吗 *(shì ma)* (is that so?). Some young people in urban areas will also acknowledge a compliment by saying 谢谢 *(xièxie)* (thanks) instead.

# Vocabulary

Audio

Flashcards

| No. | Word | Pinyin | Part of Speech | Definition |
|---|---|---|---|---|
| 1 | 说话 | *shuō huà* | vo | to talk |
| | 话 | *huà* | n | word, speech |
| 2 | 上个 | *shàng ge* | | previous, last |
| 3 | 得 | *de* | p | (a structural particle) [See Grammar 1.] |
| 4 | 复习 | *fùxí* | v | to review |
| 5 | 写 | *xiě* | v | to write |
| 6 | 字 | *zì* | n | character |
| 7 | 慢 | *màn* | adj | slow |
| 8 | 枝 | *zhī* | m | (measure word for long, thin, inflexible objects such as pens, pencils, etc.) |
| 9 | 笔 | *bǐ* | n | pen |
| 10 | 张 | *zhāng* | m | (measure word for flat objects such as paper, pictures, etc.) |
| 11 | 纸 | *zhǐ* | n | paper |
| 12 | 教 | *jiāo* | v | to teach |
| 13 | 怎么 | *zěnme* | qpr | how, how come |
| 14 | 懂 | *dǒng* | v | to understand |
| 15 | 真 | *zhēn* | adv | really [See Grammar 2.] |
| 16 | 哪里 | *nǎli* | pr | where |
| 17 | 预习 | *yùxí* | v | to preview |
| 18 | 学 | *xué* | v | to study, to learn |
| 19 | 第 | *dì* | prefix | (prefix for ordinal numbers) [See Grammar 5.] |
| 20 | 语法 | *yǔfǎ* | n | grammar |

## GET Real WITH CHINESE

*To convert a foreign driver's license in China, applicants must answer ninety out of a hundred questions correctly. If asked, could you identify this sign?*

| No. | Word | Pinyin | Part of Speech | Definition |
|---|---|---|---|---|
| 21 | 容易 | *róngyì* | adj | easy |
| 22 | 生词 | *shēngcí* | n | new words, vocabulary |
| 23 | 多 | *duō* | adj | many, much |
| 24 | 汉字 | *Hànzì* | n | Chinese characters |
| 25 | 难 | *nán* | adj | difficult |

## How About You?

我们一起练习写字吧！
你想练习什么字？

*Wǒmen yìqǐ liànxí xiě zì ba!*
*Nǐ xiǎng liànxí shénme zì?*

Let's practice writing characters!
What characters do you want to practice writing?

就慢教懂

我想练习写 ______ 字。

*Wǒ xiǎng liànxí xiě ______ zì.*

Pick any characters you'd like to practice writing.

# Grammar

## 1 Descriptive complements (I)

The particle 得 *(de)* can be used after a verb or an adjective. This lesson mainly deals with 得 *(de)* as it appears after a verb. The adjective, adverb, or verb phrase that follows 得 *(de)* in the construction below is called a descriptive complement. In this lesson, the descriptive complements are all adjectives that serve as comments on the actions expressed by the preceding verbs.

**A** 他写字写得很好。

*Tā xiě zì xiě de hěn hǎo.*

He writes characters very well.

[很好 *(hěn hǎo)* (very well) is a comment on the action 写 *(xiě)* (to write).]

**B** 他昨天睡觉睡得很晚。

*Tā zuótiān shuì jiào shuì de hěn wǎn.*

He went to bed very late last night.

[很晚 *(hěn wǎn)* (very late) is a comment on the action 睡觉 *(shuì jiào)* (to sleep).]

**C** 妹妹歌唱得很好。

*Mèimei gē chàng de hěn hǎo.*

My younger sister sings very well.

[很好 *(hěn hǎo)* (very well) is a comment on the action 唱 *(chàng)* (to sing).]

If the complement is an adjective, it is usually preceded by 很 *(hěn)* (very), as is the case when an adjective is used as a predicate. If the verb is followed by an object, the verb has to be repeated before it can be followed by the "得 *(de)* + complement" structure, e.g., 写字写得 *(xiě zì xiě de)* in (A). Repeating the verb turns the "verb + object" combination preceding it into a topic and the complement that follows serves as a comment on it. [See Grammar 1, Lesson 10.] The first verb can be omitted if the meaning is clear from the context, as in (C).

### EXERCISES

Complete the sentences below by using 得 to lead a complement. Use exercise 1 as an example.

More exercises

1 我昨天晚上睡________________。

→ 我昨天晚上睡得不错。

2 弟弟昨天吃晚饭吃__________。

3 王朋打球打________________。

## 2 The adverbs 太 (*tài*) (too), 真 (*zhēn*) (really), and 很 (*hěn*) (very)

When the adverbs 太 (*tài*) (too) and 真 (*zhēn*) (really) are used in exclamatory sentences, in most cases they convey not new factual information but the speaker's subjective judgment. If the speaker wants to make a more "objective" statement or description, other intensifiers, such as 很 (*hěn*) (very), are often used instead.

**A** Q: 他写字写得怎么样?

*Tā xiě zì xiě de zěnmeyàng?*

How well does he write characters?

One would normally answer:

A: 他写字写得很好。

*Tā xiě zì xiě de hěn hǎo.*

He writes characters very well.

Rather than:

A: 他写字写得真好。

*Tā xiě zì xiě de zhēn hǎo.*

Compare the second answer with (B).

**B** 小李，你写字写得真好！你可以教我吗？

*Xiǎo Lǐ, nǐ xiě zì xiě de zhēn hǎo! Nǐ kěyǐ jiāo wǒ ma?*

Little Li, you write characters really well! Could you teach me?

太 *(tài)* can also be used in a statement, either with or without 了 *(le)* at the end. It means "excessive in degree," pertaining to a less than satisfactory thing or situation, and the stress can fall either on 太 *(tài)* or the adjective following it.

**C** 你和我两个人吃饭，五个菜太多了。

*Nǐ hé wǒ liǎng ge rén chī fàn, wǔ ge cài tài duō le.*

It's just the two of us eating. Five dishes are too many.

**D** 这个电影太贵了，我不去看。

*Zhè ge diànyǐng tài guì le, wǒ bú qù kàn.*

It costs too much to see this movie, and I am not going to watch it.

**E** 我们是同学，你不要太客气了。

*Wǒmen shì tóngxué, nǐ bú yào tài kèqi le.*

We are classmates. There is no need for you to be so polite.

More exercises

## EXERCISES

Rewrite the declarative sentences as two exclamatory sentences, replacing 很 with 太 and 真 where appropriate. Use exercise 1 as an example.

1 那个电影很有意思。
→ 那个电影真有意思！/那个电影太有意思了！

2 第六课的语法很容易。

3 高文中的家很漂亮。

## 3 The adverb 就 *(jiù)* (I)

The adverb 就 *(jiù)* is used before a verb to suggest the earliness, brevity, or quickness of an action.

**A** 他明天七点就得上课。

*Tā míngtiān qī diǎn jiù děi shàng kè.*

He has to go to class early at 7:00 tomorrow.

**B** 我们八点看电影，他七点半就来了。

*Wǒmen bā diǎn kàn diànyǐng, tā qī diǎn bàn jiù lái le.*

We were supposed to see the movie at 8:00, but he came early at 7:30.

**就 *(jiù)* vs. 才 *(cái)***

就 *(jiù)* suggests the perceived earliness or promptness of an action, as in (C) and (E), whereas 才 *(cái)* suggests the perceived lateness of an action, as in (D) and (F). [See also Grammar 6, Lesson 5.] When commenting on a past action, 就 *(jiù)* is always used with 了 *(le)* to indicate promptness, but 才 *(cái)* is never used with 了 *(le)*.

**C** 八点上课，小白七点就来了。

*Bā diǎn shàng kè, Xiǎo Bái qī diǎn jiù lái le.*

Class started at 8:00, but Little Bai came early at 7:00.

**D** 八点上课，小张八点半才来。

*Bā diǎn shàng kè, Xiǎo Zhāng bā diǎn bàn cái lái.*

Class starts at 8:00, but Little Zhang didn't come until 8:30.

**E** 我昨天五点就回家了。

*Wǒ zuótiān wǔ diǎn jiù huí jiā le.*

Yesterday I went home early at 5:00.

**F** 我昨天五点才回家。

*Wǒ zuótiān wǔ diǎn cái huí jiā.*

Yesterday I didn't get home until 5:00.

More exercises

**EXERCISES**

Indicate the earliness or lateness of an action by inserting 就 or 才 where appropriate. Use exercise 1 as an example.

1 我明天要回家。妹妹上个星期回家了。
→ 我明天要回家，妹妹上个星期就回家了。

2 我昨天五点去打球。王朋四点去打球。

3 我们昨天晚上十一点睡觉。高文中十二点睡觉。

## 4 Double objects

Some verbs can take two objects. The object representing people or animate entities, usually the direct object, precedes the one representing inanimate things, usually the indirect object.

**A** 老师教我们生词和语法。

*Lǎoshī jiāo wǒmen shēngcí hé yǔfǎ.*

The teacher teaches us vocabulary and grammar.

**B** 大哥给了我一瓶水。

*Dà gē gěi le wǒ yì píng shuǐ.*

My big brother gave me a bottle of water.

**C** 你教我汉字，可以吗？

*Nǐ jiāo wǒ Hànzì, kěyǐ ma?*

Will you teach me Chinese characters, please?

**D** 我想问你一个问题。

*Wǒ xiǎng wèn nǐ yí ge wèntí.*

I'd like to ask you a question.

### EXERCISES

Add a direct or indirect object to the sentences below. Use exercise 1 as an example.

More exercises

1 老师给我______________。 → 老师给我一本书。

2 白英爱问______________一个问题。

3 王朋教李友______________。

## 5 Ordinal numbers

Ordinal numbers in Chinese are formed by placing 第 *(dì)* before cardinal numbers, e.g., 第一 *(dì yī)* (the first), 第二杯茶 *(dì èr bēi chá)* (the second cup of tea), 第三个月 *(dì sān ge yuè)* (the third month). However, 第 *(dì)* is not used directly before months, e.g., 一月, 二月, 三月 *(yīyuè, èryuè, sānyuè)* (January, February, March). Neither is it used to indicate the birth order of siblings, e.g., 大哥, 二哥, 三哥 *(dàgē, èrgē, sāngē)* (oldest brother, second oldest brother, third oldest brother); 大姐, 二姐, 三姐 *(dàjiě, èrjiě, sānjiě)* (oldest sister, second oldest sister, third oldest sister).

## 6 有（一）点儿 *(yǒu[yì]diǎnr)* (somewhat, rather, a little bit)

The phrase 有一点儿 *(yǒuyìdiǎnr)* precedes adjectives or verbs. It often carries a negative tone. 一 *(yī)* is optional.

**A** 我觉得中文有（一）点儿难。

*Wǒ juéde Zhōngwén yǒu(yì)diǎnr nán.*

I think Chinese is a little hard.

[✗ 我觉得中文有（一）点儿容易。]

**B** 我觉得这一课生词有（一）点儿多。

*Wǒ juéde zhè yí kè shēngcí yǒu(yì)diǎnr duō.*

I think there are a few too many new words in this lesson.

However, when the sentence describes a change in situation, the phrase 有（一）点儿 *(yǒu[yì]diǎnr)* can carry a positive tone.

**C** 我以前不喜欢他，现在有（一）点儿喜欢他了。

*Wǒ yǐqián bù xǐhuan tā, xiànzài yǒu(yì)diǎnr xǐhuan tā le.*

I used to dislike him, but now I rather like him. [以前 (*yǐqián*) (previously or before)] [See Lesson 8.]

Take care not to confuse 有（一）点儿 (*yǒu|yì|diǎnr*) (a little), which is an adverbial used to modify adjectives, with （一）点儿 (*|yì|diǎnr*) (a little), which usually modifies nouns. In the above sentences, 有（一）点儿 (*yǒu|yì|diǎnr*) is not interchangeable with （一）点儿 (*|yì|diǎnr*).

**D** 给我（一）点儿咖啡。

*Gěi wǒ (yì)diǎnr kāfēi.*

Give me a little coffee.

**E** 给我（一）点儿时间。

*Gěi wǒ (yì)diǎnr shíjiān.*

Give me a little time.

**F** 我有（一）点儿忙。 [✗ 我（一）点儿忙。]

*Wǒ yǒu(yì)diǎnr máng.*

I am kind of busy.

**G** 她有（一）点儿不高兴。

*Tā yǒu(yì)diǎnr bù gāoxìng.*

She is a little unhappy.

[✗ 她（一）点儿不高兴。]

More exercises

## EXERCISES

Rewrite the sentences below to reduce the intensity by inserting 有（一）点儿 where appropriate. Use exercise 1 as an example.

1 第七课很难。 → 第七课有（一）点儿难。

2 老师今天很忙。

3 王朋说中文说得很快。

# Language Practice

## A How well? PRESENTATIONAL

Describe Little Wang's traits based on the information given, inserting 得 *(de)* where appropriate. Pay attention to the structure of the verbs involved, e.g.:

考试 (VO) 好 — *kǎo shì* (VO) *hǎo*

小王常常考试考得很好。 — *Xiǎo Wáng chángcháng kǎo shì kǎo de hěn hǎo.*

1 睡觉 (VO) 晚 — *shuì jiào* (VO) *wǎn*

2 喝咖啡 (VO) 多 — *hē kāfēi* (VO) *duō*

3 写字 (VO) 快 — *xiě zì* (VO) *kuài*

4 说中文 (VO) 好 — *shuō Zhōngwén* (VO) *hǎo*

5 预习 (V) 不错 — *yùxí* (V) *búcuò*

6 工作 (V) 好 — *gōngzuò* (V) *hǎo*

## B Exclamations! PRESENTATIONAL

Let people know how you feel by inserting the adverb 太 *(tài)* or 真 *(zhēn)* when appropriate, e.g.:

汉字◇有意思

*Hànzì ◇ yǒu yìsi*

汉字太有意思了！/ 汉字真有意思！

*Hànzì tài yǒu yìsi le!/Hànzì zhēn yǒu yìsi!*

1 老师家◇漂亮 — *lǎoshī jiā ◇ piàoliang*

2 考试◇容易 — *kǎo shì ◇ róngyì*

3 语法◇难 — *yǔfǎ ◇ nán*

4 同学的中文◇好 *tóngxué de Zhōngwén ◇ hǎo*

5 我写字◇慢 *wǒ xiě zì ◇ màn*

## C Could be worse

PRESENTATIONAL

Moderate your view by inserting 有（一）点儿 *(yǒu[yì]diǎnr)* where appropriate e.g.:

语法◇难 *yǔfǎ ◇ nán*

语法有（一）点儿难。 *Yǔfǎ yǒu(yì)diǎnr nán.*

1 第七课的生词◇多 *dì qī kè de shēngcí ◇ duō*

2 我们的考试◇难 *wǒmen de kǎo shì ◇ nán*

3 中文课◇早 *(zǎo)* (early) *Zhōngwén kè ◇ zǎo* (early)

4 汉字◇难 *Hànzì ◇ nán*

5 老师说话◇快 *lǎoshī shuō huà ◇ kuài*

## D Runs in the family

INTERPERSONAL

In pairs, discuss how well your family members perform certain activities, e.g.:

Q: 你爸爸打球打得怎么样？
*Nǐ bàba dǎ qiú dǎ de zěnmeyàng?*

A: 我爸爸打球打得不好，我妈妈打球打得好。
*Wǒ bàba dǎ qiú dǎ de bù hǎo, wǒ māma dǎ qiú dǎ de hǎo.*

1 

2 

3 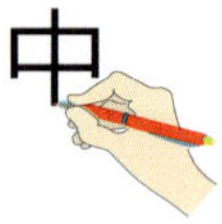

## E How's it going so far? INTERPERSONAL

In pairs, discuss your experience learning Chinese, e.g.:

你觉得中文什么难？生词、语法还是汉字？

*Nǐ juéde Zhōngwén shénme nán? Shēngcí, yǔfǎ háishi hànzì?*

### Characterize it!

- What do the characters mean?
- What is the common radical?
- What does the radical mean?
- How does the radical relate to the overall meaning of the characters?

1 快 2 慢 3 懂

More characters

### Chinese Chat

Your classmate is chatting with you on Google Hangouts about a recent test. How would you reply?

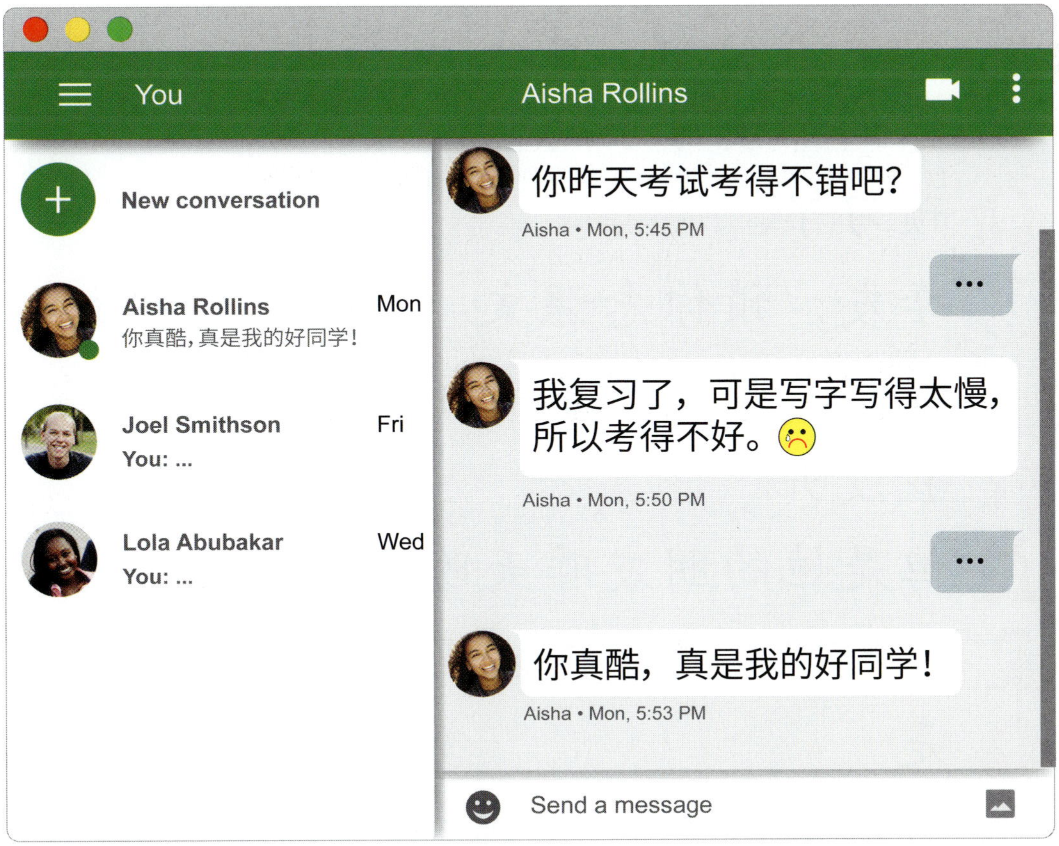

# Preparing for Chinese Class

## Dialogue 2

李友跟白英爱说话……

Audio

Video

白英爱，你平常来得很早，今天怎么[7]这么晚？

我昨天预习中文，早上[a]四点才[3]睡觉，你也睡得很晚吗？

我昨天十点就[3]睡了。因为王朋帮我练习中文，所以我功课做得很快。

有个中国朋友真好。

上中文课……

大家早[b]，现在我们开始上课。第七课你们都预习了吗？

预习了。

李友，请你念课文。……念得很好。你昨天晚上听录音了吧？

我没听。

但是她的朋友昨天晚上帮她学习了。

你的朋友是中国人吗？

是。

他是一个男的[8]，很帅[c]，很酷，叫王朋。[9]

## Pinyin Dialogue

*Lǐ Yǒu gēn Bái Yīng'ài shuō huà . . .*

*Bái Yīng'ài, nǐ píngcháng lái de hěn zǎo, jīntiān zěnme[7] zhème wǎn?*

*Wǒ zuótiān yùxí Zhōngwén, zǎoshang[a] sì diǎn cái[3] shuì jiào, nǐ yě shuì de hěn wǎn ma?*

*Wǒ zuótiān shí diǎn jiù[3] shuì le. Yīnwèi Wáng Péng bāng wǒ liànxí Zhōngwén, suǒyǐ wǒ gōngkè zuò de hěn kuài.*

*Yǒu ge Zhōngguó péngyou zhēn hǎo.*

*Shàng Zhōngwén kè . . .*

*Dàjiā zǎo[b], xiànzài wǒmen kāishǐ shàng kè. Dì qī kè nǐmen dōu yùxí le ma?*

*Yùxí le.*

*Lǐ Yǒu, qǐng nǐ niàn kèwén . . . Niàn de hěn hǎo. Nǐ zuótiān wǎnshang tīng lùyīn le ba?*

*Wǒ méi tīng.*

*Dànshì tā de péngyou zuótiān wǎnshang bāng tā xuéxí le.*

*Nǐ de péngyou shì Zhōngguó rén ma?*

*Shì.*

*Tā shì yí ge nán de[8], hěn shuài[c], hěn kù, jiào Wáng Péng.[9]*

## Language Notes

**a** 早上 *(zǎoshang)*/上午 *(shàngwǔ)*

Both words are usually translated as "morning," but the two are not interchangeable. 早上 *(zǎoshang)* refers to early morning, whereas 上午 *(shàngwǔ)* covers the entire first half of the day (until noon).

**b** 早 *(zǎo)*

This is a common Chinese greeting. Other morning greetings, such as 早上好 *(zǎoshang hǎo)* and 早安 *(zǎo'ān)*, still sound rather formal to many Chinese people.

**c** 帅 *(shuài)*

This term is usually used to describe a handsome man. 漂亮 *(piàoliang)* (pretty) is used to describe an attractive woman. The term 好看 *(hǎokàn)* (good-looking) is gender-neutral, and can be used to describe anyone.

# Vocabulary

Audio

Flashcards

| No. | Word | Pinyin | Part of Speech | Definition |
|---|---|---|---|---|
| 1 | 平常 | *píngcháng* | adv | usually |
| 2 | 早 | *zǎo* | adj | early |
| 3 | 这么 | *zhème* | pr | so, this (late, etc.) |
| 4 | 晚 | *wǎn* | adj | late |
| 5 | 早上 | *zǎoshang* | t | morning |
| 6 | 功课 | *gōngkè* | n | homework, schoolwork |
| 7 | 大家 | *dàjiā* | pr | everybody |
| 8 | 上课 | *shàng kè* | vo | to go to a class, to start a class, to be in class |
| 9 | 开始 | *kāishǐ* | v/n | to begin, to start; beginning |
| 10 | 念 | *niàn* | v | to read aloud |
| 11 | 课文 | *kèwén* | n | text of a lesson |
| 12 | 录音 | *lùyīn* | n/vo | sound recording; to record |
| 13 | 学习 | *xuéxí* | v | to study, to learn |
| 14 | 帅 | *shuài* | adj | handsome |
| 15 | 酷 | *kù* | adj | cool (appearance, behavior) |

## How About You?

你有中文书吗？

*Nǐ yǒu Zhōngwén shū ma?*

Do you have Chinese books?

我有 ________。

*Wǒ yǒu* ________.

See index for corresponding vocabulary or research another term.

# Grammar

## 7 Question pronoun: 怎么 (*zěnme*) (how, how come)

怎么 (*zěnme*) (how, how come) is an interrogative pronoun. It is used to ask about the manner of an action, as in (A), and sometimes the reason or the cause of an action, as in (B) and (C).

**A** 请你教我怎么写"懂"这个字。

*Qǐng nǐ jiāo wǒ zěnme xiě "dǒng" zhè ge zì.*

Please teach me how to write the character "懂."

**B** 你怎么才来?

*Nǐ zěnme cái lái?*

How come you've just arrived?

**C** 你怎么没去看电影?

*Nǐ zěnme méi qù kàn diànyǐng?*

How come you didn't go see the movie?

Both 怎么 (*zěnme*) (how come) and 为什么 (*wèishénme*) (why) are used to ask about the cause of or reason for something. However, 怎么 (*zěnme*) (how come) conveys the speaker's surprise, whereas 为什么 (*wèishénme*) (why) does not.

### EXERCISES

Join these sentences to express surprise by using 怎么 where appropriate. Use exercise 1 as an example.

More exercises

1 我们今天考中文。你昨天晚上九点就睡了。
→ 我们今天考中文，你昨天晚上怎么九点就睡了?

2 上个星期的考试很容易。 白英爱考得不好。

3 高小音是高文中的姐姐。 你不认识高小音。

## 8 The 的 (*de*) structure (I)

We have a 的 (*de*) structure when an adjective is followed by the structural particle 的 (*de*). Grammatically, a 的 (*de*) structure is equivalent to a noun. When Bai Ying'ai says, "他是一个男的 (*Tā shì yí ge nán de*)," it is clear from the context that she means a male (one). [See also Grammar 3, Lesson 9.]

**A** 我写了十个字，五个难的，五个容易的。

*Wǒ xiě le shí ge zì, wǔ ge nán de, wǔ ge róngyì de.*

I wrote ten characters, five difficult ones and five easy ones.

More exercises

### EXERCISES

Rewrite the sentences below by omitting repeated nouns and inserting the 的 structure where appropriate. Use exercise 1 as an example.

1 我练习写了四十个汉字，二十个难的汉字，二十个容易的汉字。

→ 我练习写了四十个汉字，二十个难的，二十个容易的。

2 学校有三个图书馆，一个大图书馆，两个小图书馆。

3 老师想给学生考两个考试，一个难的考试，一个容易的考试。

# Writing Conventions

Traditionally, Chinese was written from top to bottom and from right to left. Store signs and placards, however, were often inscribed horizontally, typically from right to left. Since a 1955 government mandate, left-to-right writing has become standard in Mainland China. However, the traditional way of writing is still kept alive in calligraphy, and occasionally it is still possible to see a store sign that reads from right to left.

For many centuries, the Chinese wrote with a 毛笔 (*máobǐ*), or "writing brush." But people have switched to more convenient Western-style writing instruments such as 铅笔 (*qiānbǐ*) (pencils), 钢笔 (*gāngbǐ*) (fountain pens), and 圆珠笔 (*yuánzhūbǐ*) (ballpoint pens), which are also known as 原子笔 (*yuánzǐbǐ*) in Taiwan. The traditional 毛笔 (*máobǐ*) is now used almost only for calligraphy. Moreover, in the digital era, typing and texting have significantly eroded the importance of handwriting in general.

# Four treasures

The term 文房四宝 (*wénfáng sì bǎo*) ("Four Treasures of the Study") is often used to refer to traditional Chinese stationery, which usually includes 笔 (*bǐ*) (writing brush), 墨 (*mò*) (ink stick), 纸 (*zhǐ*) (paper), and 砚 (*yàn*) (inkstone). The traditional paper for writing and painting is known as 宣纸 (*xuānzhǐ*), named after its most famous place of production, 宣城 (*Xuānchéng*) in Anhui Province. Ink is made by grinding an ink stick on an inkstone with water. Many inkstones are carved. Two of the most famous kinds are 端砚 (*duānyàn*) and 歙砚 (*shèyàn*), from Guangdong and Anhui, respectively. Ink sticks are typically made from burnt pinewood with a binding agent and an aromatic substance. Antique ink sticks and inkstones are highly prized as collectibles.

# Lesson Wrap-Up

## Make It Flow!

Rearrange the following sentences into a logical sequence. Then combine them into a coherent narrative. Remember to omit repetitive elements and substitute subjects with personal pronouns where appropriate. Use connective devices such as 因为 *(yīnwèi)* and 所以 *(suǒyǐ)*.

| | |
|---|---|
| __1__ 王朋昨天帮李友练习中文了。 | _____ 李友今天有中文课。 |
| _____ 李友昨天晚上功课做得很快。 | _____ 李友念得很好。 |
| _____ 李友昨天晚上十点就睡了。 | _____ 老师请李友念课文。 |

## Study Buddy

*Pre-interview:* Assess your strengths and weaknesses.

| | |
|---|---|
| 你常常听录音吗？ | 第六课的语法你懂了吗？ |
| 你的发音好吗？ | 你写汉字写得怎么样？ |
| 你觉得生词难吗？ | 你中文考试考得怎么样？ |

*Interview:* What are your classmates' strengths? Interview three classmates.

| | |
|---|---|
| 你觉得中文语法容易吗？ | 你想和同学一起学习中文吗？ |
| 你觉得汉字怎么样，难吗？ | 你什么时候有时间？ |

Can you think of any other questions that would help you find a good study partner?

## Skit

Prepare a skit based on the prompts, then perform it in front of the class.

**Student A** Your friend has been acting strangely. Usually, he/she is never late to class. You want to find out why.

**Student B** You've been very busy and going to bed very late. You've been having difficulty with your Chinese class. The grammar is very difficult. There is a lot of homework and new vocabulary. And there are many tests!

**Student A** Can you relate to your friend? What can you do to help?

## Can-Do Check List

Before proceeding to Lesson 8, be sure you can complete the following tasks in Chinese:

I can

- Describe my performance on a test
- Describe the way someone reads, writes, and speaks Chinese
- Ask someone to help me with my Chinese
- Explain how I prepare for my Chinese class
- Describe my experience learning Chinese

# Lesson 8

## 第八课

*Dì bā kè*

# 学校生活

*Xuéxiào shēnghuó*

# SCHOOL LIFE

## Learning Objectives

**In this lesson, you will learn to:**

- Describe a student's daily routine
- Write a simple diary entry or blog post
- Write a brief letter or formal email applying appropriate conventions
- Update a friend on recent activities
- Express hope that a friend will accept your invitation

## Relate & Get Ready

**In your own culture/community:**

- How do people connect with friends?
- How has technology affected letter-writing conventions?
- How do you think people will communicate about their daily lives and connect with others in the future?

# A Typical School Day

## Diary Entry

Audio

Video

李友的一篇日记

十一月三日 星期二

今天我很忙，很累。早上七点半起床[1]，洗了澡以后就[2]吃早饭。我一边吃饭，一边[3]听录音。九点到教室去上课[4]。

第一节课是中文，老师教我们发音、生词和语法，也教我们写字，还给了[5]我们一篇新课文[6]，这篇课文很有意思。第二节是电脑[a]课，很难。

中午我和同学们一起到餐厅去吃午饭。我们一边吃，一边练习说中文。下午我到图书馆去上网。四点王朋来找我打球。五点三刻吃晚饭。七点半我去白英爱的宿舍跟她聊天（儿）。到那儿的时候，她正在[7]做功课。我八点半回家。睡觉以前，高文中给我打了一个电话，告诉我明天要考试，我说我已经知道了。

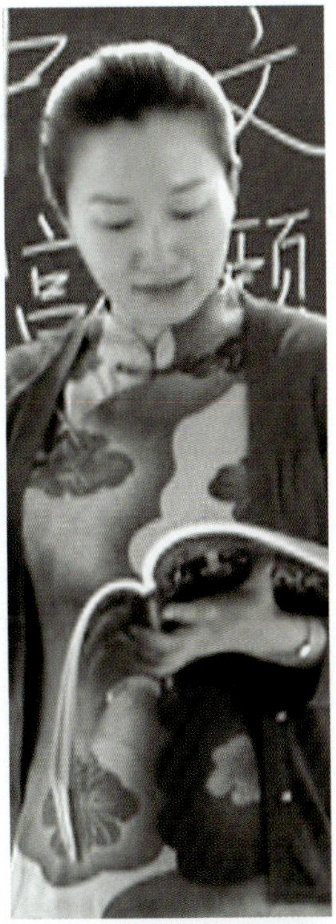

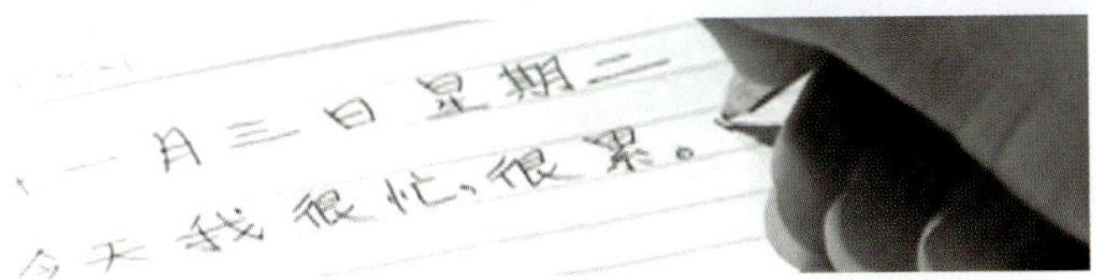


## Pinyin Diary Entry

*Lǐ Yǒu de yì piān rìjì*

*Shíyī yuè sān rì xīngqīèr*

*Jīntiān wǒ hěn máng, hěn lèi. Zǎoshang qī diǎn bàn qǐ chuáng*[1]*, xǐ le zǎo yǐhòu jiù*[2] *chī zǎofàn. Wǒ yìbiān chī fàn, yìbiān*[3] *tīng lùyīn. Jiǔ diǎn dào jiàoshì qù shàng kè*[4]*.*

*Dì yī jié kè shì Zhōngwén, lǎoshī jiāo wǒmen fāyīn, shēngcí hé yǔfǎ, yě jiāo wǒmen xiě zì, hái gěi le*[5] *wǒmen yì piān xīn kèwén*[6]*, zhè piān kèwén hěn yǒu yìsi. Dì èr jié shì diànnǎo*[a] *kè, hěn nán.*

*Zhōngwǔ wǒ hé tóngxuémen yìqǐ dào cāntīng qù chī wǔfàn. Wǒmen yìbiān chī, yìbiān liànxí shuō Zhōngwén. Xiàwǔ wǒ dào túshūguǎn qù shàng wǎng. Sì diǎn Wáng Péng lái zhǎo wǒ dǎ qiú. Wǔ diǎn sān kè chī wǎnfàn. Qī diǎn bàn wǒ qù Bái Yīng'ài de sùshè gēn tā liáo tiān(r). Dào nàr de shíhou, tā zhèngzài*[7] *zuò gōngkè. Wǒ bā diǎn bàn huí jiā. Shuì jiào yǐqián, Gāo Wénzhōng gěi wǒ dǎ le yí ge diànhuà, gàosu wǒ míngtiān yào kǎoshì, wǒ shuō wǒ yǐjīng zhīdao le.*

## Language Note

### a 电脑 (*diànnǎo*)

The usual colloquial term for a computer is 电脑 (*diànnǎo*), literally "electric brain." A more formal term, especially in Mainland China, is 电子计算机 (*diànzǐ jìsuànjī*) (electronic computing machine) or simply 计算机 (*jìsuànjī*). But in Taiwan, 计算机 (*jìsuànjī*) means a calculator. In Mainland China, a calculator is called 计算器 (*jìsuànqì*).

# Vocabulary

Audio

Flashcards

| No. | Word | Pinyin | Part of Speech | Definition |
|---|---|---|---|---|
| 1 | 篇 | *piān* | m | (measure word for essays, articles, etc.) |
| 2 | 日记 | *rìjì* | n | diary |
| 3 | 累 | *lèi* | adj | tired |
| 4 | 起床 | *qǐ chuáng* | vo | to get up |
| | 床 | *chuáng* | n | bed |
| 5 | 洗澡 | *xǐ zǎo* | vo | to take a bath/shower |
| 6 | 早饭 | *zǎofàn* | n | breakfast |
| 7 | 一边 | *yìbiān* | adv | simultaneously, at the same time [See Grammar 3.] |
| 8 | 教室 | *jiàoshì* | n | classroom |
| 9 | 发音 | *fāyīn* | n | pronunciation |
| 10 | 新 | *xīn* | adj | new |
| 11 | 电脑 | *diànnǎo* | n | computer |
| | 脑 | *nǎo* | n | brain |
| 12 | 中午 | *zhōngwǔ* | t | noon |
| 13 | 餐厅 | *cāntīng* | n | dining room, cafeteria |
| 14 | 午饭 | *wǔfàn* | n | lunch, midday meal |
| 15 | 上网 | *shàng wǎng* | vo | to go online, to surf the internet |
| 16 | 宿舍 | *sùshè* | n | dormitory |
| 17 | 那儿 | *nàr* | pr | there |
| 18 | 正在 | *zhèngzài* | adv | in the middle of (doing something) [See Grammar 7.] |

*Street food in China ranges from steamed buns to scallion pancakes. Based on the character with the smiley face, determine whether this food truck serves breakfast, lunch, or dinner.*

**GET Real WITH CHINESE**

| No. | Word | Pinyin | Part of Speech | Definition |
|---|---|---|---|---|
| 19 | 以前 | *yǐqián* | t | before |
| 20 | 告诉 | *gàosu* | v | to tell |
| 21 | 已经 | *yǐjīng* | adv | already |
| 22 | 知道 | *zhīdao* | v | to know |

## How About You?

你和朋友在哪儿见面？

*Nǐ hé péngyǒu zài nǎ'er jiànmiàn?*

Where do you meet your friends?

我们在 ________ 见面。

*Wǒmen zài ________ jiànmiàn.*

See index for corresponding vocabulary or research another term.

# Grammar

## 1 The position of time-when expressions

Time-when expressions come before the verb. They often appear after the subject, but sometimes precede the subject under certain conditions. In this lesson, we focus on practicing time-when expressions positioned after the subject.

**A** 我们十点上课。

*Wǒmen shí diǎn shàng kè.*

We start class at ten.

**B** 我们几点去?

*Wǒmen jǐ diǎn qù?*

What time are we going?

**C** 你什么时候睡觉?

*Nǐ shénme shíhou shuì jiào?*

When do you go to bed?

**D** 他明天上午八点来。

*Tā míngtiān shàngwǔ bā diǎn lái.*

He will come at eight tomorrow morning.

More exercises

### EXERCISES

Form two new sentences by inserting time-when expressions where appropriate. Use exercise 1 as an example.

1 王朋去学校看书。 昨天晚上七点

→ 王朋昨天晚上七点去学校看书了。

2 李友去高文中家玩儿。 上个星期六

3 常老师要去中国开会。 下个月

## 2 The adverb 就 (*jiù*) (II)

The adverb 就 (*jiù*) connects two verbs or verb phrases to indicate that the second action happens as soon as the first one is completed. [See also Grammar 3, Lesson 7.]

**A** 他今天早上起床以后就听中文录音了。

*Tā jīntiān zǎoshang qǐ chuáng yǐhòu jiù tīng Zhōngwén lùyīn le.*

He listened to the Chinese audio right after he got up this morning.

**B** 王朋看了电视以后就去睡觉了。

*Wáng Péng kàn le diànshì yǐhòu jiù qù shuì jiào le.*

Wang Peng went to bed right after watching TV.

**C** 我做了功课以后就去朋友家玩儿。

*Wǒ zuò le gōngkè yǐhòu jiù qù péngyou jiā wánr.*

I will go to my friend's place right after I finish my homework.

### EXERCISES

Link the two actions to form a sentence, inserting 就 where appropriate. Use exercise 1 as an example.

More exercises

1 常老师起床以后 去洗澡

→ 常老师起床以后就去洗澡。

2 李友吃了晚饭 去找人打球

3 小王给他弟弟打了电话 去学校上课

## 3 Describing simultaneity using 一边⋯ 一边⋯ (*yìbiān . . . yìbiān . . .*)

This structure describes two simultaneous actions. Typically, the first action is the principal one, which begins before the second, accompanying action.

**A** 我们一边吃晚饭，一边练习说中文。

*Wǒmen yìbiān chī wǎnfàn, yìbiān liànxí shuō Zhōngwén.*

We practiced speaking Chinese while having dinner.

**B** 他常常一边吃饭一边看电视。

*Tā chángcháng yìbiān chī fàn yìbiān kàn diànshì.*

He often eats and watches TV at the same time.

**C** 我一边洗澡一边唱歌。

*Wǒ yìbiān xǐ zǎo, yìbiān chàng gē.*

I sang while I was showering.

**D** 我妹妹喜欢一边看书一边听音乐。

*Wǒ mèimei xǐhuan yìbiān kàn shū, yìbiān tīng yīnyuè.*

My younger sister likes to listen to music while she reads.

More exercises

### EXERCISES

Form sentences to indicate the simultaneity of the two actions by inserting 一边⋯一边⋯ where appropriate. Use exercise 1 as an example.

1 高小音 看书 听音乐

→ 高小音一边看书，一边听音乐。

2 王朋和朋友 看球 聊天儿

3 白老师 看电影 喝可乐

## 4 Series of verbs/verb phrases

Some verbs and verb phrases can be used in succession to represent a series of actions. Their sequential order usually coincides with the temporal order of the actions.

**A** 他常常去高小音家吃饭。

*Tā chángcháng qù Gāo Xiǎoyīn jiā chī fàn.*

He often goes to eat at Gao Xiaoyin's place.

**B** 下午我要到图书馆去看书。

*Xiàwǔ wǒ yào dào túshūguǎn qù kàn shū.*

This afternoon, I will go to the library to read.

**C** 我明天想找同学去打球。

*Wǒ míngtiān xiǎng zhǎo tóngxué qù dǎ qiú.*

I'd like to find some classmates to play ball with tomorrow.

**D** 你明天来我家吃晚饭吧。

*Nǐ míngtiān lái wǒ jiā chī wǎnfàn ba.*

Come and have dinner at my house tomorrow.

### EXERCISES

Answer the questions by adding the given verb phrase where appropriate. Use exercise 1 as an example.

1 Q: 小王今天去哪儿吃晚饭？ 去朋友家

→ A: 他今天去朋友家吃晚饭。

2 Q: 周末我们去哪儿打球？ 去学校

3 Q: 小白在哪儿上网？ 在家

More exercises

## 5 The particle 了 *(le)* (II)

If a statement enumerates a series of realized actions or events, 了 *(le)* usually appears at the end of the series rather than after each verb. [See also Grammar 5, Lesson 5, and Grammar 2, Lesson 1, Volume 2.]

**A** 昨天第一节课是中文。老师教我们发音、生词和语法，也教我们写字，还给了我们一篇新课文。那篇课文很有意思。

*Zuótiān dì yī jié kè shì Zhōngwén. Lǎoshī jiāo wǒmen fāyīn, shēngcí hé yǔfǎ, yě jiāo wǒmen xiě zì, hái gěi le wǒmen yì piān xīn kèwén. Nà piān kèwén hěn yǒu yìsi.*

Yesterday, the first class was Chinese. Our teacher taught us pronunciation, vocabulary, and grammar. She also taught us how to write characters and gave us a new text. That text was very interesting.

## 6 The particle 的 *(de)* (III)

When a disyllabic or polysyllabic adjective modifies a noun, the particle 的 *(de)* is usually inserted between the adjective and the noun.

**A**

| 漂亮的学校 | 容易的汉字 | 有意思的电影 |
|---|---|---|
| *piàoliang de xuéxiào* | *róngyì de Hànzì* | *yǒu yìsi de diànyǐng* |
| beautiful school | easy character | interesting movie |

However, with monosyllabic adjectives, 的 *(de)* is generally not required.

**B**

| 新课文 | 新电脑 | 大教室 | 好老师 |
|---|---|---|---|
| *xīn kèwén* | *xīn diànnǎo* | *dà jiàoshì* | *hǎo lǎoshī* |
| new text | new computer | big classroom | good teacher |

If the adjective is preceded by 很 *(hěn)*, however, 的 *(de)* cannot be dropped, e. g., 很大的教室 *(hěn dà de jiàoshì)* (very big classroom), 很好的老师 *(hěn hǎo de lǎoshī)* (very good teacher).

## 7 The 正在 (*zhèngzài*) v structure (be doing . . . )

The 正在 (*zhèngzài*) v structure (be doing . . . ) denotes an ongoing or progressive action at a certain point of time. It is more emphatic than 在 (*zài*), which can serve the same function.

**A** Q: 李友，你在做什么？

*Lǐ Yǒu, nǐ zài zuò shénme?*

Li You, what are you doing?

A: 我在练习写汉字。

*Wǒ zài liànxí xiě Hànzì.*

I'm practicing writing Chinese characters.

**B** 我们现在正在上课，你别打电话。

*Wǒmen xiànzài zhèngzài shàng kè, nǐ bié dǎ diànhuà.*

We are in class right now. Don't make phone calls.

**C** 我昨天到他宿舍的时候，他正在练习发音。

*Wǒ zuótiān dào tā sùshè de shíhou, tā zhèngzài liànxí fāyīn.*

When I got to his dorm yesterday, he was in the middle of practicing pronunciation.

**D** Q: 你知道不知道王老师在哪儿？

*Nǐ zhīdao bù zhīdào Wáng lǎoshī zài nǎr?*

Do you know where Teacher Wang is?

A: 他正在办公室开会。

*Tā zhèngzài bàngōngshì kāi huì.*

He is having a meeting in his office.

### EXERCISES

Join the two sentences by inserting the "…的时候，…正在…" construction where appropriate. Use exercise 1 as an example.

More exercises

1 王朋给我打电话。 我做功课。

→ 王朋给我打电话的时候，我正在做功课。

2 我打电话回家。 爸爸妈妈吃晚饭。

3 我到她宿舍。 她上网。

# Language Practice

## A What a day! PRESENTATIONAL

Describe Little Gao's schedule using appropriate time expressions, e.g.:

小高早上八点起床。

*Xiǎo Gāo zǎoshang bā diǎn qǐ chuáng.*

| | | | | | | |
|---|---|---|---|---|---|---|
| MON 29 | TUE 30 | WED 31 | THU 01 | FRI 02 | SAT 03 | SUN 04 |
| MON 05 | TUE 06 | WED 07 | THU 08 | FRI 09 | SAT 10 | SUN 11 |
| MON 12 | TUE 13 | WED 14 | THU 15 | FRI 16 | SAT 17 | SUN 18 |
| MON 19 | TUE 20 | WED 21 | THU 22 | FRI 23 | SAT 24 | SUN 25 |

## B Multitasking INTERPERSONAL

Using the images below, practice how to describe two simultaneous actions by inserting 一边…一边… (*yìbiān . . . yìbiān . . .*) where appropriate. Then ask if your partner multitasks, e.g.:

他们一边喝茶，一边聊天儿。

*Tāmen yìbiān hē chá, yìbiān liáo tiānr.*

你也常常和朋友一边喝茶，一边聊天吗？

*Nǐ yě chángcháng hé péngyou yìbiān hē chá, yìbiān liáo tiānr ma?*

1 

2 

3 

4 

## C Putting things in order

INTERPRETIVE

Determine the logical sequence of the actions and fill in the blanks with appropriate locations or personal names. Then rearrange the phrases into complete sentences, e.g.:

王朋　去玩（儿）　到______家

*Wáng Péng　qù wán (r)　dào______jiā*

王朋到高小音家去玩（儿）。

*Wáng Péng dào Gāo Xiǎoyīn jiā qù wán(r).*

| | | | |
|---|---|---|---|
| 1 | 到______去<br>*dào ______qù* | 高文中<br>*Gāo Wénzhōng* | 问老师问题<br>*wèn lǎoshī wèntí* |
| 2 | 打球<br>*dǎ qiú* | 王朋<br>*Wáng Péng* | 找______<br>*zhǎo ______* |
| 3 | 找同学聊天<br>*zhǎo tóngxué liáo tiān* | 去______<br>*qù ______* | 小白<br>*Xiǎo Bái* |
| 4 | 教她怎么写汉字<br>*jiāo tā zěnme xiě Hànzì* | 李友<br>*Lǐ Yǒu* | 请______<br>*qǐng ______* |

## D Lesson plans

PRESENTATIONAL

Based on your class schedule, tell the class how you would organize classes on pronunciation, vocabulary, grammar, Chinese characters, and the lesson texts if you were the teacher, e.g.:

我星期一教大家生词，星期二教大家语法，……

*Wǒ xīngqīyī jiāo dàjiā shēngcí, xīngqīèr jiāo dàjiā yǔfǎ, . . .*

Which topics do students have the most questions about?

学生常常问老师发音的问题。

*Xuésheng chángcháng wèn lǎoshī fāyīn de wèntí.*

## E Keeping tabs

INTERPERSONAL

In pairs, form a question-and-answer about what people are doing based on the images below. Use 正在 (*zhèngzài*), e.g.:

Q: 他正在做什么？

*Tā zhèngzài zuò shénme?*

A: 他正在睡觉。

*Tā zhèngzài shuì jiào.*

1 

2 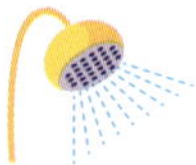

3 

4 

## F Business as usual

INTERPERSONAL

In pairs, form a question-and-answer about your partner's daily routines, e.g.:

Q: 你平常几点起床？ *Nǐ píngcháng jǐ diǎn qǐ chuáng?*

A: 我平常八点起床。 *Wǒ píngcháng bā diǎn qǐchuáng.*

你平常几点吃早饭/去上课/吃午饭/吃晚饭？

*Nǐ píngcháng jǐ diǎn chī zǎofàn/qù shàng kè/chī wǔfàn/chī wǎnfàn?*

你平常什么时候洗澡？

*Nǐ píngcháng shénme shíhou xǐ zǎo?*

你（是）起床以后还是睡觉以前洗澡？

*Nǐ (shì) qǐ chuáng yǐhòu háishi shuì jiào yǐqián xǐ zǎo?*

## G Character development

INTERPRETIVE PRESENTATIONAL

Present a day in the life of a fictional character from a screenplay or novel you'd like to write, e.g.:

王文早上九点起床，吃了早饭以后就去上课，……下午两点去找同学打球，……

*Wáng Wén zǎoshang jiǔ diǎn qǐ chuáng, chī le zǎofàn yǐhòu jiù qù shàng kè, . . .*

*Xiàwǔ liǎng diǎn qù zhǎo tóngxué dǎ qiú, . . .*

Then quiz the class about your character's day, e.g.:

王文吃了午饭以后做什么?

*Wáng Wén chī le wǔfàn yǐhòu zuò shénme?*

王文练习了中文以后做什么?

*Wáng Wén liànxí le Zhōngwén yǐhòu zuò shénme?*

王文跟朋友打了球以后做什么?

*Wáng Wén gēn péngyou dǎ le qiú yǐhòu zuò shénme?*

## Characterize it!

- What do the characters mean?
- What is the common radical?
- What does the radical mean?
- How does the radical relate to the overall meaning of the characters?

1 洗 2 澡

More characters

## Chinese Chat

Your friend is texting you through Facebook Messenger about when to hang out. How would you reply?

# Writing to a Friend

## Letter

Audio

Video

一封信

这是李友给高小音的一封信。

小音：

你好！好久不见，最近怎么样？

这个学期我很忙，除了专业课以外，还[8]得学中文。我们的中文课很有意思。因为我们的中文老师只会[9]说中文，不会说英文，所以上课的时候我们只说中文，不说英文。开始我觉得很难，后来[a]，王朋常常帮我练习中文，就[10]觉得不难了[b]。

你喜欢听音乐吗？下个星期六，我们学校有一个音乐会，希望你能[9]来。我用中文写信写得很不好，请别笑我。祝好！

你的朋友

李友

十一月十八日

*Yì fēng xìn*

*Zhè shì Lǐ Yǒu gěi Gāo Xiǎoyīn de yì fēng xìn.*

*Xiǎoyīn:*

*Nǐ hǎo! Hǎo jiǔ bú jiàn, zuìjìn zěnmeyàng?*

*Zhè ge xuéqī wǒ hěn máng, chúle zhuānyè kè yǐwài, hái*[8] *děi xué Zhōngwén. Wǒmen de Zhōngwén kè hěn yǒu yìsi. Yīnwèi wǒmen de Zhōngwén lǎoshī zhǐ huì*[9] *shuō Zhōngwén, bú huì shuō Yīngwén, suǒyǐ shàng kè de shíhou wǒmen zhǐ shuō Zhōngwén, bù shuō Yīngwén. Kāishǐ wǒ juéde hěn nán, hòulái*[a]*, Wáng Péng chángcháng bāng wǒ liànxí Zhōngwén, jiù*[10] *juéde bù nán le*[b]*.*

*Nǐ xǐhuan tīng yīnyuè ma? Xià ge xīngqīliù, wǒmen xuéxiào yǒu yí ge yīnyuèhuì, xīwàng nǐ néng*[9] *lái. Wǒ yòng Zhōngwén xiě xìn xiě de hěn bù hǎo, qǐng bié xiào wǒ. Zhù*

*Hǎo!*

*Nǐ de péngyou*

*Lǐ Yǒu*

*Shíyīyuè shíbā rì*

## Language Notes

**a** 后来 *(hòulái)*

This is usually translated as "later," but it pertains only to actions and situations in the unspecified past.

**b** 了 *(le)*

This sentence-final particle usually indicates a change in status or the realization of a new situation. [See also Grammar 2, Lesson 1, Volume 2.]

# Vocabulary

Audio

Flashcards

| No. | Word | Pinyin | Part of Speech | Definition |
|---|---|---|---|---|
| 1 | 封 | *fēng* | m | (measure word for letters) |
| 2 | 信 | *xìn* | n | letter (correspondence) |
| 3 | 最近 | *zuìjìn* | t | recently |
| | 最 | *zuì* | adv | (of superlative degree, most, -est) |
| | 近 | *jìn* | adj | close, near |
| 4 | 学期 | *xuéqī* | n | school term, semester, quarter |
| 5 | 除了……以外 | *chúle . . . yǐwài* | conj | in addition to, besides [See Grammar 8.] |
| 6 | 专业 | *zhuānyè* | n | major (in college), specialty |
| 7 | 会 | *huì* | mv | can, know how to [See Grammar 9.] |
| 8 | 后来 | *hòulái* | t | later |
| 9 | 音乐会 | *yīnyuèhuì* | n | concert |
| 10 | 希望 | *xīwàng* | v/n | to hope; hope [See Grammar 9.] |
| 11 | 能 | *néng* | mv | can, to be able to [See Grammar 9.] |
| 12 | 用 | *yòng* | v | to use |
| 13 | 笑 | *xiào* | v | to laugh at, to laugh, to smile |
| 14 | 祝 | *zhù* | v | to wish (well) |

你的专业是什么？

*Nǐ de zhuānyè shì shénme?*

What's your major?

How About You?

我的专业是____________。

*Wǒ de zhuānyè shì* ____________.

See index for corresponding vocabulary or research another term.

# Grammar

## 8 Indicating inclusiveness: 除了…以外，还/也… (*chúle . . . yǐwài, hái/ yě . . .*) (in addition to, also)

除了… 以外 (*chúle . . . yǐwài*) means “apart from” or “in addition to.” When followed by 还… (*hái . . .*) (also, too, as well) or 也 (*yě*) (too, also), it indicates inclusiveness of the content inserted between 除了 (*chúle*) and 以外 (*yǐwài*).

**A** 我除了学专业课以外，还学中文。

*Wǒ chúle xué zhuānyè kè yǐwài, hái xué Zhōngwén.*

Besides the courses in my major, I also take Chinese.

**B** 上个周末我们除了看电影以外，还听音乐了。

*Shàng ge zhōumò wǒmen chúle kàn diànyǐng yǐwài, hái tīng yīnyuè le.*

Last weekend, besides seeing a movie, we also listened to music.

**C** 他除了喜欢听音乐以外，还喜欢打球。

*Tā chúle xǐhuan tīng yīnyuè yǐwài, hái xǐhuan dǎ qiú.*

In addition to listening to music, he also likes to play ball.

The activities in (A), (B), and (C) are performed by the same subject. If activities are done by different subjects, the adverb 也 has to be used. In these cases, the first subject follows 除了, and the second subject precedes 也, as in (D).

**D** 除了小王以外，小李也喜欢唱歌、跳舞。

*Chúle Xiǎo Wáng yǐwài, Xiǎo Lǐ yě xǐhuan chàng gē, tiào wǔ.*

Like Little Wang, Little Li also enjoys singing and dancing.

### EXERCISES

Join the two sentences to indicate inclusiveness by inserting 除了… 以外，还/也… where appropriate. Use exercise 1 as an example.

More exercises

1 她这个学期学中文。她这个学期学日文。
→ 她这个学期除了学中文以外，还学日文。

2 王朋今天晚上想看球。王朋今天晚上想上网。

3 李友周末想看电影。白英爱周末想看电影。

## 9 Comparing 能 (*néng*) and 会 (*huì*) (I)

Both 能 (*néng*) and 会 (*huì*) have several meanings. The basic meaning of 能 (*néng*) is "to be capable of (doing something)," as in (A). It can also indicate the viability of an action, as in (B) and (C). Additional meanings will be introduced in later lessons. 会 (*huì*), as used in (D), (E), and (F), means having acquired the skill to do something through learning.

**A** 我能喝十杯咖啡。

*Wǒ néng hē shí bēi kāfēi.*

I can drink ten cups of coffee.

**B** 今天下午我要开会，不能去听音乐会。

*Jīntiān xiàwǔ wǒ yào kāi huì, bù néng qù tīng yīnyuèhuì.*

I have a meeting this afternoon. I cannot go to the concert.

**C** 我们不能在图书馆聊天儿。

*Wǒmen bù néng zài túshūguǎn liáo tiānr.*

We cannot chat in the library.

**D** 李友会说中文。

*Lǐ Yǒu huì shuō Zhōngwén.*

Li You can speak Chinese.

**E** 小白会唱很多美国歌。

*Xiǎo Bái huì chàng hěn duō Měiguó gē.*

Little Bai can sing many American songs.

**F** 我不会打球，请你教我。

*Wǒ bú huì dǎ qiú, qǐng nǐ jiāo wǒ.*

I don't know how to play ball. Please teach me how.

## EXERCISES

In pairs, ask about your partner's capabilities or availability by inserting 会 or 能 when appropriate.

More exercises

1 Q: 你______ 用中文写信吗? A: 我 ______。

2 Q: 明天考试，今天晚上你 ______去看电影吗?

A: 我 ______。

## 10 The conjunctions 要是 *(yàoshi)* and 因为 *(yīnwèi)* and the adverb 就 *(jiù)* (III)

In this structure, the first clause conveys a condition or reason while the second clause denotes the result or conclusion. The adverb 就 *(jiù)* indicates the close relationship between the two. The relationship is often causal, as in (A) and (B), or conditional, as in (C) and (D).

**A** （因为）小高喜欢吃中国菜，（所以）我们就吃中国菜。

*(Yīnwèi) Xiǎo Gāo xǐhuan chī Zhōngguó cài, (suǒyǐ) wǒmen jiù chī Zhōngguó cài.*

Little Gao prefers Chinese food, so we went for Chinese food.

**B** （因为）小王的专业是中文，（所以）我就请他教我怎么说中文。

*(Yīnwèi) Xiǎo Wáng de zhuānyè shì Zhōngwén, (suǒyǐ) wǒ jiù qǐng tā jiāo wǒ zěnme shuō Zhōngwén.*

Little Wang's major is Chinese, so I asked him to teach me how to speak Chinese.

**C** 要是同学帮我复习，我考试就考得很好。

*Yàoshi tóngxué bāng wǒ fùxí, wǒ kǎoshì jiù kǎo de hěn hǎo.*

If my classmates help me review, I do very well on my tests.

**D** 要是你不能来，我就去你那儿。

*Yàoshi nǐ bù néng lái, wǒ jiù qù nǐ nàr.*

If you can't come over, I will go to your place.

**E** 写汉字，开始觉得很难，（要是）常常练习，就觉得容易了。

*Xiě Hànzì, kāishǐ juéde hěn nán, (yàoshi) chángcháng liànxí, jiù juéde róngyì le.*

Learning to write Chinese characters might be very difficult at first. It becomes easier with practice.

More exercises

## EXERCISES

Join the sentences to indicate the close relationship between two actions or situations. Use exercise 1 as an example.

1 你喜欢看美国电影。我们看美国电影。
→ 你喜欢看美国电影，我们就看美国电影。

2 你不喜欢吃中国菜。我们不吃中国菜。

3 你不会用中文跟他聊天。你用英文跟他聊天。

## GET Real WITH CHINESE

*Upon enrollment, Chinese university students are given a basic ID card (学生卡) (xuéshēngkǎ) and a more detailed ID book (学生证) (xuéshēngzhèng). Based on her ID book, describe this student as best you can.*

# Language Practice

## H In addition

INTERPERSONAL

In pairs, ask each other these questions using 除了…以外，还… (*chúle . . . yǐwài, hái . . .*):

1 你今天除了上中文课以外，还上什么课？

*Nǐ jīntiān chúle shàng Zhōngwén kè yǐwài, hái shàng shénme kè?*

2 你们上中文课除了练习语法以外，还做什么？

*Wǒmen shàng Zhōngwén kè chúle liànxí yǔfǎ yǐwài, hái zuò shénme?*

3 你除了会说中文以外，还会说什么话？

*Nǐ chúle huì shuō Zhōngwén yǐwài, hái huì shuō shénme huà?*

## I Ends and means

INTERPERSONAL

In pairs, form a question-and-answer about what tools people use to perform certain actions. Use 用 (*yòng*), e.g.:

上网 ◇ 电脑

*shàng wǎng ◇ diànnǎo*

Q: 你用什么上网？
*Nǐ yòng shénme shàng wǎng?*

A: 我用电脑上网。
*Wǒ yòng diànnǎo shàng wǎng.*

1 做功课 ◇ 笔

*zuò gōngkè ◇ bǐ*

2 练习发音 ◇ 电脑

*liànxí fāyīn ◇ diànnǎo*

3 喝茶 ◇ 咖啡杯

*hē chá ◇ kāfēi bēi*

4 写日记 ◇ 中文

*xiě rìjì ◇ Zhōngwén*

5 看电影 ◇ 电脑

*kàn diànyǐng ◇ diànnǎo*

J

## Get personal

INTERPERSONAL

Survey your classmates about how they write letters and diary entries.

你写信吗?

*Nǐ xiě xìn ma?*

你常常给谁写信?

*Nǐ chángcháng gěi shéi xiě xìn?*

你会用电脑写信吗?

*Nǐ huì yòng diànnǎo xiě xìn ma?*

你写日记吗?

*Nǐ xiě rìjì ma?*

你用中文写日记还是用英文写日记?

*Nǐ yòng Zhōngwén xiě rìjì háishi yòng yīngwén xiě rìjì?*

## Characterize it!

| |
|---|
| What do the characters mean? |
| What is the common radical? |
| What does the radical mean? |
| How does the radical relate to the overall meaning of the characters? |

1 近 2 边 3 道

More characters

## Chinese Chat

Li You just published a post on Qzone (QQ空间) (*QQ kōngjiān*), a Chinese social networking site. What comment would you leave?

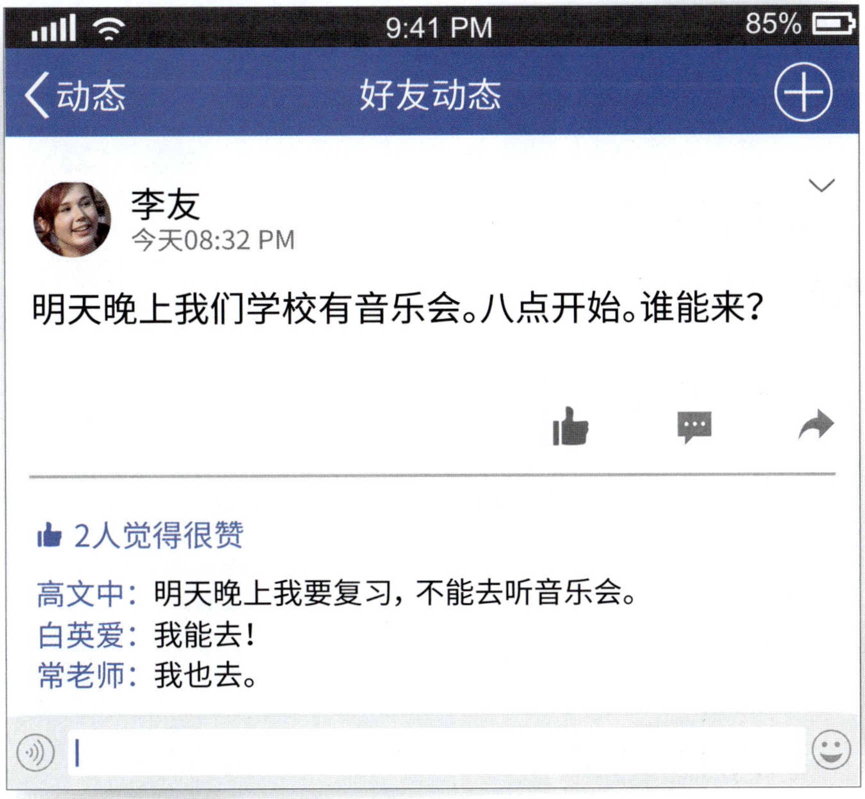

# CULTURAL LITERACY

文化
Continue to explore

## Semesters

Colleges and universities in both Mainland China and Taiwan are on the semester system. Typically, the fall semester starts in late August or early September, and ends in mid-January. The winter break lasts about a month. Since the Chinese New Year usually falls in late January or early February, college students can take advantage of the break to go home and celebrate the most important holiday of the year with their families. The spring semester starts around mid-February and lasts until early July. A semester at a Chinese college is about three weeks longer than a typical American college semester.

### COMPARE & CONTRAST

Applicants to Chinese universities and colleges are required to take the National Higher Education Entrance Examination, also known as *Gaokao* (高考) (*gāo kǎo*). In 2015, more than nine million people took the test. The admission rate was about 75%. Although the majority of applicants make it into college, only those with the highest scores are admitted into a 一本大学 (*yī běn dàxué*) (first-tier university). Others go to a 二本大学 (*èr běn dàxué*) (second-tier university), 三本大学 (*sān běn dàxué*) (third-tier university), or higher vocational college. Compare *Gaokao* and the equivalent standardized test in your own country, and discuss the advantages and disadvantages of different college admission processes.

# Yours truly

The traditional way to end a formal letter is to use the closing 祝好 (*zhù hǎo*) (I wish you well), with the character 祝 (*zhù*) (to wish) following the final sentence of the letter and the character 好 (*hǎo*) at the very beginning of the next line.

However, it is now more common to keep the two characters 祝好 (*zhù hǎo*) unseparated. With the advent of new technology like social media, formal writing conventions (including salutations and sign-offs) are changing rapidly.

# Lesson Wrap-Up

## Make It Flow!

Rearrange the following sentences into chronological order. Then combine them into a coherent narrative. Remember to avoid repeating the same nouns by replacing them with pronouns where appropriate. Use 一边⋯ 一边⋯ (*yìbiān . . . yìbiān . . .*), 除了⋯以外，还⋯ (*chúle . . . yǐwài, hái . . .*) where appropriate.

____李友早上7点起床。

____李友吃早饭的时候听录音。

____李友上午有中文课。

_1__李友今天很忙。

____李友下午3点去图书馆上网。

____李友晚上8点半和王朋一起练习说中文。

____李友11点半才睡觉。

____李友7点半吃早饭。

____李友5点半吃晚饭。

____李友上午有三节课。

____李友4点去打球。

____李友上午还有电脑课。

## Blog

Using the diary format, post a blog entry describing your day.

## Email

Write an email describing your Chinese teacher and outlining why he/she should be nominated for a teaching award. Use formal letter-writing conventions.

### Can-Do Check List

Before proceeding to Lesson 9, make sure you can complete the following tasks in Chinese:

I can

- Narrate my daily routine at school
- Update a friend on recent activities
- Write a simple diary entry or blog post using appropriate conventions
- Write a brief letter or formal email using appropriate conventions

# Lesson 9

## 第九课

*Dì jiǔ kè*

# 买东西

*Mǎi dōngxi*

# SHOPPING

## Learning Objectives

**In this lesson, you will learn to:**

- Describe the color, size, and price of a purchase
- Recognize Chinese currency
- Pay in cash or with a credit card
- Determine the proper change you should receive
- Ask for merchandise in a different size or color
- Exchange merchandise

## Relate & Get Ready

**In your own culture/community:**

- Do people haggle over prices in stores?
- Can merchandise be returned or exchanged?
- Do people typically pay for their purchases with cash?

# Shopping for Clothes

## Dialogue 1

李友在商店买东西，售货员问她……

Audio

Video

小姐，您要[1]买什么衣服？

我想买一件[2]衬衫。

您喜欢什么颜色的[3]，黄的还是红的？

我喜欢穿[a]红的。我还想买一条[2]裤子[b]。

多[4]大的？大号的、中号的、还是小号的？

中号的。不要太贵的，也不要太便宜[c]的。

这条裤子怎么样？

颜色很好。如果长短合适的话，我就买。

您试一下。

Li You checks the size on the label and measures the pants against her legs.

不用试。可以。

这件衬衫呢？

也不错。一共多少钱？

衬衫二十一块五，裤子三十二块九毛九，一共是五十四块四毛九分[5]。

好，这是一百块钱。

找您四十五块五毛一。

谢谢。

## Pinyin Dialogue

*Lǐ Yǒu zài shāngdiàn mǎi dōngxi, shòuhuòyuán wèn tā . . .*

*Xiǎojiě, nín yào[1] mǎi shénme yīfu?*

*Wǒ xiǎng mǎi yí jiàn[2] chènshān.*

*Nín xǐhuan shénme yánsè de[3], huáng de háishi hóng de?*

*Wǒ xǐhuan chuān[a] hóng de. Wǒ hái xiǎng mǎi yì tiáo[2] kùzi[b].*

*Duō[4] dà de? Dà hào de, zhōng hào de, háishi xiǎo hào de?*

*Zhōng hào de. Bú yào tài guì de, yě bú yào tài piányi[c] de.*

*Zhè tiáo kùzi zěnmeyàng?*

*Yánsè hěn hǎo, rúguǒ chángduǎn héshì de huà, wǒ jiù mǎi.*

*Nín shì yí xia.*

Li You checks the size on the label and measures the pants against her legs.

*Búyòng shì, kěyǐ.*

*Zhè jiàn chènshān ne?*

*Yě búcuò. Yígòng duōshao qián?*

*Chènshān èrshíyī kuài wǔ, kùzi sānshí'èr kuài jiǔ máo jiǔ, yígòng shì wǔshísì kuài sì máo jiǔ fēn[5].*

*Hǎo, zhè shì yìbǎi kuài qián.*

*Zhǎo nín sìshíwǔ kuài wǔ máo yī.*

*Xièxie.*

## Language Notes

### a 穿 *(chuān)*

Note that this verb can mean both "to wear" and "to put on." However, for most accessories, 戴 *(dài)* (to wear, to put on) is used instead.

### b 一条裤子 *(yì tiáo kùzi)*

In Chinese, a pair of pants is considered a single piece of clothing. Hence, it is 一条裤子 *(yì tiáo kùzi)* (lit. a trouser) instead of ✖ 一双裤子 *(yì shuāng kùzi)* (lit. a pair of trousers).

### c 便宜 *(piányi)*

The first character of 便宜 *(piányi)* (inexpensive) is pronounced "*pián*." But in 方便 *(fāngbiàn)* (convenient), the same character is pronounced "*biàn*." Sometimes the same character can have different pronunciations that carry different meanings. Other examples include 乐 *(yuè* or *lè)* and 觉 *(jué* or *jiào)*: 音乐 *(yīnyuè)* (music), 可乐 *(kělè)* (cola), 觉得 *(juéde)* (to feel), and 睡觉 *(shuì jiào)* (to sleep).

# Vocabulary

Audio

Flashcards

| No. | Word | Pinyin | Part of Speech | Definition |
|---|---|---|---|---|
| 1 | 商店 | *shāngdiàn* | n | store, shop |
| 2 | 买 | *mǎi* | v | to buy |
| 3 | 东西 | *dōngxi* | n | things, objects |
| 4 | 售货员 | *shòuhuòyuán* | n | shop assistant, salesclerk |
| 5 | 衣服 | *yīfu* | n | clothes |
| 6 | 件 | *jiàn* | m | (measure word for shirts, dresses, jackets, coats, etc.) |
| 7 | 衬衫 | *chènshān* | n | shirt |
| 8 | 颜色 | *yánsè* | n | color |
| 9 | 黄 | *huáng* | adj | yellow |
| 10 | 红 | *hóng* | adj | red |
| 11 | 穿 | *chuān* | v | to wear, to put on |
| 12 | 裤子 | *kùzi* | n | pants |
| 13 | 号 | *hào* | n | size |
| 14 | 中 | *zhōng* | adj | medium, middle |
| 15 | 便宜 | *piányi* | adj | cheap, inexpensive |
| 16 | 如果 | *rúguǒ* | conj | if |
| | 的话 | *de huà* | | |
| 17 | 长短 | *chángduǎn* | n | length |
| | 长 | *cháng* | adj | long |
| | 短 | *duǎn* | adj | short |
| 18 | 合适 | *héshì* | adj | suitable |
| 19 | 试 | *shì* | v | to try |
| 20 | 不用 | *búyòng* | | need not |
| 21 | 一共 | *yígòng* | adv | altogether |
| 22 | 多少 | *duōshao* | qpr | how much/many |

You are wandering the Shilin Night Market in Taipei and come across this vendor selling *imagawayaki* (车轮饼) (*chēlúnbǐng*). How many can you buy with 100 yuan?

**GET Real WITH CHINESE**

| No. | Word | Pinyin | Part of Speech | Definition |
|---|---|---|---|---|
| 23 | 钱 | *qián* | n | money |
| 24 | 块 | *kuài* | m | (measure word for the basic Chinese monetary unit [equivalent of a dollar]) |
| 25 | 毛 | *máo* | m | (measure word for 1/10 of a kuai [equivalent of a dime]) |
| 26 | 分 | *fēn* | m | (measure word for 1/100 of a kuai [equivalent of a cent]) |
| 27 | 百 | *bǎi* | nu | hundred |
| 28 | 找（钱） | *zhǎo (qián)* | v(o) | to give change |

## 您要买什么衣服？

*Nín yào mǎi shénme yīfu?*

What would you like to buy?

### How About You?

我想买__________。

*Wǒ xiǎng mǎi* __________.

See index for corresponding vocabulary or research another term.

# Grammar

## 1 The modal verb 要 (*yào*) (want to do) (II)

要 (*yào*) can also mean "to desire to do something." [See also Grammar 2, Lesson 6.]

**A** 明天是周末，你要做什么？

*Míngtiān shì zhōumò, nǐ yào zuò shénme?*

Tomorrow is the weekend. What do you want to do?

**B** 我要去图书馆看书，你去不去？

*Wǒ yào qù túshūguǎn kàn shū, nǐ qù bu qù?*

I want to go to the library to read. Do you want to come?

**C** 我要喝可乐，他要喝茶。

*Wǒ yào hē kělè, tā yào hē chá.*

I want to drink cola. He wants to drink tea.

To negate it, use 不想 (*bù xiǎng*).

**D** 我不想去图书馆。

*Wǒ bù xiǎng qù túshūguǎn.*

I don't want to go to the library.

**E** 今天我不想做功课。

*Jīntiān wǒ bù xiǎng zuò gōngkè.*

I don't want to do my homework today.

Both of the modal verbs 想 (*xiǎng*) and 要 (*yào*) can express a desire or an intention, but 要 (*yào*) carries a stronger tone.

More exercises

### EXERCISES

Answer the following questions using 要 where appropriate.

1 李友要去商店买什么？

2 你这个周末要做什么？

## 2 Measure words (II)

These are useful "measure word + noun" combinations. [See also Grammar 2, Lesson 2.]

| Word | Pinyin | Definition |
|---|---|---|
| 一个人 | *yí ge rén* | a person |
| 一位先生 | *yí wèi xiānsheng* | a gentleman |
| 一杯茶 | *yì bēi chá* | a cup of tea |
| 一瓶可乐 | *yì píng kělè* | a bottle of cola |
| 一枝笔 | *yì zhī bǐ* | a pen |
| 一张纸 | *yì zhāng zhǐ* | a piece of paper |
| 一节课 | *yì jié kè* | a class period |
| 一篇课文 | *yì piān kèwén* | the text of a lesson |
| 一件衬衫 | *yí jiàn chènshān* | a shirt |
| 一条裤子 | *yì tiáo kùzi* | a pair of pants |
| 一双鞋 | *yì shuāng xié* | a pair of shoes [See Dialogue 2.] |
| 一块钱 | *yí kuài qián* | one yuan |
| 一毛钱 | *yì máo qián* | one mao (1/10 of a yuan) |
| 一分钱 | *yì fēn qián* | one fen (1/100 of a yuan) |
| 一本书 | *yì běn shū* | a book |
| 一只鞋 | *yì zhī xié* | a shoe (one of a pair) [See also "a pair of shoes," above.] |

### EXERCISES

Fill in the blanks with the proper measure words.

More exercises

1 两______咖啡

2 三______衬衫

## 3 The 的 (*de*) structure (II)

We have a 的 (*de*) structure when a noun, a pronoun, an adjective, or a verb is followed by the structural particle 的 (*de*). Grammatically, a 的 (*de*) structure is equivalent to a noun, e.g., 老师的 (*lǎoshī de*) (the teacher's), 我的 (*wǒ de*) (mine), 大的 (*dà de*) (the big one), 吃的 (*chī de*) (things to eat). [See also Grammar 8, Lesson 7.]

More exercises

### EXERCISES

Answer the following questions using the 的 structure where appropriate.

1 你的衬衫是大号的、中号的还是小号的？

2 你爸爸喜欢穿什么颜色的裤子？

## 4 Using 多 (*duō*) interrogatively

The adverb 多 (*duō*) is often used in questions asking about degree or extent. The adjectives that follow 多 (*duō*) typically suggest an expansive quality, such as 大 (*dà*) (big), as in (A) and (B), and 高 (*gāo*) (tall, high), as in (C). Note that words that denote a diminutive quality, such as 小 (*xiǎo*) (small, little) and 矮 (*ǎi*) (short), are not used in this construction.

**A** 你今年多大？ [See Lesson 3.]

*Nǐ jīnnián duō dà?*

How old are you this year?

**B** 你穿多大的衣服？

*Nǐ chuān duō dà de yīfu?*

What size clothes do you wear?

**C** 你弟弟多高？

*Nǐ dìdi duō gāo?*

How tall is your younger brother?

More exercises

### EXERCISES

Form questions asking about degree or extent by inserting 多 where appropriate.

1 高文中　高

2 你弟弟　大

## 5 Denominations of currency

The denominations of Chinese currency are as follows.

| Usage | Unit of Currency | 1/10 of a Unit | 1/100 of a Unit |
|---|---|---|---|
| Standard[a] | 元 *(yuán)* | 角 *(jiǎo)* | 分 *(fēn)* |
| Colloquial | 块 *(kuài)* | 毛 *(máo)* | 分 *(fēn)* |

[a]Store prices are typically listed in 元 *(yuán)* and 角 *(jiǎo)*.

In colloquial speech, ¥5.99 is 五块九毛九分钱 *(wǔ kuài jiǔ máo jiǔ fēn qián)*. In conversation, abbreviated forms are also used, e.g., 五块九毛九分 (omitting 钱 *[qián]* [money]) and 五块九毛九 (omitting 钱 *[qián]* and the last unit). If 钱 *(qián)* is included, the preceding measure (e.g., 分 *[fēn]*) must also be included. ✖ 五块九毛九钱.

One or more zeroes occurring internally in a complex number are read as 〇 *(líng)* (zero). To avoid ambiguity, 毛 *(máo)* and 分 *(fēn)* must be retained, as in (D) or (E).

**A** 八块五毛五（分）（钱）

*bā kuài wǔ máo wǔ (fēn) (qián)*

¥8.55

**B** 十五块三（毛）（钱）

*shíwǔ kuài sān (máo) (qián)*

¥15.30

**C** 一百〇三块（钱）

*yìbǎi líng sān kuài (qián)*

¥103

**D** 一百块〇三毛（钱）

*yìbǎi kuài líng sān máo (qián)*

¥100.30

**E** 一百块〇三分（钱）

*yìbǎi kuài líng sān fēn (qián)*

¥100.03

### EXERCISES

Say the following amounts of money in Chinese.

1 ¥9.99 2 ¥135.20 3 ¥86.04

More exercises

# Language Practice

## A I'll check my calendar INTERPERSONAL

In pairs, form a question-and-answer about what Little Wang wants to do next week based on the following calendar. [See also Grammar 2, Lesson 6.] Insert 要 *(yào)* where appropriate, e.g.:

星期一 *(xīngqīyī)*

Q: 小王下个星期一要做什么？

*Xiǎo Wáng xià ge xīngqīyī yào zuò shénme?*

A: 小王下个星期一要去上课。

*Xiǎo Wáng xià ge xīngqīyī yào qù shàng kè.*

Then discuss your partner's plans for next week, e.g.:

Q: 你呢？你下个星期要做什么？

*Nǐ ne? Nǐ xià ge xīngqī yào zuò shénme?*

A: 我下个星期一…… 星期二……

*Wǒ xià ge xīngqīyī . . . xīngqīèr . . .*

## B Online shopping spree

PRESENTATIONAL

Little Li is an avid online shopper. Recap what's in her shopping cart based on the images below, using 想 *(xiǎng)* where appropriate, e.g.:

小李想买一件新衣服。

*Xiǎo Lǐ xiǎng mǎi yí jiàn xīn yīfu.*

1 

2 

3 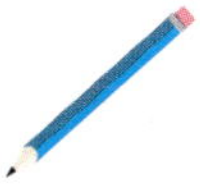

4 

Then share what's on your online wish list with the class and explain why you want the items, e.g.:

我喜欢白色/我没有白色的裤子，
所以我想买一条白色的裤子。

*Wǒ xǐhuān báisè/Wǒ méiyǒu báisè de kùzi, suǒyǐ wǒ xiǎng mǎi yì tiáo báisè de kùzi.*

## C Lost and found

INTERPERSONAL

In pairs, identify to whom the objects belong. Use 的 *(de)*, e.g.:

Q: 这瓶可乐是谁的？

*Zhè píng kělè shì shéi de?*

A: 这瓶可乐是高文中的。

*Zhè píng kělè shì Gāo Wénzhōng de.*

1  

2  

3  

Then identify the colors of Little Wang's belongings, using 的 *(de)*, e.g.:

Q: 小王的笔是什么颜色的？

*Xiǎo Wáng de bǐ shì shénme yánsè de?*

A: 小王的笔是黄色的。

*Xiǎo Wáng de bǐ shì huángsè de.*

1 

2 

3 

## D Questions, questions, questions! INTERPERSONAL

In pairs, ask questions about your friend's sibling's age, the price of your friend's pants, etc., by using 多 *(duō)*.

## E Shopping poll INTERPERSONAL

Poll your classmates on their shopping habits for the student newspaper, e.g.:

你喜欢买东西吗?

*Nǐ xǐhuan mǎi dōngxi ma?*

你喜欢买什么东西?

*Nǐ xǐhuan mǎi shénme dōngxi?*

你常常去买东西吗?

*Nǐ chángcháng qù mǎi dōngxi ma?*

你喜欢买衣服吗?

*Nǐ xǐhuan mǎi yīfu ma?*

你常常去哪儿买东西?

*Nǐ chángcháng qù nǎr mǎi dōngxi?*

你常常跟谁一起去买东西?

*Nǐ chángcháng gēn shéi yìqǐ qù mǎi dōngxi?*

你有几件衬衫?

*Nǐ yǒu jǐ jiàn chènshān?*

你有几条裤子?

*Nǐ yǒu jǐ tiáo kùzi?*

## F INTERPERSONAL Fashion blogger PRESENTATIONAL

Present a popular fashion blogger to the class, then start a dialogue about his/her sense of style, e.g.:

(Fashion blogger's name) 喜欢什么颜色?

(Fashion blogger's name) *xǐhuan shénme yánsè?*

她/他喜欢穿什么颜色的衣服?

*Tā xǐhuan chuān shénme yánsè de yīfu?*

她/他今天的衣服是什么颜色的?

*Tā jīntiān de yīfu shì shénme yánsè de?*

你觉得她/他今天的衣服长短合适不合适？

*Nǐ juéde tā jīntiān de yīfu chángduǎn héshì bù héshì?*

她/他的衣服多吗？

*Tā de yīfu duō ma?*

## Characterize it!

- What do the characters mean?
- What is the common radical?
- What does the radical mean?
- How does the radical relate to the overall meaning of the characters?

1 衬 2 衫 3 裤

More characters

## Chinese Chat

Your friend is messaging you on LINE while shopping. How would you reply?

# Exchanging Shoes

## Dialogue 2

王朋想换一双鞋，他问售货员……

Audio

Video

对不起，这双鞋太小了。
能不能换一双？

没问题。您看，这双怎么样？

也不行，这双**跟**那双**一样**[6]大。

那这双黑的呢？

这双鞋**虽然**大小合适，**可是**[7]颜色不好。
有没有咖啡色的？

对不起，这种鞋只有黑的。

这双鞋样子**挺好的**[a]，**就是它吧**[b]。
你们这儿可以刷卡吗？

对不起，我们不收信用卡。
不过，这双的钱跟那双一样，
您不用再付钱了。

## Pinyin Dialogue

*Wáng Péng xiǎng huàn yì shuāng xié, tā wèn shòuhuòyuán . . .*

*Duìbuqǐ, zhè shuāng xié tài xiǎo le. Néng bu néng huàn yì shuāng?*

*Méi wèntí. Nín kàn, zhè shuāng zěnmeyàng?*

*Yě bù xíng, zhè shuāng gēn nà shuāng yíyàng*[6] *dà.*

*Nà zhè shuāng hēi de ne?*

*Zhè shuāng xié suīrán dàxiǎo héshì, kěshì*[7] *yánsè bù hǎo. Yǒu méiyǒu kāfēisè de?*

*Duìbuqǐ, zhè zhǒng xié zhǐ yǒu hēi de.*

*Zhè shuāng xié yàngzi tíng hǎo de*[a], *jiù shì tā ba*[b]. *Nǐmen zhèr kěyǐ shuā kǎ ma?*

*Duìbuqǐ, wǒmen bù shōu xìnyòngkǎ. Búguò, zhè shuāng de qián gēn nà shuāng yíyàng, nín búyòng zài fù qián le.*

## Language Notes

**a** 挺 *(tǐng)*

The construction 挺 + adj + 的 *(tǐng + adj + de)* means "it's rather + adj." 的 *(de)* is optional.

**b** 就是它吧 *(jiù shì tā ba)*

This expression is often used to indicate the completion of a selection. It means "I'll take this one." [See Keeping It Casual (L5–L10).]

# Vocabulary

Audio

Flashcards

| No. | Word | Pinyin | Part of Speech | English |
|---|---|---|---|---|
| 1 | 双 | *shuāng* | m | (measure word for a pair) |
| 2 | 鞋 | *xié* | n | shoes |
| 3 | 换 | *huàn* | v | to exchange, to change |
| 4 | 一样 | *yíyàng* | adj | same, alike [See Grammar 6.] |
| 5 | 虽然 | *suīrán* | conj | although [See Grammar 7.] |
| 6 | 大小 | *dàxiǎo* | n | size |
| 7 | 咖啡色 | *kāfēisè* | n | brown, coffee color |
| 8 | 种 | *zhǒng* | m | (measure word for kinds, sorts, types) |
| 9 | 黑 | *hēi* | adj | black |
| 10 | 样子 | *yàngzi* | n | style |
| 11 | 挺 | *tǐng* | adv | very, rather |
| 12 | 它 | *tā* | pr | it |
| 13 | 这儿 | *zhèr* | pr | here |
| 14 | 刷卡 | *shuā kǎ* | vo | to pay with a credit card |
| | 刷 | *shuā* | v | to brush, to swipe |
| | 卡 | *kǎ* | n | card |
| 15 | 收 | *shōu* | v | to receive, to accept |
| 16 | 信用卡 | *xìnyòngkǎ* | n | credit card |
| 17 | 不过 | *búguò* | conj | however, but |
| 18 | 再 | *zài* | adv | again |
| 19 | 付钱 | *fù qián* | vo | to pay money |
| | 付 | *fù* | v | to pay |

In many countries, there is heated debate over who should appear on currency. In China, many figures used to appear but, since 1999, all have been replaced with Chairman Mao. What are the denominations of these fourth edition bills (on the right)? Research the names of the ethnic groups depicted.

**GET Real WITH CHINESE**

## How About You?

# 你喜欢什么颜色?

*Nǐ xǐhuan shénme yánsè?*

What color do you like?

我喜欢________。

*Wǒ xǐhuan ________.*

See index for corresponding vocabulary or research another term.

## Characterize it!

- What do the characters mean?
- What is the common radical?
- What does the radical mean?
- How does the radical relate to the overall meaning of the characters?

1 果 2 床 3 杯 4 末

More characters

# Grammar

## 6 Comparing using 跟/和…（不）一样 (*gēn/hé...[bù] yíyàng*) ([not] the same as . . . )

To express similarity or dissimilarity between objects, people, or actions, use the structure 跟/和…（不）一样 (*gēn/hé . . . [bù] yíyàng*) ([not] the same as . . . ). Following 一样 (*yíyàng*) (same, alike) an adjective can be used, as in (C), (D), and (E).

**A** 你的衬衫跟我的一样。

*Nǐ de chènshān gēn wǒ de yíyàng.*

Your shirt is the same as mine.

**B** 贵的衣服和便宜的衣服不一样。

*Guì de yīfu hé piányi de yīfu bù yíyàng.*

Expensive clothes are different from cheap ones.

**C** 弟弟跟哥哥一样高。

*Dìdi gēn gēge yíyàng gāo.*

The younger brother is as tall as the older one.

**D** 这个电脑跟那个电脑一样新。

*Zhè ge diànnǎo gēn nà ge diànnǎo yíyàng xīn.*

This computer is as new as that one.

**E** 常老师写汉字写得跟王老师（写汉字写得）一样漂亮。

*Cháng lǎoshī xiě Hànzì xiě de gēn Wáng lǎoshī (xiě Hànzì xiě de) yíyàng piàoliang.*

Teacher Chang writes Chinese characters as beautifully as Teacher Wang does.

More exercises

### EXERCISES

Form sentences by combining these words and inserting the A 跟/和 B 一样 structure where appropriate. Use exercise 1 as an example.

1 妹妹　　姐姐　　高

→ 妹妹和/跟姐姐一样高。

2 这件衬衫　那件衬衫　漂亮

3 你的电脑　我的电脑　贵

## 7 The conjunctions 虽然…，可是/但是… (*suīrán . . . , kěshì/dànshì . . .*) (although . . . yet . . . )

This pair of conjunctions links two clauses to form a complex sentence. Note, however, that 虽然 (*suīrán*) (although) is often optional.

**A** 虽然这双鞋很便宜，可是大小不合适。

*Suīrán zhè shuāng xié hěn piányi, kěshì dàxiǎo bù héshì.*

Although this pair of shoes is very inexpensive, they're not the right size.

**B** 这件衬衫大小很合适，可是太贵了。

*Zhè jiàn chènshān dàxiǎo hěn héshì, kěshì tài guì le.*

This shirt is the right size, but it's too expensive.

**C** 学中文不容易，但是很有意思。

*Xué Zhōngwén bù róngyì, dànshì hěn yǒu yìsi.*

Learning Chinese is not easy, but it's very interesting.

Whether or not 虽然 (*suīrán*) is used in the first clause, 可是/但是 (*kěshì/dànshì*) (but) cannot be omitted in the second.

[⊗ 虽然学中文不容易，很有意思。]

### EXERCISES

Join these sentences by using the 虽然…，可是/但是… structure and deleting identical nouns and pronouns where appropriate. Use exercise 1 as an example.

More exercises

1 这个电脑很快。 这个电脑很贵。

→ 虽然这个电脑很快，可是（这个电脑）很贵。

2 这条裤子大小很合适。 这条裤子颜色不好。

3 这个商店的东西很便宜。这个商店不收信用卡。

# Language Practice

## G Just the same

PRESENTATIONAL

Form sentences by combining these words and inserting the A 跟/和 *(gēn/hé)* B 一样 *(yíyàng)* structure in the ◇, e.g.:

这件衣服 ◇ 那件衣服 ◇ 漂亮

*zhè jiàn yīfu ◇ nà jiàn yīfu ◇ piàoliang*

这件衣服跟那件衣服一样漂亮。

*Zhè jiàn yīfu gēn nà jiàn yīfu yíyàng piàoliang.*

1 这枝笔 ◇ 那枝笔 ◇ 便宜 — *zhè zhī bǐ ◇ nà zhī bǐ ◇ piányi*

2 这条裤子 ◇ 那条裤子 ◇ 贵 — *zhè tiáo kùzi ◇ nà tiáo kùzi ◇ guì*

3 这双鞋 ◇ 那双鞋 ◇ 合适 — *zhè shuāng xié ◇ nà shuāng xié ◇ héshì*

4 这件衬衫 ◇ 那件衬衫 ◇ 大 — *zhè jiàn chènshān ◇ nà jiàn chènshān ◇ dà*

5 第九课的语法 ◇ — *dì jiǔ kè de yǔfǎ ◇*
第八课的语法 ◇ 难 — *dì bā kè de yǔfǎ ◇ nán*

## H All shopped out

PRESENTATIONAL

Form sentences expressing shopping frustrations by using the 虽然 *(suīrán)* …，可是/但是 *(kěshì/dànshì)* … structure where appropriate, e.g.:

虽然这个商店的鞋都很漂亮，可是她都不喜欢。

*Suīrán zhè ge shāngdiàn de xié dōu hěn piàoliang, kěshi tā dōu bù xǐhuan.*

1 他的新衣服很多 ◇ — *tā de xīn yīfu hěn duō ◇*
他都不穿 — *tā dōu bù chuān*

2 这条裤子很便宜 ◇ — *zhè tiáo kùzi hěn piányi ◇*
长短不合适 — *chángduǎn bù héshì*

3 这件衬衫的颜色很好看 ◇ — *zhè jiàn chènshān de yánsè hěn hǎokàn ◇*

有一点儿小 yǒu yìdiǎnr xiǎo

4 这双鞋样子挺不错的 ◇ zhè shuāng xié yàngzi tǐng búcuò de ◇

太贵了 tài guì le

5 这个商店不小 ◇ zhè ge shāngdiàn bù xiǎo ◇

不能刷卡 bù néng shuā kǎ

## I Double trouble

PRESENTATIONAL

Here's some information about two sisters who are identical twins. Describe what they have in common, using 跟/和 *(gēn/hé)* …一样 *(yíyàng)* where appropriate, e.g.:

王文京跟王文英一样大。 *Wáng Wénjīng gēn Wáng Wényīng yíyàng dà.*

1 Height: 5'5" 5'5"

2 Shirts: size 6 size 6

3 Pants: red red

## J Taking stock

INTERPERSONAL INTERPRETIVE

You're starting your own fashion line. To determine your business strategy, survey your classmates about their color preferences and sizes. Then jot down your findings.

鞋/衬衫/裤子 *xié/chènshān/kùzi*

你喜欢穿什么颜色的? *Nǐ xǐhuan chuān shénme yánsè de?*

你穿多大的? *Nǐ chuān duō dà de?*

**Chinese Chat**

Li You just updated her status on Facebook, and Wang Peng left a comment. What do you think Wang Peng is hinting at?

文化
Continue to explore

# Traditional Clothes

Contemporary Chinese fashion is largely similar to that of the West. On formal occasions, Chinese men wear suits and ties and women wear Western-style dresses. When dressing casually, many young people wear jeans and T-shirts. However, more traditional clothing from the early tewntieth century can still be seen around China.

One of the most enduring examples of traditional Chinese fashion is 旗袍 (*qípáo*), a close-fitting woman's dress with a high collar and a slit skirt. It was extremely popular among urban women until 1949 in Mainland China and into the 1960s and 70s in Taiwan. Today, you can still see women in *qipao* at weddings and formal parties. Specialized stores offer *qipao* designs in both modernized and traditional versions. They are popular among foreign tourists, and several fashion brands in Europe and North America have introduced *qipao*-influenced designs.

For Chinese men in the early twentieth century, the traditional formal attire was a long robe called 长袍 (*chángpáo*) (lit. long gown) and a short jacket called 马褂 (*mǎguà*) (Mandarin jacket). Today they have disappeared from city streets, but remain an important part of Chinese visual culture. Characters in popular period dramas and films, as well as performers of 相声 (*xiàngsheng*) (cross-talk), a type of traditional stand-up comedy involving two comics, and storytelling arts such as 评弹 (*píngtán*) (Suzhou-style ballad singing), are frequently seen in 长袍 (*chángpáo*). Until the 1990s, almost every Chinese man wore the 中山装 (*Zhōngshānzhuāng*) ("Sun Yat-sen suit"), better known in the West as the "Mao suit." Even today, Chinese leaders wear the high-collared jacket in place of a Western-style suit jacket on some formal occasions, and padded versions can still be seen in rural China in winter.

# Prices

In Mainland China, prices are usually non-negotiable in supermarkets and large department stores, but bargaining is routine at street-side stalls and small shops. It is also not customary to tip at a restaurant, although upscale restaurants often charge a service fee.

## Compare & Contrast

E-commerce is becoming prevalent in China. For many people, online shopping, 网上购物 (*wǎngshang gòuwù*) or 网购 (*wǎng gòu*), is the preferred way to find the best deal. Two of the most popular sites, 天猫 (*Tiānmāo*: www.tmall.com) and 淘宝 (*Táobǎo*: www.taobao.com), are owned by Alibaba. Alibaba's sales dwarf those of Amazon and eBay combined.

Search for an item on one of these sites, put it in the shopping cart, and describe how the experience compares with your usual online shopping.

# Forms of Address

In Mainland China, a salesperson in a department store is usually addressed as 售货员 (*shòuhuòyuán*), and a server in a restaurant is usually called 服务员 (*fúwùyuán*) (service person). Both male and female taxi drivers and bus drivers are commonly addressed as 师傅 (*shīfu*) (an old term of respect for a master craftsman or skilled worker). However, these forms of address vary according to the age and preference of the speaker as well as the status or function of the person spoken to, and usage has very much been in flux.

Students should carefully observe actual usage and follow suit. In Taiwan, 小姐 (*xiǎojiě*) (Miss) and 先生 (*xiānsheng*) (Mr.) are the preferred terms in all these contexts. Most recently, 老师 (*lǎoshī*) (teacher) has come to be used as a respectful form of address for people in the arts (such as writers, painters, and actors) on both sides of the Taiwan Strait, regardless of whether they teach professionally.

# Lesson Wrap-Up

## Make It Flow!

Rearrange the following sentences into a logical sequence. Then combine them into a coherent narrative. Remember to omit repetitive elements and substitute subjects with personal pronouns where appropriate. Time expressions and place words can also serve as useful connective devices.

_____售货员找给李友四十五块五毛一。

_____李友买的衬衫是中号的。

_____李友买了一件衬衫。

__1__李友在商店买衣服。

_____李友买的衬衫是红的。

_____李友还买了一条裤子。

_____李友一共得付五十四块四毛九。

_____李友给了售货员一百块钱。

## Role-Play

It's your younger brother's birthday next week. You want to get him a shirt. His favorite color is blue and his size is medium. You want to buy something that's stylish yet not too expensive, but the salesperson tries to get you to buy the most expensive shirt in the store. Create a short skit with your partner, and perform it in class or make a video and post it on social media.

## Social Media

On social media, post three items of clothing you are considering buying. Tell your friends what you like about them (style, color, etc.). See which item gets the most likes.

## Can-Do Check List

**Before proceeding to Lesson 10, make sure you can complete the following tasks in Chinese:**

I can

- Name my favorite color and other common colors
- Talk about clothing and shoe sizes
- Count money and determine proper change
- Return or exchange items at a store

# Lesson 10

第十课

*Dì shí kè*

## 交通

*Jiāotōng*

# TRANSPORTATION

## Learning Objectives

**In this lesson, you will learn to:**

- Discuss different means of transportation
- Explain how to transfer from one subway or bus line to another
- Navigate public transit
- Express gratitude after receiving a favor
- Offer New Year wishes

## Relate & Get Ready

**In your own culture/community:**

- How often do people use public transportation?
- Do people hail taxis or do they order rides on their phone?
- How do people express gratitude?
- What do people say to each other on New Year's Day?

# Going Home for Winter Vacation

## Dialogue

李友跟王朋说话……

Audio

Video

李友，寒假你回家吗？

对，我要回家。

飞机票你买了吗[1]？

已经买了。是二十一号的。

飞机是几点的？

晚上八点的。

你怎么去[a]机场？

我想坐公共汽车或者[2]坐地铁。你知道怎么走[a]吗？

你先坐一路汽车，坐三站下车，然后换地铁。先坐红线，再[3]换绿线，最后换蓝线。

不行，不行，太麻烦了。我还是[4]打车[b]吧。

出租汽车太贵，我开车送你去吧。

谢谢你。

不用客气。

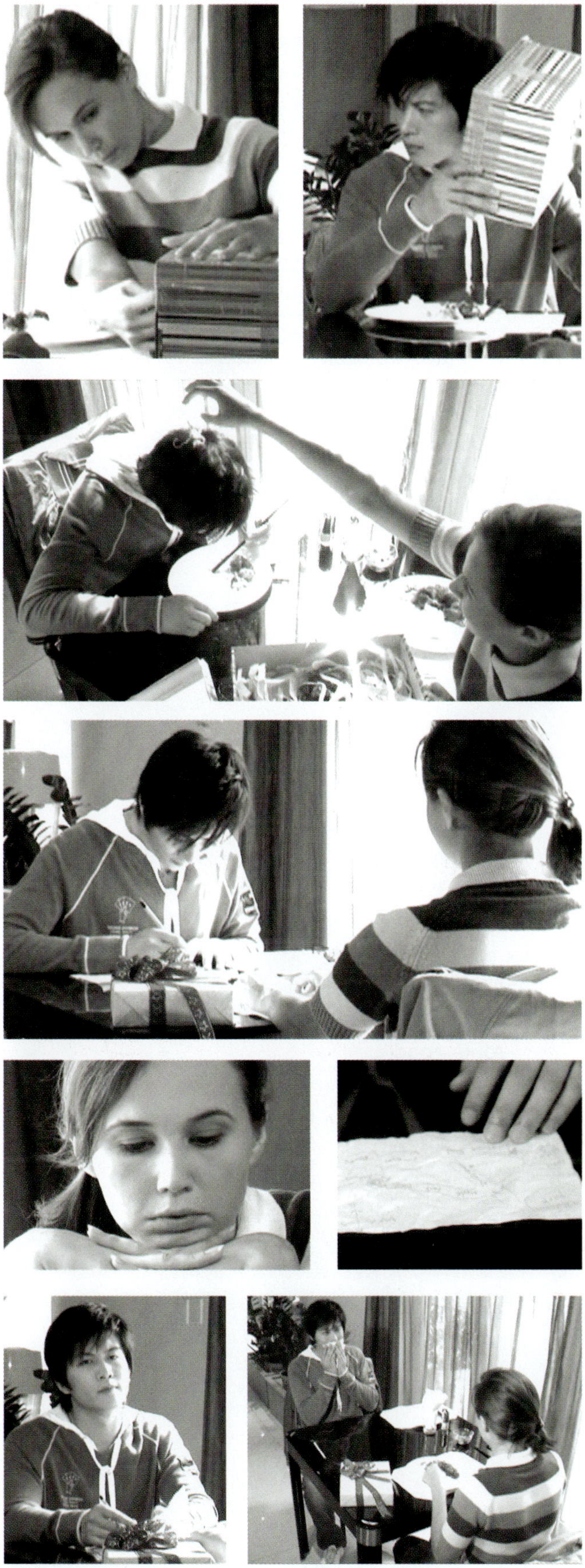

*Lǐ Yǒu gēn Wáng Péng shuō huà . . .*

*Lǐ Yǒu, hánjià nǐ huí jiā ma?*

*Duì, wǒ yào huí jiā.*

*Fēijī piào nǐ mǎi le ma*[1]*?*

*Yǐjīng mǎi le. Shì èrshíyī hào de.*

*Fēijī shì jǐ diǎn de?*

*Wǎnshang bā diǎn de.*

*Nǐ zěnme qù*[a] *jīchǎng?*

*Wǒ xiǎng zuò gōnggòng qìchē huòzhě*[2] *zuò dìtiě. Nǐ zhīdao zěnme zǒu*[a] *ma?*

*Nǐ xiān zuò yī lù qìchē, zuò sān zhàn xià chē, ránhòu huàn dìtiě. Xiān zuò hóng xiàn, zài*[3] *huàn lǜ xiàn, zuìhòu huàn lán xiàn.*

*Bù xíng, bù xíng, tài máfan le. Wǒ háishi*[4] *dǎ chē*[b] *ba.*

*Chūzū qìchē tài guì, wǒ kāi chē sòng nǐ qù ba.*

*Xièxie nǐ.*

*Búyòng kèqi.*

## Language Notes

**a** 怎么去 (*zěnme qù*) and 怎么走 (*zěnme zǒu*)

怎么去 (*zěnme qù*) is used to ask about the means of transportation, whereas 怎么走 (*zěnme zǒu*) is used to ask for directions.

**b** 打车 (*dǎ chē*)

This means "to take a taxi." A common variant is 打的 (*dǎ dī*). Taxis are 出租（汽）车 (*chūzū [qì]chē*) in Mainland China, but 计程车 (*jìchéng chē*) (metered cars) in Taiwan.

# Vocabulary

Audio

Flashcards

| No. | Word | Pinyin | Part of Speech | Definition |
|---|---|---|---|---|
| 1 | 寒假 | *hánjià* | n | winter vacation |
| 2 | 飞机 | *fēijī* | n | airplane |
| | 飞 | *fēi* | v | to fly |
| | 机 | *jī* | n | machine |
| 3 | 票 | *piào* | n | ticket |
| 4 | （飞）机场 | *(fēi)jīchǎng* | n | airport |
| 5 | 坐 | *zuò* | v | to travel by |
| 6 | 公共汽车 | *gōnggòng qìchē* | n | bus |
| | 公共 | *gōnggòng* | adj | public |
| | 汽车 | *qìchē* | n | automobile |
| | 车 | *chē* | n | vehicle, car |
| 7 | 或者 | *huòzhě* | conj | or [See Grammar 2.] |
| 8 | 地铁 | *dìtiě* | n | subway |
| 9 | 走 | *zǒu* | v | to go by way of, to walk |
| 10 | 先 | *xiān* | adv | first [See Grammar 3.] |
| 11 | 路 | *lù* | n | route, road |
| 12 | 站 | *zhàn* | m | (measure word for bus stops, train stops, etc.) |
| 13 | 下车 | *xià chē* | vo | to get off (a bus, train, etc.) |
| 14 | 然后 | *ránhòu* | adv | then |
| 15 | 绿 | *lǜ* | adj | green |
| 16 | 线 | *xiàn* | n | line |
| 17 | 最后 | *zuìhòu* | | final, last |
| 18 | 蓝 | *lán* | adj | blue |
| 19 | 麻烦 | *máfan* | adj | troublesome |

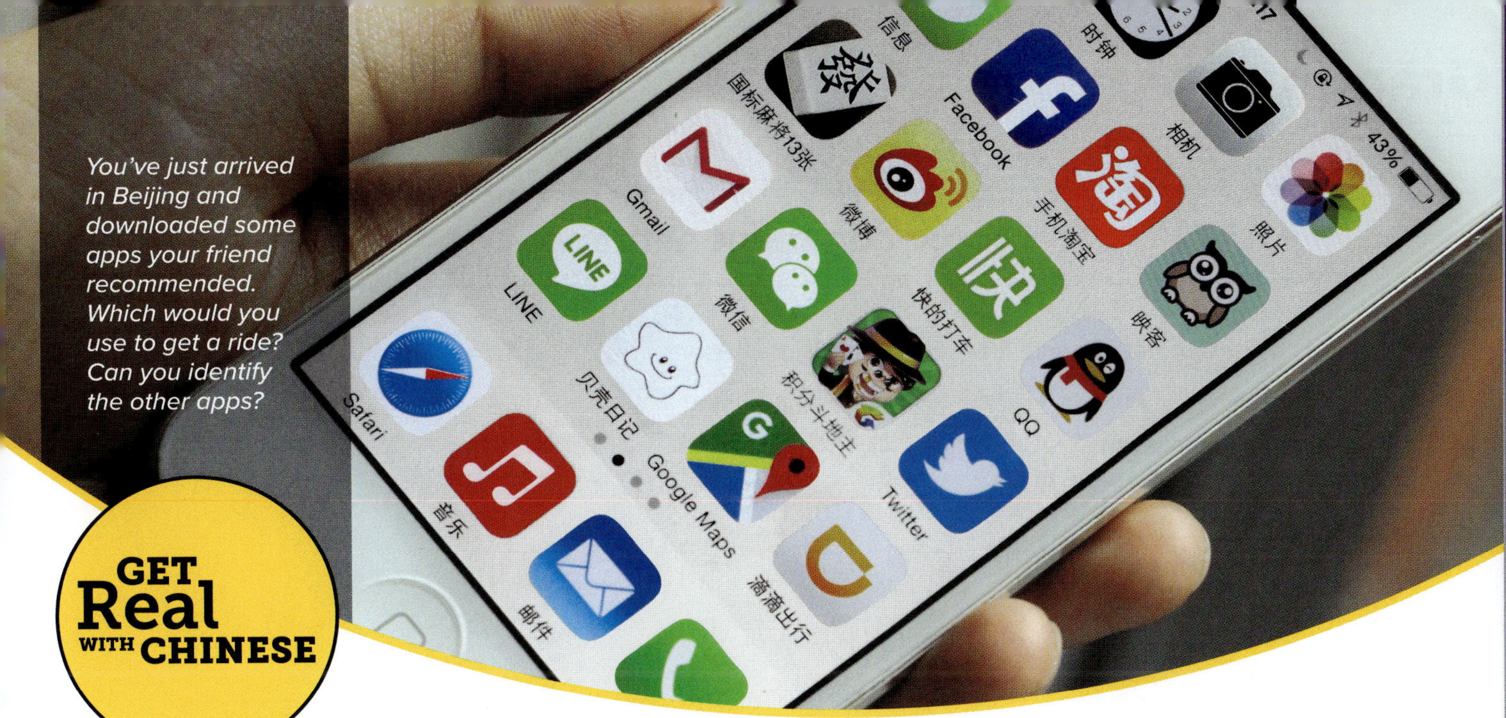


*You've just arrived in Beijing and downloaded some apps your friend recommended. Which would you use to get a ride? Can you identify the other apps?*

## GET Real WITH CHINESE

| No. | Word | Pinyin | Part of Speech | Definition |
|---|---|---|---|---|
| 20 | 打车 | *dǎ chē* | vo | to take a taxi |
| 21 | 出租汽车 | *chūzū qìchē* | n | taxi |
| | 出租 | *chūzū* | v | to rent out, to let |
| | 租 | *zū* | v | to rent |
| 22 | 开车 | *kāi chē* | vo | to drive a car |
| | 开 | *kāi* | v | to drive, to operate |
| 23 | 送 | *sòng* | v | to see off or out, to take (someone somewhere) |

## How About You?

### 你怎么回家？

*Nǐ zěnme huí jiā?*

How do you get home?

我 ________________。

*Wǒ* ________________.

See index for corresponding vocabulary or research another term.

# Grammar

## 1 Topic-comment sentences (I)

In a topic-comment sentence, the previously established noun, noun phrase, or object of the verb becomes the topic, and moves to the beginning of the sentence. The rest of the sentence serves as the comment.

**A**

**Student A** 我昨天买了一枝笔。

*Wǒ zuótiān mǎi le yì zhī bǐ.*

I bought a pen yesterday.

**Student B** 那枝笔你用了吗？

*Nà zhī bǐ nǐ yòng le ma?*

Have you used it?

**B**

Q: 你知道我的衬衫在哪儿吗？

*Nǐ zhīdao wǒ de chènshān zài nǎr ma?*

Do you know where my shirt is?

A: 你的衬衫我给你妈妈了。

*Nǐ de chènshān wǒ gěi nǐ māma le.*

I gave your shirt to your mother.

**C**

Q: 你有朋友吗？

*Nǐ yǒu péngyou ma?*

Do you have any friends?

A: 朋友我有很多，可是都不在这儿。

*Péngyou wǒ yǒu hěn duō, kěshì dōu bú zài zhèr.*

I have many friends, but none of them are here.

**D** 她不想去纽约，可是飞机票她妈妈已经帮她买了。

*Tā bù xiǎng qù Niǔyuē, kěshì fēijī piào tā māma yǐjīng bāng tā mǎi le.*

She does not want to go to New York, but her mother has already bought her a plane ticket.

### EXERCISES

Join these sentences to form a topic-comment sentence. Use exercise 1 as an example.

More exercises

1 我昨天买了一件衬衫。
我很喜欢那件衬衫。
→ 我昨天买了一件衬衫。那件衬衫我很喜欢。

2 学校有一个商店。
我常常去那个商店。

3 Q: 李友买飞机票了吗？
A: 李友已经买飞机票了。

## 2 Indicating alternatives: 或者 (*huòzhě*) (or) and 还是 (*háishi*) (or)

Both 或者 (*huòzhě*) (or) and 还是 (*háishi*) (or) connect words or phrases to indicate alternatives. The former usually appears in statements, the latter in questions.

**A** Q: 你今天晚上做什么？

*Nǐ jīntiān wǎnshang zuò shénme?*

What are you going to do tonight?

A: 听音乐或者看电影。

*Tīng yīnyuè huòzhě kàn diànyǐng.*

Listen to music or watch a movie.

**B** Q: 你周末想看电影还是跳舞?

*Nǐ zhōumò xiǎng kàn diànyǐng háishi tiào wǔ?*

Would you like to see a movie or go dancing this weekend?

A: 看电影或者跳舞都行。

*Kàn diànyǐng huòzhě tiào wǔ dōu xíng.*

Either seeing a movie or going dancing would be fine with me.

**C** Q: 你喜欢什么颜色的鞋? 黑色的还是咖啡色的?

*Nǐ xǐhuan shénme yánsè de xié? Hēisè de háishi kāfēisè de?*

What color shoes do you like? Black or brown?

A: 黑色的或者咖啡色的我都不喜欢,
我喜欢白的。

*Hēisè de huòzhě kāfēisè de wǒ dōu bù xǐhuan, wǒ xǐhuan bái de.*

I don't like either black or brown; I like white ones.

**D** 明天你去开会或者小高去开会都可以。

*Míngtiān nǐ qù kāi huì huòzhě Xiǎo Gāo qù kāi huì dōu kěyǐ.*

Either you or Little Gao may attend tomorrow's meeting.

More exercises

## EXERCISES

Connect these words to form a question or a statement by inserting either 或者 or 还是 as appropriate. Use exercise 1 as an example.

1 今天晚上我们 去跳舞 去打球
→ 今天晚上我们去跳舞或者去打球。

2 白医生想 坐地铁 坐公共汽车 去机场

3 高文中 星期五 星期六 请客

## 3 Indicating sequence: 先⋯再⋯ (*xiān . . . zài . . .*) (first . . . , then . . . )

In this structure, 再 (*zài*) (then) indicates a sequence of actions rather than repetition.

**A** 我想先打球再去图书馆。

*Wǒ xiǎng xiān dǎ qiú zài qù túshūguǎn.*

I'd like to play ball and then go to the library.

**B** 弟弟常常先做功课再上网聊天儿。

*Dìdi chángcháng xiān zuò gōngkè zài shàng wǎng liáo tiānr.*

My little brother often does his homework first and then chats online.

**C** Q: 你什么时候给妈妈打电话?

*Nǐ shénme shíhou gěi māma dǎ diànhuà?*

When are you going to call Mom?

A: 下课以后再打。

*Xià kè yǐhòu zài dǎ.*

I'll call her after class.

As adverbs, 先 (*xiān*) and 再 (*zài*) must come before a verb. They should not be placed in front of the subject.

**D** 小王先买东西再吃晚饭。

*Xiǎo Wáng xiān mǎi dōngxi zài chī wǎnfàn.*

Little Wang will shop first before having dinner.

[✖ 先小王买东西再吃晚饭。]

More exercises

## EXERCISES

Combine these words to indicate sequence by inserting 先…再… where appropriate. Use exercise 1 as an example.

1 小王 坐公共汽车 坐地铁 去学校上课

→ 小王先坐公共汽车，再坐地铁去学校上课。

2 王朋常常 看电视 做功课

3 张律师今天 吃晚饭 开车 去机场

## 4 Pondering alternatives: 还是…（吧） (*háishi . . . [ba]*) (had better)

The structure 还是…（吧） (*háishi . . . [ba]*) (had better) can be used to suggest an alternative.

**A**

Q: 我们星期五去看电影，好不好?

*Wǒmen xīngqīwǔ qù kàn diànyǐng, hǎo bù hǎo?*

Let's go to a movie on Friday. How's that?

A: 还是星期六去吧。

*Háishi xīngqīliù qù ba.*

Let's go on Saturday instead.

**B**

**Student A** 我们今天晚上去听音乐会吧。

*Wǒmen jīntiān wǎnshang qù tīng yīnyuèhuì ba.*

How about we go to a concert tonight?

**Student B** 可是我明天考试。

*Kěshì wǒ míngtiān kǎo shì.*

But I have a test tomorrow.

**Student A** 那别去听音乐会了。你**还是**在家复习功课**吧**。

*Nà bié qù tīng yīnyuèhuì le. Nǐ **háishi** zài jiā fùxí gōngkè **ba**.*

Let's not go to the concert then. You'd better stay home and review.

## EXERCISES

More exercises

In pairs, use these words to discuss alternatives by inserting 还是…吧 where appropriate. Use exercise 1 as an example.

1 打球　　有点儿累　　明天

**Student A** 我想打球，可是有点儿累。

**Student B** 你有点儿累，还是明天打吧。

2 打车去学校　　打车太贵　　坐公共汽车

3 看球　　明天考中文　　复习生词语法

### Chinese Chat

You're about to post this picture of your trip on Instagram. What caption would you write? Use the hashtag #寒假.

# Language Practice

## A On topic

INTERPERSONAL

In pairs, answer the questions in the affirmative or negative using the topic-comment structure, e.g.:

Q: 你喜欢我这件衣服吗？
*Nǐ xǐhuan wǒ zhè jiàn yīfu ma?*

A: 这件衣服我不喜欢。
*Zhè jiàn yīfu wǒ bù xǐhuan.*

1 你会不会打球？
*Nǐ huì bu huì dǎ qiú?*

2 你复习课文了吗？
*Nǐ fùxí kèwén le ma?*

3 你现在想不想喝咖啡？
*Nǐ xiànzài xiǎng bu xiǎng hē kāfēi?*

4 你认识白英爱吗？
*Nǐ rènshi Bái Yīng'ài ma?*

## B Fine either way

INTERPERSONAL

In pairs, suggest and accept alternatives, inserting 或者 (*huòzhě*) or 还是 (*háishi*) where appropriate, e.g.:

今天晚上做什么 ◇ 听音乐/看电视
*jīntiān wǎnshang zuò shénme ◇ tīng yīnyuè/kàn diànshì*

Q: 我们今天晚上做什么？听音乐还是看电视？
*Wǒmen jīntiān wǎnshang zuò shénme? Tīng yīnyuè háishi kàn diànshì?*

A: 听音乐或者看电视都行。
*Tīng yīnyuè huòzhě kàn diànshì dōu xíng.*

1 明天下午做什么 ◇ 去打球/去跳舞
*míngtiān xiàwǔ zuò shénme ◇ qù dǎ qiú/qù tiào wǔ*

2 明天晚上做什么 ◇ 去商店买东西/去朋友家聊天儿
*míngtiān wǎnshang zuò shénme ◇ qù shāngdiàn mǎi dōngxi/qù péngyou jiā liáo tiānr*

3 这个周末怎么去机场◇坐地铁/打车

*zhège zhōumò zěnme qù jīchǎng ◇ zuò dìtiě/dǎ chē*

4 喝什么茶◇中国茶/英国茶

*hē shénme chá ◇ Zhōngguó chá/Yīngguó chá*

5 买什么颜色的车◇蓝的/黑的

*mǎi shénme yánsè de chē ◇ lán de/hēi de*

## C First things first

PRESENTATIONAL

Based on the images, sequence these actions using 先 (*xiān*) … 再 (*zài*) … where appropriate, e.g.:

他先吃早饭，再去图书馆学习。

*Tā xiān chī zǎofàn, zài qù túshūguǎn xuéxí.*

1 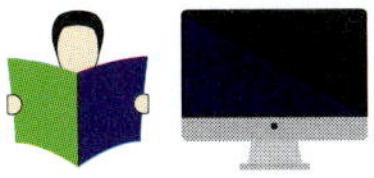

2 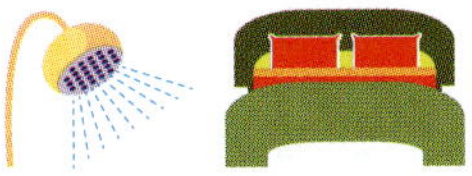

3 

4 

5 

## Characterize it!

| What do the characters mean? |
| --- |
| What is the common radical? |
| What does the radical mean? |
| How does the radical relate to the overall meaning of the characters? |

1 地 2 场 3 坐 4 在

More characters

## D Plan B

INTERPERSONAL

Use 还是…吧 (*háishi . . . ba*) and the information below to form question-and-answers. The answers should propose alternatives to the original suggestions, e.g.:

听音乐◇看电视

*tīng yīnyuè ◇ kàn diànshì*

Q: 我们听音乐，好吗？
*Wǒmen tīng yīnyuè, hǎo ma?*

A: 我们还是看电视吧。
*Wǒmen háishi kàn diànshì ba.*

1 坐地铁去机场◇开车

*zuò dìtiě qù jīchǎng ◇ kāi chē*

2 坐公共汽车去买东西◇打车

*zuò gōnggòng qìchē qù mǎi dōngxi ◇ dǎ chē*

3 买黑色的衬衫◇买红色的

*mǎi hēisè de chènshān ◇ mǎi hóngsè de*

4 学中文专业◇学电脑专业

*xué Zhōngwén zhuānyè ◇ xué diànnǎo zhuānyè*

## E En route

INTERPERSONAL

In pairs, take turns asking and giving directions to the following destinations by using 先 (*xiān*) ··· 再 (*zài*) ··· where appropriate.

1 Dr. Wang's office: Take the subway—the Red Line. Get off after five stops.

2 Sofia's house: Take Bus #5. Get off after four stops. Then change to the subway. Take the Green Line first and then switch to the Red Line. Get off after six stops.

3 Mark's school: Take Bus #29. Get off after six stops. Then switch to the subway. Take the Red Line first and then switch to the Blue Line. Get off after three stops.

## F Exchange student

PRESENTATIONAL

You will be studying Chinese at Peking University next summer. How will you get to Tian'anmen Square from campus? After researching transportation options, share your plan with your partner. Use expressions such as 先 *(xiān)* ···, 再 *(zài)* ···, and 然后 *(ránhòu)*···.

**Chinese Chat**

Your friend is sending you WeChat messages from the subway. How would you reply?

# Thanks for the Ride

## Email

Audio

Video

李友给王朋写电子邮件[a]：

Date: 12月20日

From: 李友

To: 王朋

Subject: 谢谢！

王朋：

谢谢你那天开车送我到机场。不过，让你花那么多时间，真不好意思。我这几天每天都[5]开车出去看老朋友。这个城市的人开车开得特别快。我在高速公路上开车，真有点儿紧张。可是这儿没有公共汽车，也没有地铁，只能自己开车，很不方便。

有空儿的话打我的手机或者给我发短信，我想跟你聊天儿。

新年快要到了[6]，祝你新年快乐！

李友

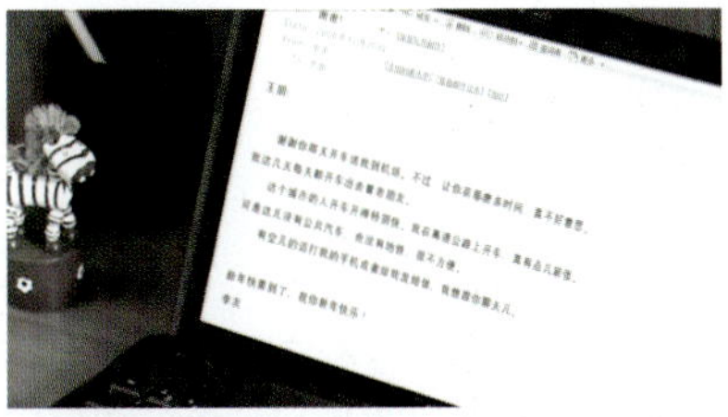

*Lǐ Yǒu gěi Wáng Péng xiě diànzǐ yóujiàn*[a]:

Date: *12 yuè 20 rì*

From: *Lǐ Yǒu*

To: *Wáng Péng*

Subject: *Xièxie!*

*Wáng Péng:*

*Xièxie nǐ nà tiān kāi chē sòng wǒ dào jīchǎng. Búguò, ràng nǐ huā nàme duō shíjiān, zhēn bù hǎoyìsi. Wǒ zhè jǐ tiān měi tiān dōu*[5] *kāi chē chūqu kàn lǎo péngyou. Zhè ge chéngshì de rén kāi chē kāi de tèbié kuài. Wǒ zài gāosù gōnglù shang kāi chē, zhēn yǒudiǎn(r) jǐnzhāng. Kěshì zhèr méiyǒu gōnggòng qìchē, yě méiyǒu dìtiě, zhǐ néng zìjǐ kāi chē, hěn bù fāngbiàn.*

*Yǒu kòngr de huà dǎ wǒ de shǒujī huòzhě gěi wǒ fā duǎnxìn, wǒ xiǎng gēn nǐ liáo tiānr.*

*Xīnnián kuài yào dào le*[6], *zhù nǐ xīnnián kuàilè!*

*Lǐ Yǒu*

## Language Note

**a 电子邮件** *(diànzǐ yóujiàn)*

As in English, the Chinese word for electronic mail, 电子邮件 *(diànzǐ yóujiàn)*, is often abbreviated as 电邮 *(diàn yóu)* (email).

# Vocabulary

Audio

Flashcards

| No. | Word | Pinyin | Part of Speech | Definition |
|---|---|---|---|---|
| 1 | 电子邮件 | *diànzǐ yóujiàn* | n | email/electronic mail |
| | 电子 | *diànzǐ* | n | electron |
| 2 | 让 | *ràng* | v | to allow or cause (somebody to do something) |
| 3 | 花 | *huā* | v | to spend |
| 4 | 不好意思 | *bù hǎoyìsi* | | to feel embarrassed |
| 5 | 出去 | *chū qu* | vc | to go out |
| 6 | 每 | *měi* | pr | every, each [See Grammar 5.] |
| 7 | 城市 | *chéngshì* | n | city |
| 8 | 特别 | *tèbié* | adv | especially |
| 9 | 高速公路 | *gāosù gōnglù* | n | highway |
| | 高速 | *gāosù* | adj | high speed |
| | 公路 | *gōnglù* | n | highway, public road |
| | 路 | *lù* | n | road, path |
| 10 | 紧张 | *jǐnzhāng* | adj | nervous, anxious |
| 11 | 自己 | *zìjǐ* | pr | oneself |
| 12 | 手机 | *shǒujī* | n | cell phone |
| 13 | 发短信 | *fā duǎnxìn* | vo | to send a text message (lit. to send a short message) |
| 14 | 新年 | *xīnnián* | n | new year |
| 15 | 快乐 | *kuàilè* | adj | happy |

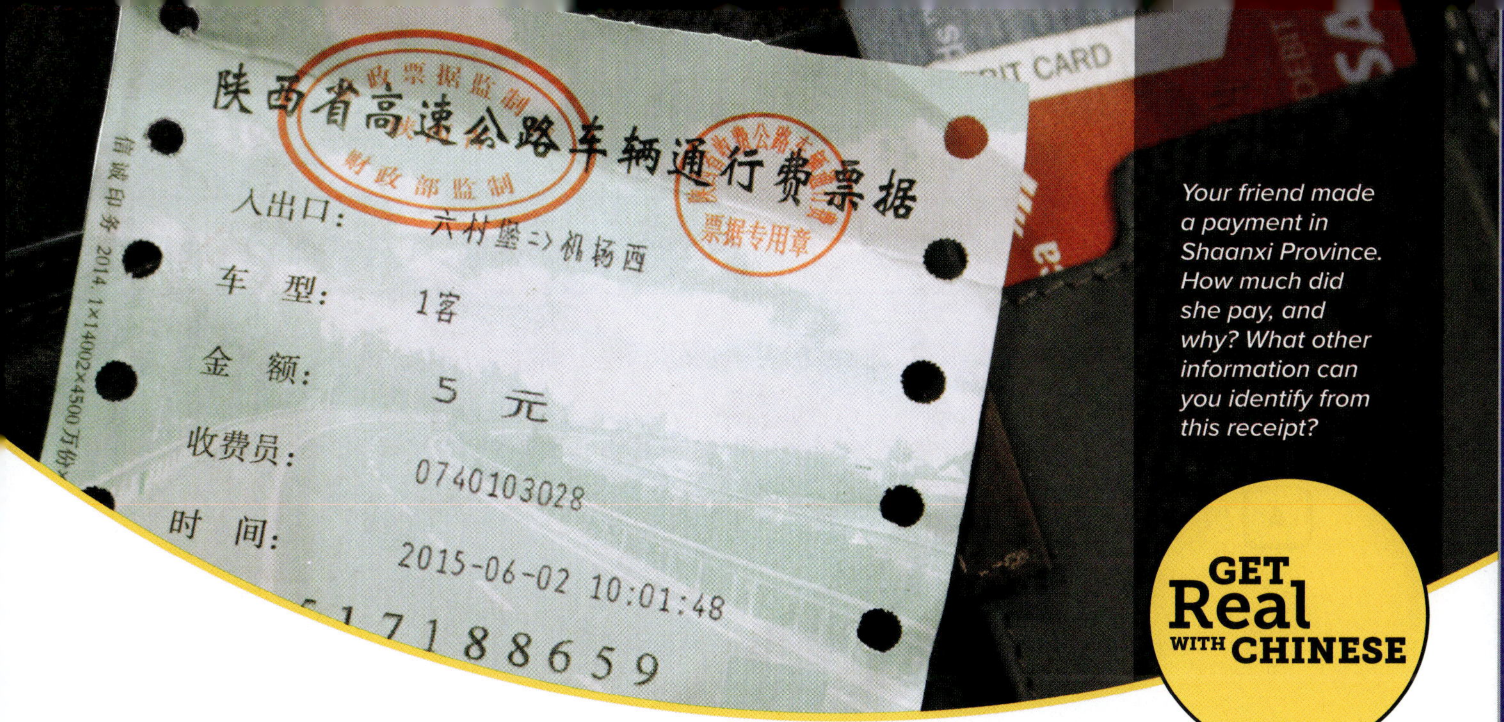


Your friend made a payment in Shaanxi Province. How much did she pay, and why? What other information can you identify from this receipt?

**GET Real WITH CHINESE**

## Characterize it!

| What do the characters mean? |
|---|
| What is the common radical? |
| What does the radical mean? |
| How does the radical relate to the overall meaning of the characters? |

1 跳 2 跟 3 路

More characters

## How About You?

你怎么去机场?

*Nǐ zěnme qù jīchǎng?*

How do you get to the airport?

我__________。

*Wǒ* __________.

See index for corresponding vocabulary or research another term.

# Grammar

## 5 Indicating totality: 每…都… (*měi . . . dōu . . .*) (every)

In sentences that contains the term 每 (*měi*) (every), the adverb 都 (*dōu*) (both, all) is usually inserted before the verb.

**A** 他每天晚上都预习课文。

*Tā měi tiān wǎnshang dōu yùxí kèwén.*

He studies the lessons in advance every night.

**B** 我每节课都来。

*Wǒ měi jié kè dōu lái.*

I come to every class.

**C** 这儿每个人我都认识。

*Zhèr měi gè rén wǒ dōu rènshi.*

I know everyone here.

**D** 常老师的字每个都好看。

*Cháng lǎoshī de zì měi ge dōu hǎokàn.*

Every one of Teacher Chang's characters looks good.

More exercises

### EXERCISES

Translate the English phrase by using 每 and add it to the sentence, inserting 都 where appropriate. Use exercise 1 as an example.

1 我在高速公路上开车。 Every day

→ 我每天都在高速公路上开车。

2 王律师坐飞机去纽约。 Every month

3 白英爱的鞋很漂亮。 Each pair

## 6 Indicating imminence: 要…了 (*yào . . . le*) (soon)

The 要…了 (*yào . . . le*) (soon) structure indicates the imminence of an anticipated action or situation. It also appears in the form of 快要…了 (*kuài yào . . . le*).

**A** 新年快要到了，我们给爸爸妈妈打一个电话吧。

*Xīnnián kuài yào dào le, wǒmen gěi bàba māma dǎ yí ge diànhuà ba.*

New Year is around the corner. Let's call Mom and Dad.

**B** 寒假要到了，你要做什么？

*Hánjià yào dào le, nǐ yào zuò shénme?*

It'll be winter break soon. What do you want to do?

**C** 电影快要开始了，你买票了吗？

*Diànyǐng kuài yào kāishǐ le, nǐ mǎi piào le ma?*

The movie is going to start soon. Did you get the tickets?

**D** 快要考试了，我们大家得准备一下。

*Kuài yào kǎo shì le, wǒmen dàjiā děi zhǔnbèi yí xià.*

The exam is coming. We have to prepare.

### EXERCISES

Form a new sentence to indicate the imminence of an action or situation by inserting (快) 要…了 where appropriate. Use exercise 1 as an example.

1 新年到 → 新年快要到了。

2 我们考中文

3 我们上课

More exercises

# Language Practice

## G Creature of habit

INTERPERSONAL

Use 每···都··· (*měi . . . dōu . . .*) and the words below to form a sentence describing Little Bai's lifestyle, e.g.:

晚上◇复习生词语法

*wǎnshang ◇ fùxí shēngcí yǔfǎ*

小白每天晚上都复习生词语法。

*Xiǎo Bái měi tiān wǎnshang dōu fùxí shēngcí yǔfǎ.*

1 早上◇洗澡 — *zǎoshang ◇ xǐ zǎo*

2 衬衫◇是白色的 — *chènshān ◇ shì báisè de*

3 裤子◇是三十二号的 — *kùzi ◇ shì sānshíèr hào de*

4 周末◇去商店买东西 — *zhōumò ◇ qù shāngdiàn mǎi dōngxi*

5 寒假◇坐飞机回家 — *hánjià ◇ zuò fēijī huí jiā*

Then take turns finding out if your partner also follows a routine.

1 你每天都吃早饭吗？

*Nǐ měi tiān dōu chī zǎofàn ma?*

2 你每天都给同学发短信吗？

*Nǐ měi tiān dōu gěi tóngxué fā duǎnxìn ma?*

3 你每个星期都上网跟朋友聊天儿吗？

*Nǐ měi ge xīngqī dōu shàng wǎng gēn péngyǒu liáotiānr ma?*

4 你每年都换手机吗？

*Nǐ měi nián dōu huàn shǒujī ma?*

## H INTERPERSONAL — Behind the wheel — PRESENTATIONAL

Use the following questions to survey your classmates about their driving habits, then present the results to the class.

你会开车吗？

*Nǐ huì kāi chē ma?*

你每天都开车吗？

*Nǐ měitiān dōu kāi chē ma?*

你开车开得快不快？

*Nǐ kāi chē kāi de kuài bu kuài?*

在高速公路上开车让你紧张吗？

*Zài gāosù gōnglù shang kāi chē ràng nǐ jǐnzhāng ma?*

### Chinese Chat

Li You just published a post on Renren Network 人人网 (*Rénrénwǎng*), a Chinese social networking service, and Wang Peng left a comment with questions. Why do you think he's asking these questions?

# CULTURAL LITERACY

文化

Continue to explore

## HIGH-SPEED RAIL

For many decades before the early 1990s, the railroad system was the principal means of travel and transport in China. However, both the highway system and air travel infrastructure grew rapidly around the turn of the century. China now has seventy thousand miles of highway, the most of any country in the world, and is second only to the United States in total number of air passengers per year. In the 1990s, passenger train service rapidly lost market share to airlines and highway travel, but it soon made an astonishing comeback with the construction of an expansive high-speed railroad network, referred to as 高速铁路 (*gāosù tiělù*) or 高铁 (*gāotiě*). As of December 2014, the system had more track in service than the rest of the world combined. Now, about two and a half million people take *gaotie* every day. Traveling by train between Beijing and Shanghai, which took as long as seventeen hours in 1980, now takes only five hours.

## TAXI DRIVERS

Taxi drivers in China, especially those in Beijing, are known for being very outgoing. If you visit China and your taxi driver happens to be chatty, you might find yourself with a good opportunity to learn about ordinary Chinese people's lives and their opinions on current affairs.

## COMPARE & CONTRAST

To get a sense of the scale of human movement over the Chinese New Year, look up 春运 *(chūnyùn)* on Google Images. What is the busiest travel day in your country? How do most people travel? Discuss holiday travel with a Chinese friend or a Chinese student on campus. Your conversation can include such questions as: How do you get around? Do you like driving? Is it easy for you to buy plane or train tickets online? How do you get to the airport or train station?

# NEW YEAR TRAFFIC

Chinese New Year, also known as 春节 *(Chūnjié)* (Spring Festival), is the most important annual holiday in Chinese communities. The date is determined by the lunar calendar and usually falls in late January or early February. However, nowadays, the international New Year on January 1 is also recognized. The most common New Year greetings are 新年好 *(xīnnián hǎo)* and 新年快乐 *(xīnnián kuàilè)*, which can be used for both New Years. However, many people still prefer the traditional Chinese New Year greeting 恭喜发财 *(gōngxǐ fācái)*. This phrase, which literally means "Congratulations and may you make a fortune," can be translated as "May you be happy and prosperous!"

The largest human migration on earth is known as 春运 *(chūnyùn)* (Spring Festival traffic) in Chinese. Over a forty-day period around the time of the Chinese New Year, millions of Chinese people return home by train or long-distance bus to reunite with their families and then make their way back to their places of work. In 2015, the total number of trips taken was estimated to be around 3.7 billion; migrant laborers from inland provinces accounted for a significant portion of this figure.

# Lesson Wrap-Up

## Make It Flow!

Rearrange the following sentences into a logical sequence. Then combine them into a coherent narrative. If the subject remains the same, replace it with a personal pronoun. Remember to avoid unnecessary repetitions of identical elements. Add **但是** (*dànshì*), **再** (*zài*), or **最后** (*zuìhòu*) where appropriate.

_____李友得先坐三站汽车，然后换地铁。

_____李友坐绿线地铁以后得换蓝线地铁。

__1__李友寒假要回家。

_____李友买了二十一号晚上8点的机票。

_____李友想坐公共汽车和地铁去机场。

_____李友坐红线地铁以后得换绿线地铁。

_____王朋说他可以开车送李友去。

_____李友得先坐红线地铁。

_____李友觉得太麻烦。

_____王朋说打车太贵。

_____李友想打车。

## Research

You work for a travel company catering to Chinese tourists. They've asked you to provide directions for taking public transportation from Boston's Logan Airport to Harvard Square. Research the information online, summarize it in Chinese, and post it on social media. **从洛根** (*Luògēn*) (Logan) **机场到哈佛广场** (*Hāfó Guángchǎng*) (Harvard Square) **怎么走?**

## Presentation

In your opinion, which city in your country has the best transportation system? Consider:

这个城市大吗?

这个城市有没有地铁?

这个城市地铁有几条线?

这个城市有几个机场? 机场大吗?

在这个城市里开车容易吗? 为什么?

在这个城市没有车方便吗? 为什么?

Present your case to the class using a slideshow. After everyone finishes, have a vote.

**Can-Do Check List**

Before proceeding to the next Volume, make sure you can complete the following tasks in Chinese:

I can

- Talk about common means of transportation
- Discuss the most/least convenient way to get to a destination
- Thank someone for a favor
- Extend New Year greetings, both oral and written

# Keeping It Casual (L6–L10)

**Before you progress to the next volume, we'll review how some of the functional expressions from Lessons 6–10 are used in casual Chinese. After you complete the review, note any other casual expressions you would like to learn, then share the list with your teacher.**

## 1 喂 *(wéi)* (hello [on the phone])

Say this to start a phone conversation. [See Lesson 6.]

**A**

**Li You's Roommate** 喂，你好，请问哪位？
*Wéi, nǐ hǎo, qǐng wèn nǎ wèi?*
Hello! May I ask who's calling?

**Wang Peng** 你好，我是王朋。请问，李友在吗？
*Nǐ hǎo, wǒ shì Wáng Péng. Qǐng wèn, Lǐ Yǒu zài ma?*
Hello! This is Wang Peng. Is Li You there, please?

**Li You's Roommate** 在，你等等，我去叫她。
*Zài, nǐ děngdeng, wǒ qù jiào tā.*
Yes. Wait a minute. I'll go get her.

**B**

**Little Li** 喂，你找谁？
*Wéi, nǐ zhǎo shéi?*
Hello! Who would you like to speak to?

**Teacher Chang** 我找小李。
*Wǒ zhǎo Xiǎo Lǐ.*
I'd like to speak to Little Li.

**Little Li** 我就是。你是哪位？
*Wǒ jiù shì. Nǐ shì nǎ wèi?*
This is she. Who's speaking?

**Teacher Chang** 我是常老师。
*Wǒ shì Cháng lǎoshī.*
This is Teacher Chang.

**C**

**Little Li** 喂，请问小王在吗？

*Wéi, qǐng wèn Xiǎo Wáng zài ma?*

Hello! Is Little Wang there, please?

**Old Wang** 在，你是哪位？

*Zài, nǐ shì nǎ wèi?*

Yes, he is. Who is this, please?

**Little Li** 我是小李。

*Wǒ shì Xiǎo Lǐ.*

This is Little Li.

**Old Wang** 好，请等一下。

*Hǎo, qǐng děng yí xià.*

OK. Please wait a minute.

## 2 没问题 *(méi wèntí)* (no problem)

Say this to put someone at ease that you will agree to do something, or to assure someone that there is no need to worry. [See Lesson 6.]

**A**

**Li You** 王朋，你今天晚上帮我练习中文，好吗？

*Wáng Péng, nǐ jīntiān wǎnshang bāng wǒ liànxí Zhōngwén, hǎo ma?*

Wang Peng, would you help me practice Chinese this evening?

**Wang Peng** 没问题。晚上见。

*Méi wèntí. Wǎnshang jiàn.*

No problem. See you this evening.

**B**

**Little Li** 英爱，坐地铁太麻烦了。
你开车送我去机场，好吗？

*Yīng'ài, zuò dìtiě tài máfan le.*
*Nǐ kāi chē sòng wǒ qù jīchǎng, hǎo ma?*

Ying'ai, it's too much trouble to take the subway.
Would you drive me to the airport instead?

**Bai Ying'ai** 没问题。

*Méi wèntí.*

Sure thing.

**C**

**Li You** 你下午有空儿帮我准备考试吗？要是你没时间，就算了。

*Nǐ xiàwǔ yǒu kòngr bāng wǒ zhǔnbèi kǎoshì ma?*

*Yàoshi nǐ méi shíjiān, jiù suàn le.*

Do you have time this afternoon to help me prepare for my test?

Never mind if you're too busy.

**Wang Peng** 没问题，我有空儿。

*Méi wèntí, wǒ yǒu kòngr.*

Don't worry, I have time.

## 3 Expressions of gratitude

Say these phrases to express and acknowledge gratitude.

**A**

**Wang Peng** 小李，这是你的手机吗？

*Xiǎo Lǐ, zhèshì nǐ de shǒujī ma?*

Little Li, is this cell phone yours?

**Little Li** 谢谢！

*Xièxie!*

Thanks!

**Wang Peng** 不客气。

*Bú kèqi.*

You're welcome.

**B**

**Little Bai** 小高，请喝茶。

*Xiǎo Gāo, qǐng hē chá.*

Please have some tea, Little Gao.

**Little Gao** 多谢！

*Duō xiè.*

Thanks a lot.

**Little Bai** 不谢。

*Bú xiè.*

No thanks needed.

**C**

**Waitress** 王小姐，这是你的咖啡。

*Wáng xiǎojiě, zhè shì nǐ de kāfēi.*

Miss Wang, here's your coffee.

**Miss Wang** 谢谢！

*Xièxie!*

Thanks!

**Waitress** 没事儿。

*Méi shìr.*

No problem.

**D**

**Dr. Wang** 白医生，你的书。

*Bái Yīshēng, nǐ de shū.*

Dr. Bai, your book.

**Dr. Bai** 谢了。

*Xiè le.*

Thanks.

**Dr. Wang** 不用谢。

*Búyòng xiè.*

No thanks needed.

## 4 哪里，哪里 *(nǎli, nǎli)* **(I'm flattered)** or 是吗 *(shì ma)* **(is that so?)**

When receiving a compliment, Chinese people often express modesty by saying 哪里 *(nǎli)* or 是吗 *(shì ma)*. Nowadays, however, some people say 谢谢 *(xièxie)* instead. [See Lesson 7.]

**A**

**Student A** 你今天很漂亮。

*Nǐ jīntiān hěn piàoliang.*

You look very pretty today.

**Student B** 哪里，哪里。

*Nǎli, nǎli.*

I'm flattered.

**B**

**Student A** 你写汉字写得很漂亮。

*Nǐ xiě Hànzì xiě de hěn piàoliang.*

You write Chinese characters beautifully.

**Student B** 哪里，写得不好。

*Nǎli, xiě de bù hǎo.*

I wish that were true. My writing isn't good.

**C**

**Student A** 你说中文说得真好！

*Nǐ shuō Zhōngwén shuō de zhēn hǎo!*

You speak Chinese really well!

**Student B** 是吗？我觉得我说得不好。

*Shì ma? Wǒ juéde wǒ shuō de bù hǎo.*

You think so? I don't think I speak very well.

## 5 就是它吧 *(jiù shì tā ba)* **(let's go with that)** or 就是他/她了 *(jiù shì tā le)* **(we'll go with him/her)**

Say these when you've made a decision. [See Lesson 9.]

**A**

**Salesperson** 先生，你知道要哪一双了吗？

*Xiānsheng, nǐ zhīdao yào nǎ yì shuāng le ma?*

Sir, do you know which pair you'd like?

**Mr. Gao** 就是它吧。

*Jiù shì tā ba.*

I'll take that one.

**B**

**Li You** 王老师，小李打球打得不太好，
你找别人跟你一起练习吧。

*Wáng lǎoshī, Xiǎo Lǐ dǎ qiú dǎ de bú tài hǎo,*
*nǐ zhǎo bié rén gēn nǐ yìqǐ liànxí ba.*

Teacher Wang, Little Li is not a very good ball player.
Why don't you find someone else to practice with?

**Teacher Wang** 就是他了。别人都没空儿。

*Jiù shì tā le. Biérén dōu méi kòngr.*

I'll have to go with him. Everyone else is busy.

## 6 祝 *(zhù)* (I wish . . . )

To express good wishes, say the verb 祝 *(zhù)* at the beginning of a sentence. [See Lesson 10.]

**A**

祝你新年快乐!

*Zhù nǐ xīnnián kuàilè!*

Happy New Year!

**B**

祝你生日快乐!

*Zhù nǐ shēngrì kuàilè!*

Happy birthday!

**C**

祝你考试考得好!

*Zhù nǐ kǎo shì kǎo de hǎo!*

I hope you do well on the exam!

**D**

祝寒假快乐!

*Zhù hánjià kuàilè!*

Have a pleasant winter break!

**E**

祝感恩节快乐!

*Zhù Gǎn'ēnjié kuàilè!*

Happy Thanksgiving!

**F**

祝春节快乐!

*Zhù Chūnjié kuàilè!*

Happy Chinese New Year!

**G**

祝一路平安!

*Zhù yí lù píng'ān!*

Have a safe trip!

**H**

祝旅途愉快!

*Zhù lǚtú yúkuài!*

Bon voyage!

# Vocabulary Index (Chinese-English)

The Chinese-English index is alphabetized according to *pinyin*. Words containing the same Chinese characters are grouped together first. Homonyms appear in the order of their tonal pronunciation (i.e., first tones first, second tones second, third tones third, fourth tones fourth, and neutral tones last).

| Simplified | Traditional | Pinyin | Part of Speech | Definition | Lesson |
|---|---|---|---|---|---|
| **A** | | | | | |
| 啊 | | *a* | p | (a sentence-final particle of exclamation, interrogation, etc.) | 6 |
| **B** | | | | | |
| 爸爸 | | *bàba* | n | father, dad | 2 |
| 吧 | | *ba* | p | (a sentence-final particle) | 5 |
| 白英爱 | 白英愛 | *Bái Yīng'ài* | pn | (a personal name) | 2 |
| 百 | | *bǎi* | nu | hundred | 9 |
| 半 | | *bàn* | nu | half, half an hour | 3 |
| 办公室 | 辦公室 | *bàngōngshì* | n | office | 6 |
| 帮 | 幫 | *bāng* | v | to help | 6 |
| 杯 | | *bēi* | m | (measure word for things contained in a cup or glass) | 5 |
| 北京 | | *Běijīng* | pn | Beijing | 1 |
| 笔 | 筆 | *bǐ* | n | pen | 7 |
| 别 | 別 | *bié* | adv | don't | 6 |
| 别人 | 別人 | *biérén* | n | other people, another person | 4 |
| 不 | | *bù* | adv | not, no | 1 |
| 不错 | 不錯 | *búcuò* | adj | pretty good | 4 |
| 不过 | 不過 | *búguò* | conj | however, but | 9 |
| 不好意思 | | *bù hǎoyìsi* | | to feel embarrassed | 10 |
| 不用 | | *bú yòng* | | need not | 9 |

| Simplified | Traditional | Pinyin | Part of Speech | Definition | Lesson |
|---|---|---|---|---|---|
| **C** | | | | | |
| 才 | | *cái* | adv | not until, only then | 5 |
| 菜 | 菜 | *cài* | n | dish, cuisine | 3 |
| 餐厅 | 餐廳 | *cāntīng* | n | dining room, cafeteria | 8 |
| 茶 | 茶 | *chá* | n | tea | 5 |
| 常常 | | *chángcháng* | adv | often | 4 |
| 常老师 | 常老師 | *Cháng lǎoshī* | pn | Teacher Chang | 6 |
| 长短 | 長短 | *chángduǎn* | n | length | 9 |
| 唱歌（儿） | 唱歌（兒） | *chàng gē(r)* | vo | to sing (a song) | 4 |
| 衬衫 | 襯衫 | *chènshān* | n | shirt | 9 |
| 城市 | | *chéngshì* | n | city | 10 |
| 吃 | | *chī* | v | to eat | 3 |
| 除了…以外 | | *chúle . . . yǐwài* | conj | in addition to, besides | 8 |
| 出去 | | *chūqu* | vc | to go out | 10 |
| 出租汽车 | 出租汽車 | *chūzū qìchē* | n | taxi | 10 |
| 穿 | | *chuān* | v | to wear, to put on | 9 |
| **D** | | | | | |
| 打车 | 打車 | *dǎ chē* | vo | to take a taxi | 10 |
| 打电话 | 打電話 | *dǎ diànhuà* | vo | to make a phone call | 6 |
| 打球 | | *dǎ qiú* | vo | to play ball | 4 |
| 大 | | *dà* | adj | big, old | 3 |
| 大哥 | | *dàgē* | n | eldest/oldest brother | 2 |
| 大家 | | *dàjiā* | pr | everybody | 7 |
| 大姐 | | *dàjiě* | n | eldest/oldest sister | 2 |

| Simplified | Traditional | Pinyin | Part of Speech | Definition | Lesson |
|---|---|---|---|---|---|
| 大小 | | *dàxiǎo* | n | size | 9 |
| 大学生 | 大學生 | *dàxuéshēng* | n | college student | 2 |
| 但是 | | *dànshì* | conj | but | 6 |
| 到 | | *dào* | v | to go to, to arrive | 6 |
| 的 | | *de* | p | (a possessive or descriptive particle) | 2 |
| 得 | | *de* | p | (a structural particle) | 7 |
| 得 | | *děi* | av | must, to have to | 6 |
| 等 | | *děng* | v | to wait, to wait for | 6 |
| 第 | | *dì* | prefix | (prefix for ordinal numbers) | 7 |
| 弟弟 | | *dìdi* | n | younger brother | 2 |
| 地铁 | 地鐵 | *dìtiě* | n | subway | 10 |
| 点 | 點 | *diǎn* | m | o'clock (lit. dot, point, thus "points on the clock") | 3 |
| 点（儿） | 點（兒） | *diǎn(r)* | m | a little, a bit, some | 5 |
| 电脑 | 電腦 | *diànnǎo* | n | computer | 8 |
| 电视 | 電視 | *diànshì* | n | television | 4 |
| 电影 | 電影 | *diànyǐng* | n | movie | 4 |
| 电子邮件 | 電子郵件 | *diànzǐ yóujiàn* | n | email/electronic mail | 10 |
| 东西 | 東西 | *dōngxi* | n | things, objects | 9 |
| 懂 | 懂 | *dǒng* | v | to understand | 7 |
| 都 | | *dōu* | adv | both, all | 2 |
| 对 | 對 | *duì* | adj | right, correct | 4 |
| 对不起 | 對不起 | *duìbuqǐ* | v | sorry | 5 |
| 多 | | *duō* | adv | how many/much, to what extent | 3 |

| Simplified | Traditional | Pinyin | Part of Speech | Definition | Lesson |
|---|---|---|---|---|---|
| 多 | | *duō* | adj | many, much | 7 |
| 多少 | | *duōshao* | qpr | how much/how many | 9 |
| | | | **E** | | |
| 儿子 | 兒子 | *érzi* | n | son | 2 |
| 二姐 | | *èrjiě* | n | second oldest sister | 2 |
| | | | **F** | | |
| 发短信 | 發短信 | *fā duǎnxìn* | vo | to send a text message (lit. to send a short message) | 10 |
| 发音 | 發音 | *fāyīn* | n | pronunciation | 8 |
| 饭 | 飯 | *fàn* | n | meal, (cooked) rice | 3 |
| 方便 | | *fāngbiàn* | adj | convenient | 6 |
| 飞机 | 飛機 | *fēijī* | n | airplane | 10 |
| （飞）机场 | （飛）機場 | *(fēi)jīchǎng* | n | airport | 10 |
| 分 | | *fēn* | m | (measure word for 1/100 of a kuai [equivalent of a cent]) | 9 |
| 封 | | *fēng* | m | (measure word for letters) | 8 |
| 付钱 | 付錢 | *fù qián* | vo | to pay money | 9 |
| 复习 | 復習 | *fùxí* | v | to review | 7 |
| | | | **G** | | |
| 高速公路 | | *gāosù gōnglù* | n | highway | 10 |
| 高文中 | | *Gāo Wénzhōng* | pn | (a personal name) | 2 |
| 高小音 | | *Gāo Xiǎoyīn* | pn | (a personal name) | 5 |
| 高兴 | 高興 | *gāoxìng* | adj | happy, pleased | 5 |
| 告诉 | 告訴 | *gàosu* | v | to tell | 8 |
| 哥哥 | | *gēge* | n | older brother | 2 |
| 个 | 個 | *gè/ge* | m | (measure word for many common everyday objects) | 2 |

| Simplified | Traditional | Pinyin | Part of Speech | Definition | Lesson |
|---|---|---|---|---|---|
| 给 | 給 | *gěi* | v | to give | 5 |
| 给 | 給 | *gěi* | prep | to, for | 6 |
| 跟 | | *gēn* | prep | with | 6 |
| 公共汽车 | 公共汽車 | *gōnggòng qìchē* | n | bus | 10 |
| 功课 | 功課 | *gōngkè* | n | homework, schoolwork | 7 |
| 工作 | | *gōngzuò* | n/v | job; to work | 2 |
| 贵 | 貴 | *guì* | adj | honorable, expensive | 1 |
| **H** | | | | | |
| 还 | 還 | *hái* | adv | also, too, as well | 3 |
| 还是 | 還是 | *háishi* | conj | or | 3 |
| 孩子 | | *háizi* | n | child | 2 |
| 寒假 | | *hánjià* | n | winter vacation | 10 |
| 汉字 | 漢字 | *Hànzì* | n | Chinese characters | 7 |
| 好 | | *hǎo* | adj | fine, good, nice, OK, it's settled | 1 |
| 好久 | | *hǎojiǔ* | | a long time | 4 |
| 号 | 號 | *hào* | m | (measure word for a position in a numerical series, day of the month) | 3 |
| 号 | 號 | *hào* | n | size | 9 |
| 喝 | | *hē* | v | to drink | 5 |
| 和 | | *hé* | conj | and | 2 |
| 合适 | 合適 | *héshì* | adj | suitable | 9 |
| 黑 | | *hēi* | adj | black | 9 |
| 很 | | *hěn* | adv | very | 3 |
| 红 | 紅 | *hóng* | adj | red | 9 |

| Simplified | Traditional | Pinyin | Part of Speech | Definition | Lesson |
|---|---|---|---|---|---|
| 后来 | 後來 | *hòulái* | t | later | 8 |
| 花 | 花 | *huā* | v | to spend | 10 |
| 换 | 換 | *huàn* | v | to exchange, to change | 9 |
| 黄 | 黃 | *huáng* | adj | yellow | 9 |
| 回家 | | *huí jiā* | vo | to go home | 5 |
| 回来 | 回來 | *huí lai* | vc | to come back | 6 |
| 会 | 會 | *huì* | mv | can, know how to | 8 |
| 或者 | | *huòzhě* | conj | or | 10 |
| | | **J** | | | |
| 几 | 幾 | *jǐ* | nu | how many, some, a few | 2 |
| 家 | | *jiā* | n | family, home | 2 |
| 件 | | *jiàn* | m | (measure word for shirts, dresses, jackets, coats, etc.) | 9 |
| 见 | 見 | *jiàn* | v | to see | 3 |
| 见面 | 見面 | *jiàn miàn* | vo | to meet up, to meet with | 6 |
| 教 | | *jiāo* | v | to teach | 7 |
| 教室 | | *jiàoshì* | n | classroom | 8 |
| 叫 | | *jiào* | v | to be called, to call | 1 |
| 节 | 節 | *jié* | m | (measure word for class periods) | 6 |
| 姐姐 | | *jiějie* | n | older sister | 2 |
| 介绍 | 介紹 | *jièshào* | v | to introduce | 5 |
| 今年 | | *jīnnián* | t | this year | 3 |
| 今天 | | *jīntiān* | t | today | 3 |
| 紧张 | 緊張 | *jǐnzhāng* | adj | nervous, anxious | 10 |
| 进 | 進 | *jìn* | v | to enter | 5 |

| Simplified | Traditional | Pinyin | Part of Speech | Definition | Lesson |
|---|---|---|---|---|---|
| 进来 | 進來 | *jìn lai* | vc | to come in | 5 |
| 九月 | | *jiǔyuè* | n | September | 3 |
| 就 | | *jiù* | adv | precisely, exactly | 6 |
| 觉得 | 覺得 | *juéde* | v | to feel, to think | 4 |
| | | **K** | | | |
| 咖啡 | | *kāfēi* | n | coffee | 5 |
| 咖啡色 | | *kāfēisè* | n | brown, coffee color | 9 |
| 开车 | 開車 | *kāi chē* | vo | to drive a car | 10 |
| 开会 | 開會 | *kāi huì* | vo | to have a meeting | 6 |
| 开始 | 開始 | *kāishǐ* | v/n | to begin, to start; beginning | 7 |
| 看 | | *kàn* | v | to watch, to look, to read | 4 |
| 考试 | 考試 | *kǎo shì* | vo/n | to give or take a test; test | 6 |
| 可乐 | 可樂 | *kělè* | n | cola | 5 |
| 可是 | | *kěshì* | conj | but | 3 |
| 可以 | | *kěyǐ* | mv | can, may | 5 |
| 刻 | | *kè* | m | quarter (of an hour) | 3 |
| 课 | 課 | *kè* | n | class, course, lesson | 6 |
| 课文 | 課文 | *kèwén* | n | text of a lesson | 7 |
| 客气 | 客氣 | *kèqi* | adj | polite | 6 |
| 空（儿） | 空（兒） | *kòng(r)* | n | free time | 6 |
| 口 | | *kǒu* | m | (measure word for number of family members) | 2 |
| 酷 | | *kù* | adj | cool (appearance, behavior) | 7 |
| 裤子 | 褲子 | *kùzi* | n | pants | 9 |
| 快 | | *kuài* | adj/adv | fast, quick; quickly | 5 |

| Simplified | Traditional | Pinyin | Part of Speech | Definition | Lesson |
|---|---|---|---|---|---|
| 快乐 | 快樂 | *kuàilè* | adj | happy | 10 |
| 块 | 塊 | *kuài* | m | (measure word for the basic Chinese monetary unit [equivalent of a dollar]) | 9 |
| | | | **L** | | |
| 来 | 來 | *lái* | v | to come | 5 |
| 蓝 | 藍 | *lán* | adj | blue | 10 |
| 老师 | 老師 | *lǎoshī* | n | teacher | 1 |
| 了 | | *le* | p | (a dynamic particle) | 5 |
| 累 | | *lèi* | adj | tired | 8 |
| 李友 | | *Lǐ Yǒu* | pn | (a personal name) | 1 |
| 练习 | 練習 | *liànxí* | v | to practice | 6 |
| 两 | 兩 | *liǎng* | nu | two, a couple of | 2 |
| 聊天（儿） | 聊天（兒） | *liáo tiān(r)* | vo | to chat | 5 |
| 路 | | *lù* | n | route, road | 10 |
| 录音 | 錄音 | *lùyīn* | n/vo | sound recording; to record | 7 |
| 绿 | 綠 | *lǜ* | adj | green | 10 |
| 律师 | 律師 | *lǜshī* | n | lawyer | 2 |
| | | | **M** | | |
| 妈妈 | 媽媽 | *māma* | n | mother, mom | 2 |
| 吗 | 嗎 | *ma* | qp | (question particle) | 1 |
| 麻烦 | 麻煩 | *máfan* | adj | troublesome | 10 |
| 买 | 買 | *mǎi* | v | to buy | 9 |
| 慢 | | *màn* | adj | slow | 7 |
| 忙 | | *máng* | adj | busy | 3 |
| 毛 | | *máo* | m | (measure word for 1/10 of a kuai [equivalent of a dime]) | 9 |

| Simplified | Traditional | Pinyin | Part of Speech | Definition | Lesson |
|---|---|---|---|---|---|
| 没 | 沒 | *méi* | adv | not | 2 |
| 每 | | *měi* | pr | every, each | 10 |
| 美国 | 美國 | *Měiguó* | pn | America | 1 |
| 妹妹 | | *mèimei* | n | younger sister | 2 |
| 明天 | | *míngtiān* | t | tomorrow | 3 |
| 名字 | | *míngzi* | n | name | 1 |
| **N** | | | | | |
| 哪 | | *nǎ/něi* | qpr | which | 6 |
| 哪里 | 哪裡 | *nǎli* | pr | where | 7 |
| 哪儿 | 哪兒 | *nǎr* | qpr | where | 5 |
| 那 | | *nà* | pr | that | 2 |
| 那 | | *nà* | conj | in that case, then | 4 |
| 那儿 | 那兒 | *nàr* | pr | there | 8 |
| 男 | | *nán* | adj | male | 2 |
| 难 | 難 | *nán* | adj | difficult question | 7 |
| 呢 | | *ne* | qp | (question particle) | 1 |
| 能 | | *néng* | mv | can, to be able to | 8 |
| 你 | | *nǐ* | pr | you | 1 |
| 年级 | 年級 | *niánjí* | n | grade in school | 6 |
| 念 | | *niàn* | v | to read aloud | 7 |
| 您 | | *nín* | pr | you (honorific for 你) | 6 |
| 纽约 | 紐約 | *Niǔyuē* | pn | New York | 1 |
| 女 | | *nǚ* | adj | female | 2 |
| 女儿 | 女兒 | *nǚ'ér* | n | daughter | 2 |

| Simplified | Traditional | Pinyin | Part of Speech | Definition | Lesson |
|---|---|---|---|---|---|
| | | | **P** | | |
| 朋友 | | *péngyou* | n | friend | 3 |
| 篇 | | *piān* | m | (measure word for essays, articles, etc.) | 8 |
| 便宜 | | *piányi* | adj | cheap, inexpensive | 9 |
| 票 | | *piào* | n | ticket | 10 |
| 漂亮 | 漂亮 | *piàoliang* | adj | pretty | 5 |
| 瓶 | | *píng* | m/n | (measure word for bottled liquid, etc.) | 5 |
| 平常 | | *píngcháng* | adv | usually | 7 |
| | | | **Q** | | |
| 起床 | 起床 | *qǐ chuáng* | vo | to get up | 8 |
| 钱 | 錢 | *qián* | n | money | 9 |
| 请 | 請 | *qǐng* | v | please (polite form of request), to treat or to invite (somebody) | 1 |
| 请客 | 請客 | *qǐng kè* | vo | to invite someone (to dinner, coffee, etc.), to play the host | 4 |
| 去 | | *qù* | v | to go | 4 |
| | | | **R** | | |
| 然后 | 然後 | *ránhòu* | adv | then | 10 |
| 让 | 讓 | *ràng* | v | to allow or cause (somebody to do something) | 10 |
| 人 | | *rén* | n | people, person | 1 |
| 认识 | 認識 | *rènshi* | v | to be acquainted with, to recognize | 3 |
| 日记 | 日記 | *rìjì* | n | diary | 8 |
| 容易 | | *róngyì* | adj | easy | 7 |
| 如果…的话 | 如果…的話 | *rúguǒ . . . de huà* | conj | if | 9 |

| Simplified | Traditional | Pinyin | Part of Speech | Definition | Lesson |
|---|---|---|---|---|---|
| **S** | | | | | |
| 商店 | | *shāngdiàn* | n | store, shop | 9 |
| 上个 | 上個 | *shàng ge* | | previous, last | 7 |
| 上课 | 上課 | *shàng kè* | vo | to go to a class, to start a class, to be in class | 7 |
| 上网 | 上網 | *shàng wǎng* | vo | to go online, to surf the internet | 8 |
| 上午 | | *shàngwǔ* | t | morning | 6 |
| 谁 | 誰 | *shéi* | qpr | who, whom | 2 |
| 什么 | 什麼 | *shénme* | qpr | what | 1 |
| 生词 | 生詞 | *shēngcí* | n | new words, vocabulary | 7 |
| 生日 | | *shēngrì* | n | birthday | 3 |
| 十八 | | *shíbā* | nu | eighteen | 3 |
| 十二 | | *shí'èr* | nu | twelve | 3 |
| 时候 | 時候 | *shíhou* | n | (a point in) time, moment, (a duration of) time | 4 |
| 时间 | 時間 | *shíjiān* | n | time | 6 |
| 试 | 試 | *shì* | v | to try | 9 |
| 事（儿） | 事（兒） | *shì(r)* | n | matter, affair, event | 3 |
| 是 | | *shì* | v | to be | 1 |
| 收 | | *shōu* | v | to receive, to accept | 9 |
| 手机 | 手機 | *shǒujī* | n | cell phone | 10 |
| 售货员 | 售貨員 | *shòuhuòyuán* | n | shop assistant, salesclerk | 9 |
| 书 | 書 | *shū* | n | book | 4 |
| 刷卡 | | *shuā kǎ* | vo | to pay with a credit card | 9 |
| 帅 | 帥 | *shuài* | adj | handsome | 7 |

| Simplified | Traditional | Pinyin | Part of Speech | Definition | Lesson |
|---|---|---|---|---|---|
| 双 | 雙 | *shuāng* | m | (measure word for a pair) | 9 |
| 水 | | *shuǐ* | n | water | 5 |
| 睡觉 | 睡覺 | *shuì jiào* | vo | to sleep | 4 |
| 说 | 說 | *shuō* | v | to say, to speak | 6 |
| 说话 | 說話 | *shuō huà* | vo | to talk | 7 |
| 送 | | *sòng* | v | to see off or out, to take (someone somewhere) | 10 |
| 宿舍 | | *sùshè* | n | dormitory | 8 |
| 算了 | | *suàn le* | | forget it, never mind | 4 |
| 虽然 | 雖然 | *suīrán* | conj | although | 9 |
| 岁 | 歲 | *suì* | n | year (of age) | 3 |
| 所以 | | *suǒyǐ* | conj | so | 4 |
| | | **T** | | | |
| 他 | | *tā* | pr | he, him | 2 |
| 她 | | *tā* | pr | she, her | 2 |
| 它 | | *tā* | pr | it | 9 |
| 太⋯了 | | *tài . . . le* | | too, extremely | 3 |
| 特别 | 特別 | *tèbié* | adv | especially | 10 |
| 天 | | *tiān* | n | day | 3 |
| 条 | 條 | *tiáo* | m | (measure word for pants and long, thin objects) | 9 |
| 跳舞 | | *tiào wǔ* | vo | to dance | 4 |
| 听 | 聽 | *tīng* | v | to listen | 4 |
| 挺 | | *tǐng* | adv | very, rather | 9 |
| 同学 | 同學 | *tóngxué* | n | classmate | 3 |
| 图书馆 | 圖書館 | *túshūguǎn* | n | library | 5 |

| Simplified | Traditional | Pinyin | Part of Speech | Definition | Lesson |
|---|---|---|---|---|---|
| **W** | | | | | |
| 外国 | 外國 | *wàiguó* | n | foreign country | 4 |
| 玩（儿） | 玩（兒） | *wán(r)* | v | to have fun, to play | 5 |
| 晚 | | *wǎn* | adj | late | 7 |
| 晚饭 | 晚飯 | *wǎnfàn* | n | dinner, supper | 3 |
| 晚上 | | *wǎnshang* | t | evening, night | 3 |
| 王朋 | | *Wáng Péng* | pn | (a personal name) | 1 |
| 喂 | | *wéi/wèi* | interj | (on the phone) Hello!, Hey! | 6 |
| 位 | | *wèi* | m | (polite measure word for people) | 6 |
| 为什么 | 為什麼 | *wèishénme* | qpr | why | 3 |
| 问 | 問 | *wèn* | v | to ask (a question) | 1 |
| 问题 | 問題 | *wèntí* | n | question, problem | 6 |
| 我 | | *wǒ* | pr | I, me | 1 |
| 我们 | 我們 | *wǒmen* | pr | we, us | 3 |
| 午饭 | 午飯 | *wǔfàn* | n | lunch, midday meal | 8 |
| **X** | | | | | |
| 希望 | 希望 | *xīwàng* | v/n | to hope; hope | 8 |
| 喜欢 | 喜歡 | *xǐhuan* | v | to like | 3 |
| 洗澡 | | *xǐ zǎo* | vo | to take a bath/shower | 8 |
| 下车 | 下車 | *xià chē* | vo | to get off (a bus, train, etc.) | 10 |
| 下个 | 下個 | *xià ge* | | next | 6 |
| 下午 | | *xiàwǔ* | t | afternoon | 6 |
| 先 | | *xiān* | adv | first | 10 |
| 先生 | | *xiānsheng* | n | Mr., husband, teacher | 1 |
| 线 | 線 | *xiàn* | n | line | 10 |

| Simplified | Traditional | Pinyin | Part of Speech | Definition | Lesson |
|---|---|---|---|---|---|
| 现在 | 現在 | *xiànzài* | t | now | 3 |
| 想 | | *xiǎng* | av | to want to, would like to | 4 |
| 小 | | *xiǎo* | adj | small, little | 4 |
| 小姐 | | *xiǎojiě* | n | Miss, young lady | 1 |
| 笑 | | *xiào* | v | to laugh at, to laugh, to smile | 8 |
| 鞋 | | *xié* | n | shoes | 9 |
| 写 | 寫 | *xiě* | v | to write | 7 |
| 谢谢 | 謝謝 | *xièxie* | v | to thank | 3 |
| 新 | | *xīn* | adj | new | 8 |
| 新年 | | *xīnnián* | n | new year | 10 |
| 信 | | *xìn* | n | letter (correspondence) | 8 |
| 信用卡 | | *xìnyòngkǎ* | n | credit card | 9 |
| 星期 | | *xīngqī* | n | week | 3 |
| 星期四 | | *xīngqīsì* | n | Thursday | 3 |
| 行 | | *xíng* | v | all right, OK | 6 |
| 姓 | | *xìng* | v/n | (one's ) family name is . . . ; family name | 1 |
| 学 | 學 | *xué* | v | to study, to learn | 7 |
| 学期 | 學期 | *xuéqī* | n | school term, semester, quarter | 8 |
| 学生 | 學生 | *xuésheng* | n | student | 1 |
| 学习 | 學習 | *xuéxí* | v | to study, to learn | 7 |
| 学校 | 學校 | *xuéxiào* | n | school | 5 |
| | | | **Y** | | |
| 呀 | | *ya* | p | (interjectory particle used to soften a question) | 5 |
| 颜色 | 顏色 | *yánsè* | n | color | 9 |
| 样子 | 樣子 | *yàngzi* | n | style | 9 |

| Simplified | Traditional | Pinyin | Part of Speech | Definition | Lesson |
|---|---|---|---|---|---|
| 要 | | *yào* | v | to want | 5 |
| 要 | | *yào* | mv | will, to be going to; to want to, to have a desire to | 6 |
| 要是 | | *yàoshi* | conj | if | 6 |
| 也 | | *yě* | adv | too, also | 1 |
| 一边 | 一邊 | *yìbiān* | adv | simultaneously, at the same time | 8 |
| 一共 | | *yígòng* | adv | altogether | 9 |
| 一起 | 一起 | *yìqǐ* | adv | together | 5 |
| 一下 | | *yí xià* | n+m | once, a bit | 5 |
| 一样 | 一樣 | *yíyàng* | adj | same, alike | 9 |
| 衣服 | | *yīfu* | n | clothes | 9 |
| 医生 | 醫生 | *yīshēng* | n | doctor, physician | 2 |
| 以后 | 以後 | *yǐhòu* | t | after, from now on, later on | 6 |
| 以前 | | *yǐqián* | t | before | 8 |
| 已经 | 已經 | *yǐjīng* | adv | already | 8 |
| 因为 | 因為 | *yīnwèi* | conj | because | 3 |
| 音乐 | 音樂 | *yīnyuè* | n | music | 4 |
| 音乐会 | 音樂會 | *yīnyuèhuì* | n | concert | 8 |
| 英国 | 英國 | *Yīngguó* | pn | Britain | 3 |
| 英文 | 英文 | *Yīngwén* | n | the English language | 2 |
| 用 | | *yòng* | v | to use | 8 |
| 有 | | *yǒu* | v | to have, to exist | 2 |
| 有的 | | *yǒude* | pr | some | 4 |
| 有意思 | | *yǒu yìsi* | adj | interesting | 4 |
| 语法 | 語法 | *yǔfǎ* | n | grammar | 7 |

| Simplified | Traditional | Pinyin | Part of Speech | Definition | Lesson |
|---|---|---|---|---|---|
| 预习 | 預習 | *yùxí* | v | to preview | 7 |
| 月 | | *yuè* | n | month | 3 |
| | | | **Z** | | |
| 在 | | *zài* | prep | at, in, on | 5 |
| 在 | | *zài* | v | to be present, to be at (a place) | 6 |
| 再 | | *zài* | adv | again | 9 |
| 再见 | 再見 | *zàijiàn* | v | goodbye, see you again | 3 |
| 早 | | *zǎo* | adj | early | 7 |
| 早饭 | 早飯 | *zǎofàn* | n | breakfast | 8 |
| 早上 | | *zǎoshang* | t | morning | 7 |
| 怎么 | 怎麼 | *zěnme* | qpr | how, how come | 7 |
| 怎么样 | 怎麼樣 | *zěnmeyàng* | qpr | Is it OK? How is that? How does that sound? | 3 |
| 站 | | *zhàn* | m | (measure word for bus stops, train stops, etc.) | 10 |
| 张 | 張 | *zhāng* | m | (measure word for flat objects such as paper, pictures, etc.) | 7 |
| 找 | | *zhǎo* | v | to look for | 4 |
| 找（钱） | 找（錢） | *zhǎo (qián)* | v(o) | to give change | 9 |
| 照片 | | *zhàopiàn* | n | picture, photo | 2 |
| 这 | 這 | *zhè* | pr | this | 2 |
| 这么 | 這麼 | *zhème* | pr | so, this (late, etc.) | 7 |
| 这儿 | 這兒 | *zhèr* | pr | here | 9 |
| 真 | | *zhēn* | adv | really | 7 |
| 正在 | | *zhèngzài* | adv | in the middle of (doing something) | 8 |
| 枝 | | *zhī* | m | (measure word for long, thin, inflexible objects such as pens, pencils, etc.) | 7 |

| Simplified | Traditional | Pinyin | Part of Speech | Definition | Lesson |
|---|---|---|---|---|---|
| 知道 | | *zhīdao* | v | to know | 8 |
| 只 | | *zhǐ* | adv | only | 4 |
| 纸 | 紙 | *zhǐ* | n | paper | 7 |
| 中 | | *zhōng* | adj | medium, middle | 9 |
| 中国 | 中國 | *Zhōngguó* | pn | China | 1 |
| 中文 | | *Zhōngwén* | n | the Chinese language | 6 |
| 中午 | | *zhōngwǔ* | t | noon | 8 |
| 种 | 種 | *zhǒng* | m | (measure word for kinds, sorts, types) | 9 |
| 周末 | 週末 | *zhōumò* | n | weekend | 4 |
| 祝 | | *zhù* | v | to wish (well) | 8 |
| 专业 | 專業 | *zhuānyè* | n | major (in college), specialty | 8 |
| 准备 | 準備 | *zhǔnbèi* | v | to prepare | 6 |
| 字 | | *zì* | n | character | 7 |
| 自己 | | *zìjǐ* | pr | oneself | 10 |
| 走 | | *zǒu* | v | to go by way of, to walk | 10 |
| 最后 | 最後 | *zuìhòu* | | final, last | 10 |
| 最近 | | *zuìjìn* | t | recently | 8 |
| 昨天 | | *zuótiān* | t | yesterday | 4 |
| 做 | | *zuò* | v | to do | 2 |
| 坐 | | *zuò* | v | to sit | 5 |
| 坐 | | *zuò* | v | to travel by | 10 |

# Vocabulary Index (English-Chinese)

The English-Chinese index is organized based on the alphabetical order of the English definitions. For ease of reference, indefinite articles and definite articles are omitted when they are at the beginning of a phrase.

| English | Simplified | Traditional | Pinyin | Part of Speech | Lesson |
|---|---|---|---|---|---|
| **A** | | | | | |
| after, from now on, later on | 以后 | 以後 | *yǐhòu* | t | 6 |
| afternoon | 下午 | | *xiàwǔ* | t | 6 |
| again | 再 | | *zài* | adv | 9 |
| airplane | 飞机 | 飛機 | *fēijī* | n | 10 |
| airport | （飞）机场 | （飛）機場 | *(fēi)jīchǎng* | n | 10 |
| all right, OK | 行 | | *xíng* | v | 6 |
| allow or cause (somebody to do something) | 让 | 讓 | *ràng* | v | 10 |
| already | 已经 | 已經 | *yǐjīng* | adv | 8 |
| also, too, as well | 还 | 還 | *hái* | adv | 3 |
| although | 虽然 | 雖然 | *suīrán* | conj | 9 |
| altogether | 一共 | | *yígòng* | adv | 9 |
| America | 美国 | 美國 | *Měiguó* | pn | 1 |
| and | 和 | | *hé* | conj | 2 |
| ask (a question) | 问 | 問 | *wèn* | v | 1 |
| at, in, on | 在 | | *zài* | prep | 5 |
| **B** | | | | | |
| Bai Ying'ai | 白英爱 | 白英愛 | *Bái Yīng'ài* | pn | 2 |
| be | 是 | | *shì* | v | 1 |
| be acquainted with, recognize | 认识 | 認識 | *rènshi* | v | 3 |

| English | Simplified | Traditional | Pinyin | Part of Speech | Lesson |
|---|---|---|---|---|---|
| be called, call | 叫 | | *jiào* | v | 1 |
| be present, be at (a place) | 在 | | *zài* | v | 6 |
| because | 因为 | 因為 | *yīnwèi* | conj | 3 |
| before | 以前 | | *yǐqián* | t | 8 |
| begin, start; beginning | 开始 | 開始 | *kāishǐ* | v/n | 7 |
| Beijing | 北京 | | *Běijīng* | pn | 1 |
| big, old | 大 | | *dà* | adj | 3 |
| birthday | 生日 | | *shēngrì* | n | 3 |
| black | 黑 | | *hēi* | adj | 9 |
| blue | 蓝 | 藍 | *lán* | adj | 10 |
| book | 书 | 書 | *shū* | n | 4 |
| both, all | 都 | | *dōu* | adv | 2 |
| breakfast | 早饭 | 早飯 | *zǎofàn* | n | 8 |
| Britain | 英国 | 英國 | *Yīngguó* | pn | 3 |
| brown, coffee color | 咖啡色 | | *kāfēisè* | n | 9 |
| bus | 公共汽车 | 公共汽車 | *gōnggòng qìchē* | n | 10 |
| busy | 忙 | | *máng* | adj | 3 |
| but | 但是 | | *dànshì* | conj | 6 |
| but | 可是 | | *kěshì* | conj | 3 |
| buy | 买 | 買 | *mǎi* | v | 9 |
| | | **C** | | | |
| can, able to | 能 | | *néng* | mv | 8 |
| can, know how to | 会 | 會 | *huì* | mv | 8 |
| can, may | 可以 | | *kěyǐ* | mv | 5 |

| English | Simplified | Traditional | Pinyin | Part of Speech | Lesson |
| --- | --- | --- | --- | --- | --- |
| cell phone | 手机 | 手機 | *shǒujī* | n | 10 |
| character | 字 | | *zì* | n | 7 |
| chat | 聊天（儿） | 聊天（兒） | *liáo tiān(r)* | vo | 5 |
| cheap, inexpensive | 便宜 | | *piányi* | adj | 9 |
| child | 孩子 | | *háizi* | n | 2 |
| China | 中国 | 中國 | *Zhōngguó* | pn | 1 |
| Chinese characters | 汉字 | 漢字 | *Hànzì* | n | 7 |
| Chinese language | 中文 | | *Zhōngwén* | n | 6 |
| city | 城市 | | *chéngshì* | n | 10 |
| class, course, lesson | 课 | 課 | *kè* | n | 6 |
| classmate | 同学 | 同學 | *tóngxué* | n | 3 |
| classroom | 教室 | | *jiàoshì* | n | 8 |
| clothes | 衣服 | | *yīfu* | n | 9 |
| coffee | 咖啡 | | *kāfēi* | n | 5 |
| cola | 可乐 | 可樂 | *kělè* | n | 5 |
| college student | 大学生 | 大學生 | *dàxuéshēng* | n | 2 |
| color | 颜色 | 顏色 | *yánsè* | n | 9 |
| come | 来 | 來 | *lái* | v | 5 |
| come back | 回来 | 回來 | *huí lai* | vc | 6 |
| come in | 进来 | 進來 | *jìn lai* | vc | 5 |
| computer | 电脑 | 電腦 | *diànnǎo* | n | 8 |
| concert | 音乐会 | 音樂會 | *yīnyuèhuì* | n | 8 |
| convenient | 方便 | | *fāngbiàn* | adj | 6 |
| cool (appearance, behavior) | 酷 | | *kù* | adj | 7 |
| credit card | 信用卡 | | *xìnyòngkǎ* | n | 9 |

| English | Simplified | Traditional | Pinyin | Part of Speech | Lesson |
|---|---|---|---|---|---|
| **D** | | | | | |
| dance | 跳舞 | | *tiào wǔ* | vo | 4 |
| daughter | 女儿 | 女兒 | *nǚ'ér* | n | 2 |
| day | 天 | | *tiān* | n | 3 |
| diary | 日记 | 日記 | *rìjì* | n | 8 |
| difficult | 难 | 難 | *nán* | adj | 7 |
| dining room, cafeteria | 餐厅 | 餐廳 | *cāntīng* | n | 8 |
| dinner, supper | 晚饭 | 晚飯 | *wǎnfàn* | n | 3 |
| dish, cuisine | 菜 | 菜 | *cài* | n | 3 |
| do | 做 | | *zuò* | v | 2 |
| doctor, physician | 医生 | 醫生 | *yīshēng* | n | 2 |
| don't | 别 | 別 | *bié* | adv | 6 |
| dormitory | 宿舍 | | *sùshè* | n | 8 |
| drink | 喝 | | *hē* | v | 5 |
| drive a car | 开车 | 開車 | *kāi chē* | vo | 10 |
| (dynamic particle) | 了 | | *le* | p | 5 |
| **E** | | | | | |
| early | 早 | | *zǎo* | adj | 7 |
| easy | 容易 | | *róngyì* | adj | 7 |
| eat | 吃 | | *chī* | v | 3 |
| eighteen | 十八 | | *shíbā* | nu | 3 |
| eldest/oldest brother | 大哥 | | *dàgē* | n | 2 |
| eldest/oldest sister | 大姐 | | *dàjiě* | n | 2 |
| email/electronic mail | 电子邮件 | 電子郵件 | *diànzǐ yóujiàn* | n | 10 |

| English | Simplified | Traditional | Pinyin | Part of Speech | Lesson |
|---|---|---|---|---|---|
| English language | 英文 | 英文 | *Yīngwén* | n | 2 |
| enter | 进 | 進 | *jìn* | v | 5 |
| especially | 特别 | 特別 | *tèbié* | adv | 10 |
| evening, night | 晚上 | | *wǎnshang* | t | 3 |
| every, each | 每 | | *měi* | pr | 10 |
| everybody | 大家 | | *dàjiā* | pr | 7 |
| exchange, change | 换 | 換 | *huàn* | v | 9 |
| **F** | | | | | |
| family, home | 家 | | *jiā* | n | 2 |
| fast, quick; quickly | 快 | | *kuài* | adj/adv | 5 |
| father, dad | 爸爸 | | *bàba* | n | 2 |
| feel, think | 觉得 | 覺得 | *juéde* | v | 4 |
| feel embarrassed | 不好意思 | | *bù hǎoyìsi* | | 10 |
| female | 女 | | *nǚ* | adj | 2 |
| final, last | 最后 | 最後 | *zuìhòu* | | 10 |
| fine, good, nice, OK, it's settled | 好 | | *hǎo* | adj | 1 |
| first | 先 | | *xiān* | adv | 10 |
| foreign country | 外国 | 外國 | *wàiguó* | n | 4 |
| forget it, never mind | 算了 | | *suàn le* | | 4 |
| free time | 空（儿） | 空（兒） | *kòng(r)* | n | 6 |
| friend | 朋友 | | *péngyou* | n | 3 |
| **G** | | | | | |
| Gao Wenzhong | 高文中 | | *Gāo Wénzhōng* | pn | 2 |
| Gao Xiaoyin | 高小音 | | *Gāo Xiǎoyīn* | pn | 5 |
| get off (a bus, train, etc.) | 下车 | 下車 | *xià chē* | vo | 10 |

| English | Simplified | Traditional | Pinyin | Part of Speech | Lesson |
|---|---|---|---|---|---|
| get up | 起床 | 起床 | *qǐ chuáng* | vo | 8 |
| give | 给 | 給 | *gěi* | v | 5 |
| give change | 找（钱） | 找（錢） | *zhǎo (qián)* | v(o) | 9 |
| give or take a test; test | 考试 | 考試 | *kǎo shì* | vo/n | 6 |
| go | 去 | | *qù* | v | 4 |
| go by way of, walk | 走 | | *zǒu* | v | 10 |
| go home | 回家 | | *huí jiā* | vo | 5 |
| go online, surf the internet | 上网 | 上網 | *shàng wǎng* | vo | 8 |
| go out | 出去 | | *chūqu* | vc | 10 |
| go to, arrive | 到 | | *dào* | v | 6 |
| go to a class, start a class, be in class | 上课 | 上課 | *shàng kè* | vo | 7 |
| goodbye, see you again | 再见 | 再見 | *zàijiàn* | v | 3 |
| grade in school | 年级 | 年級 | *niánjí* | n | 6 |
| grammar | 语法 | 語法 | *yǔfǎ* | n | 7 |
| green | 绿 | 綠 | *lǜ* | adj | 10 |
| **H** | | | | | |
| half, half an hour | 半 | | *bàn* | nu | 3 |
| handsome | 帅 | 帥 | *shuài* | adj | 7 |
| happy | 快乐 | 快樂 | *kuàilè* | adj | 10 |
| happy, pleased | 高兴 | 高興 | *gāoxìng* | adj | 5 |
| have, exist | 有 | | *yǒu* | v | 2 |
| have a meeting | 开会 | 開會 | *kāi huì* | vo | 6 |
| have fun, play | 玩（儿） | 玩（兒） | *wán(r)* | v | 5 |
| he, him | 他 | | *tā* | pr | 2 |

| English | Simplified | Traditional | Pinyin | Part of Speech | Lesson |
|---|---|---|---|---|---|
| Hello!, Hey! (on the phone) | 喂 | | *wéi/wèi* | interj | 6 |
| help | 帮 | 幫 | *bāng* | v | 6 |
| here | 这儿 | 這兒 | *zhèr* | pr | 9 |
| highway | 高速公路 | | *gāosù gōnglù* | n | 10 |
| homework, schoolwork | 功课 | 功課 | *gōngkè* | n | 7 |
| honorable, expensive | 贵 | 貴 | *guì* | adj | 1 |
| hope; hope | 希望 | 希望 | *xīwàng* | v/n | 8 |
| how, how come | 怎么 | 怎麼 | *zěnme* | qpr | 7 |
| how many, some, a few | 几 | 幾 | *jǐ* | nu | 2 |
| how many/much, to what extent | 多 | | *duō* | adv | 3 |
| how much/many | 多少 | | *duōshao* | qpr | 9 |
| however, but | 不过 | 不過 | *búguò* | conj | 9 |
| hundred | 百 | | *bǎi* | nu | 9 |
| | | **I** | | | |
| I, me | 我 | | *wǒ* | pr | 1 |
| if | 如果…的话 | 如果…的話 | *rúguǒ . . . de huà* | conj | 9 |
| if | 要是 | | *yàoshi* | conj | 6 |
| in addition to, besides | 除了…以外 | | *chúle . . . yǐwài* | conj | 8 |
| in that case, then | 那 | | *nà* | conj | 4 |
| in the middle of (doing something) | 正在 | | *zhèngzài* | adv | 8 |
| interesting | 有意思 | | *yǒu yìsi* | adj | 4 |
| (interjectory particle used to soften a question) | 呀 | | *ya* | p | 5 |
| introduce | 介绍 | 介紹 | *jièshào* | v | 5 |

| English | Simplified | Traditional | Pinyin | Part of Speech | Lesson |
|---|---|---|---|---|---|
| invite someone (to dinner, coffee, etc.), play the host | 请客 | 請客 | *qǐng kè* | vo | 4 |
| Is it OK? How is that? How does that sound? | 怎么样 | 怎麼樣 | *zěnmeyàng* | qpr | 3 |
| it | 它 | | *tā* | pr | 9 |
| | | **J** | | | |
| job; to work | 工作 | | *gōngzuò* | n/v | 2 |
| | | **K** | | | |
| know | 知道 | | *zhīdao* | v | 8 |
| | | **L** | | | |
| late | 晚 | | *wǎn* | adj | 7 |
| later | 后来 | 後來 | *hòulái* | t | 8 |
| laugh at, laugh, smile | 笑 | | *xiào* | v | 8 |
| lawyer | 律师 | 律師 | *lǜshī* | n | 2 |
| length | 长短 | 長短 | *chángduǎn* | n | 9 |
| letter (correspondence) | 信 | | *xìn* | n | 8 |
| Li You | 李友 | | *Lǐ Yǒu* | pn | 1 |
| library | 图书馆 | 圖書館 | *túshūguǎn* | n | 5 |
| like | 喜欢 | 喜歡 | *xǐhuan* | v | 3 |
| line | 线 | 線 | *xiàn* | n | 10 |
| listen | 听 | 聽 | *tīng* | v | 4 |
| little, a bit, some | 点（儿） | 點（兒） | *diǎn(r)* | m | 5 |
| long time | 好久 | | *hǎojiǔ* | | 4 |
| look for | 找 | | *zhǎo* | v | 4 |
| lunch, midday meal | 午饭 | 午飯 | *wǔfàn* | n | 8 |

| English | Simplified | Traditional | Pinyin | Part of Speech | Lesson |
|---|---|---|---|---|---|
| **M** | | | | | |
| major (in college), specialty | 专业 | 專業 | *zhuānyè* | n | 8 |
| make a phone call | 打电话 | 打電話 | *dǎ diànhuà* | vo | 6 |
| male | 男 | | *nán* | adj | 2 |
| many, much | 多 | | *duō* | adj | 7 |
| matter, affair, event | 事（儿） | 事（兒） | *shì(r)* | n | 3 |
| meal, (cooked) rice | 饭 | 飯 | *fàn* | n | 3 |
| (measure word for a pair) | 双 | 雙 | *shuāng* | m | 9 |
| (measure word for a position in a numerical series, day of the month) | 号 | 號 | *hào* | m | 3 |
| (measure word for bottled liquid, etc.) | 瓶 | | *píng* | m/n | 5 |
| (measure word for bus stops, train stops, etc.) | 站 | | *zhàn* | m | 10 |
| (measure word for class periods) | 节 | 節 | *jié* | m | 6 |
| (measure word for essays, articles, etc.) | 篇 | | *piān* | m | 8 |
| (measure word for flat objects such as paper, pictures, etc.) | 张 | 張 | *zhāng* | m | 7 |
| (measure word for kinds, sorts, types) | 种 | 種 | *zhǒng* | m | 9 |
| (measure word for letters) | 封 | | *fēng* | m | 8 |
| (measure word for long, thin, inflexible objects such as pens, pencils, etc.) | 枝 | | *zhī* | m | 7 |
| (measure word for many common everyday objects) | 个 | 個 | *gè/ge* | m | 2 |
| (measure word for number of family members) | 口 | | *kǒu* | m | 2 |
| (measure word for 1/100 of a kuai [equivalent of a cent]) | 分 | | *fēn* | m | 9 |
| (measure word for 1/10 of a kuai [equivalent of a dime]) | 毛 | | *máo* | m | 9 |

| English | Simplified | Traditional | Pinyin | Part of Speech | Lesson |
|---|---|---|---|---|---|
| (measure word for pants and long, thin objects) | 条 | 條 | *tiáo* | m | 9 |
| (measure word for people [polite]) | 位 | | *wèi* | m | 6 |
| (measure word for shirts, dresses, jackets, coats, etc.) | 件 | | *jiàn* | m | 9 |
| (measure word for the basic Chinese monetary unit [equivalent of a dollar]) | 块 | 塊 | *kuài* | m | 9 |
| (measure word for things contained in a cup or glass) | 杯 | | *bēi* | m | 5 |
| medium, middle | 中 | | *zhōng* | adj | 9 |
| meet up/with | 见面 | 見面 | *jiàn miàn* | vo | 6 |
| Miss, young lady | 小姐 | | *xiǎojiě* | n | 1 |
| money | 钱 | 錢 | *qián* | n | 9 |
| month | 月 | | *yuè* | n | 3 |
| morning | 上午 | | *shàngwǔ* | t | 6 |
| morning | 早上 | | *zǎoshang* | t | 7 |
| mother, mom | 妈妈 | 媽媽 | *māma* | n | 2 |
| movie | 电影 | 電影 | *diànyǐng* | n | 4 |
| Mr., husband, teacher | 先生 | | *xiānsheng* | n | 1 |
| music | 音乐 | 音樂 | *yīnyuè* | n | 4 |
| must, have to | 得 | | *děi* | av | 6 |
| | | **N** | | | |
| name | 名字 | | *míngzi* | n | 1 |
| need not | 不用 | | *bú yòng* | | 9 |
| nervous, anxious | 紧张 | 緊張 | *jǐnzhāng* | adj | 10 |
| new | 新 | | *xīn* | adj | 8 |
| new words, vocabulary | 生词 | 生詞 | *shēngcí* | n | 7 |

| English | Simplified | Traditional | Pinyin | Part of Speech | Lesson |
|---|---|---|---|---|---|
| new year | 新年 | | *xīnnián* | n | 10 |
| New York | 纽约 | 紐約 | *Niǔyuē* | pn | 1 |
| next one | 下个 | 下個 | *xià ge* | | 6 |
| noon | 中午 | | *zhōngwǔ* | t | 8 |
| not | 没 | 沒 | *méi* | adv | 2 |
| not, no | 不 | | *bù* | adv | 1 |
| not until, only then | 才 | | *cái* | adv | 5 |
| now | 现在 | 現在 | *xiànzài* | t | 3 |
| | | **O** | | | |
| o'clock (lit. dot, point, thus "points on the clock") | 点 | 點 | *diǎn* | m | 3 |
| office | 办公室 | 辦公室 | *bàngōngshì* | n | 6 |
| often | 常常 | | *chángcháng* | adv | 4 |
| older brother | 哥哥 | | *gēge* | n | 2 |
| older sister | 姐姐 | | *jiějie* | n | 2 |
| once, a bit | 一下 | | *yí xià* | n+m | 5 |
| (one's ) family name is . . . ; family name | 姓 | | *xìng* | v/n | 1 |
| oneself | 自己 | | *zìjǐ* | pr | 10 |
| only | 只 | | *zhǐ* | adv | 4 |
| or | 还是 | 還是 | *háishi* | conj | 3 |
| or | 或者 | | *huòzhě* | conj | 10 |
| other people, another person | 别人 | 別人 | *biérén* | n | 4 |
| | | **P** | | | |
| pants | 裤子 | 褲子 | *kùzi* | n | 9 |
| paper | 纸 | 紙 | *zhǐ* | n | 7 |

| English | Simplified | Traditional | Pinyin | Part of Speech | Lesson |
|---|---|---|---|---|---|
| pay money | 付钱 | 付錢 | *fù qián* | vo | 9 |
| pay with a credit card | 刷卡 | | *shuā kǎ* | vo | 9 |
| pen | 笔 | 筆 | *bǐ* | n | 7 |
| people, person | 人 | | *rén* | n | 1 |
| picture, photo | 照片 | | *zhàopiàn* | n | 2 |
| play ball | 打球 | | *dǎ qiú* | vo | 4 |
| please (polite form of request), to treat or to invite (somebody) | 请 | 請 | *qǐng* | v | 1 |
| polite | 客气 | 客氣 | *kèqi* | adj | 6 |
| (possessive or descriptive particle) | 的 | | *de* | p | 2 |
| practice | 练习 | 練習 | *liànxí* | v | 6 |
| precisely, exactly | 就 | | *jiù* | adv | 6 |
| (prefix for ordinal numbers) | 第 | | *dì* | prefix | 7 |
| prepare | 准备 | 準備 | *zhǔnbèi* | v | 6 |
| pretty | 漂亮 | 漂亮 | *piàoliang* | adj | 5 |
| pretty good | 不错 | 不錯 | *búcuò* | adj | 4 |
| preview | 预习 | 預習 | *yùxí* | v | 7 |
| previous one | 上个 | 上個 | *shàng ge* | | 7 |
| pronunciation | 发音 | 發音 | *fāyīn* | n | 8 |
| **Q** | | | | | |
| quarter (of an hour) | 刻 | | *kè* | m | 3 |
| (question particle) | 吗 | 嗎 | *ma* | qp | 1 |
| (question particle) | 呢 | | *ne* | qp | 1 |
| question, problem | 问题 | 問題 | *wèntí* | n | 6 |

| English | Simplified | Traditional | Pinyin | Part of Speech | Lesson |
|---|---|---|---|---|---|
| | | **R** | | | |
| read aloud | 念 | | *niàn* | v | 7 |
| really | 真 | | *zhēn* | adv | 7 |
| receive, accept | 收 | | *shōu* | v | 9 |
| recently | 最近 | | *zuìjìn* | t | 8 |
| red | 红 | 紅 | *hóng* | adj | 9 |
| review | 复习 | 復習 | *fùxí* | v | 7 |
| right, correct | 对 | 對 | *duì* | adj | 4 |
| route, road | 路 | | *lù* | n | 10 |
| | | **S** | | | |
| same, alike | 一样 | 一樣 | *yíyàng* | adj | 9 |
| say, speak | 说 | 說 | *shuō* | v | 6 |
| school | 学校 | 學校 | *xuéxiào* | n | 5 |
| school term, semester, quarter | 学期 | 學期 | *xuéqī* | n | 8 |
| second oldest sister | 二姐 | | *èrjiě* | n | 2 |
| see | 见 | 見 | *jiàn* | v | 3 |
| see off or out, take (someone somewhere) | 送 | | *sòng* | v | 10 |
| send a text message (lit. send a short message) | 发短信 | 發短信 | *fā duǎnxìn* | vo | 10 |
| (sentence-final particle of exclamation, interrogation, etc.) | 啊 | | *a* | p | 6 |
| (sentence-final particle) | 吧 | | *ba* | p | 5 |
| September | 九月 | | *jiǔyuè* | p | 3 |
| she, her | 她 | | *tā* | pr | 2 |
| shirt | 衬衫 | 襯衫 | *chènshān* | n | 9 |
| shoes | 鞋 | | *xié* | n | 9 |

| English | Simplified | Traditional | Pinyin | Part of Speech | Lesson |
|---|---|---|---|---|---|
| shop assistant, salesclerk | 售货员 | 售貨員 | *shòuhuòyuán* | n | 9 |
| simultaneously, at the same time | 一边 | 一邊 | *yìbiān* | adv | 8 |
| sing (a song) | 唱歌（儿） | 唱歌（兒） | *chàng gē(r)* | vo | 4 |
| sit | 坐 | | *zuò* | v | 5 |
| size | 大小 | | *dàxiǎo* | n | 9 |
| size | 号 | 號 | *hào* | n | 9 |
| sleep | 睡觉 | 睡覺 | *shuì jiào* | vo | 4 |
| slow | 慢 | | *màn* | adj | 7 |
| small, little | 小 | | *xiǎo* | adj | 4 |
| so | 所以 | | *suǒyǐ* | conj | 4 |
| so, this (late, etc.) | 这么 | 這麼 | *zhème* | pr | 7 |
| some | 有的 | | *yǒude* | pr | 4 |
| son | 儿子 | 兒子 | *érzi* | n | 2 |
| sorry | 对不起 | 對不起 | *duìbuqǐ* | v | 5 |
| sound recording; record | 录音 | 錄音 | *lùyīn* | n/vo | 7 |
| spend | 花 | 花 | *huā* | v | 10 |
| store, shop | 商店 | | *shāngdiàn* | n | 9 |
| (structural particle) | 得 | | *de* | p | 7 |
| student | 学生 | 學生 | *xuésheng* | n | 1 |
| study, learn | 学 | 學 | *xué* | v | 7 |
| study, learn | 学习 | 學習 | *xuéxí* | v | 7 |
| style | 样子 | 樣子 | *yàngzi* | n | 9 |
| subway | 地铁 | 地鐵 | *dìtiě* | n | 10 |
| suitable | 合适 | 合適 | *héshì* | adj | 9 |

| English | Simplified | Traditional | Pinyin | Part of Speech | Lesson |
|---|---|---|---|---|---|
| **T** | | | | | |
| take a bath/shower | 洗澡 | | *xǐ zǎo* | vo | 8 |
| take a taxi | 打车 | 打車 | *dǎ chē* | vo | 10 |
| talk | 说话 | 說話 | *shuō huà* | vo | 7 |
| taxi | 出租汽车 | 出租汽車 | *chūzū qìchē* | n | 10 |
| tea | 茶 | 茶 | *chá* | n | 5 |
| teach | 教 | | *jiāo* | v | 7 |
| teacher | 老师 | 老師 | *lǎoshī* | n | 1 |
| Teacher Chang | 常老师 | 常老師 | *Cháng lǎoshī* | pn | 6 |
| television | 电视 | 電視 | *diànshì* | n | 4 |
| tell | 告诉 | 告訴 | *gàosu* | v | 8 |
| text of a lesson | 课文 | 課文 | *kèwén* | n | 7 |
| thank | 谢谢 | 謝謝 | *xièxie* | v | 3 |
| that | 那 | | *nà* | pr | 2 |
| then | 然后 | 然後 | *ránhòu* | adv | 10 |
| there | 那儿 | 那兒 | *nàr* | pr | 8 |
| things, objects | 东西 | 東西 | *dōngxi* | n | 9 |
| this | 这 | 這 | *zhè* | pr | 2 |
| this year | 今年 | | *jīnnián* | t | 3 |
| Thursday | 星期四 | | *xīngqīsì* | n | 3 |
| ticket | 票 | | *piào* | n | 10 |
| time | 时间 | 時間 | *shíjiān* | n | 6 |
| time (a point in), moment, time (a duration of) | 时候 | 時候 | *shíhou* | n | 4 |
| tired | 累 | | *lèi* | adj | 8 |

| English | Simplified | Traditional | Pinyin | Part of Speech | Lesson |
|---|---|---|---|---|---|
| to, for | 给 | 給 | *gěi* | prep | 6 |
| today | 今天 | | *jīntiān* | t | 3 |
| together | 一起 | 一起 | *yìqǐ* | adv | 5 |
| tomorrow | 明天 | | *míngtiān* | t | 3 |
| too, also | 也 | | *yě* | adv | 1 |
| too, extremely | 太…了 | | *tài…le* | | 3 |
| travel by | 坐 | | *zuò* | v | 10 |
| troublesome | 麻烦 | 麻煩 | *máfan* | adj | 10 |
| try | 试 | 試 | *shì* | v | 9 |
| twelve | 十二 | | *shí'èr* | nu | 3 |
| two, a couple of | 两 | 兩 | *liǎng* | nu | 2 |
| | | **U** | | | |
| understand | 懂 | 懂 | *dǒng* | v | 7 |
| use | 用 | | *yòng* | v | 8 |
| usually | 平常 | | *píngcháng* | adv | 7 |
| | | **V** | | | |
| very | 很 | | *hěn* | adv | 3 |
| very, rather | 挺 | | *tǐng* | adv | 9 |
| | | **W** | | | |
| wait, wait for | 等 | | *děng* | v | 6 |
| Wang Peng | 王朋 | | *Wáng Péng* | pn | 1 |
| want | 要 | | *yào* | v | 5 |
| want to, would like to | 想 | | *xiǎng* | av | 4 |
| watch, look, read | 看 | | *kàn* | v | 4 |
| water | 水 | | *shuǐ* | n | 5 |

| English | Simplified | Traditional | Pinyin | Part of Speech | Lesson |
|---|---|---|---|---|---|
| we, us | 我们 | 我們 | *wǒmen* | pr | 3 |
| wear, put on | 穿 | | *chuān* | v | 9 |
| week | 星期 | | *xīngqī* | n | 3 |
| weekend | 周末 | 週末 | *zhōumò* | n | 4 |
| what | 什么 | 什麼 | *shénme* | qpr | 1 |
| where | 哪里 | 哪裡 | *nǎli* | pr | 7 |
| where | 哪儿 | 哪兒 | *nǎr* | qpr | 5 |
| which | 哪 | | *nǎ/něi* | qpr | 6 |
| who, whom | 谁 | 誰 | *shéi* | qpr | 2 |
| why | 为什么 | 為什麼 | *wèishénme* | qpr | 3 |
| will, be going to; want to, have a desire to | 要 | | *yào* | mv | 6 |
| winter vacation | 寒假 | | *hánjià* | n | 10 |
| wish (well) | 祝 | | *zhù* | v | 8 |
| with | 跟 | | *gēn* | prep | 6 |
| write | 写 | 寫 | *xiě* | v | 7 |
| | | **Y** | | | |
| year (of age) | 岁 | 歲 | *suì* | n | 3 |
| yellow | 黄 | 黃 | *huáng* | adj | 9 |
| yesterday | 昨天 | | *zuótiān* | t | 4 |
| you | 你 | | *nǐ* | pr | 1 |
| you (honorific for 你) | 您 | | *nín* | pr | 6 |
| younger brother | 弟弟 | | *dìdi* | n | 2 |
| younger sister | 妹妹 | | *mèimei* | n | 2 |

# Vocabulary by Lesson and Grammar Category

## Lesson 1

### L1-1

**Noun:** 小姐，名字，先生
**Pronoun:** 你，我，什么
**Verb:** 请，问，姓，叫
**Adjective:** 好，贵
**Particle:** 呢
**Proper Noun:** 王朋，李友

### L1-2

**Noun:** 老师，学生，人
**Verb:** 是
**Adverb:** 不，也
**Particle:** 吗
**Proper Noun:** 中国，北京，美国，纽约

## Lesson 2

### L2-1

**Noun:** 照片，爸爸，妈妈，孩子，姐姐，弟弟，大哥，儿子，女儿
**Measure Word:** 个
**Pronoun:** 那，这，谁，她，他
**Verb:** 有
**Adjective:** 女，男
**Adverb:** 没
**Particle:** 的
**Proper Noun:** 高文中

### L2-2

**Noun:** 家，哥哥，妹妹，大姐，二姐，工作，律师，英文，大学生，医生
**Measure Word:** 口
**Numeral:** 几，两
**Verb:** 做
**Adverb:** 都
**Conjunction:** 和
**Proper Noun:** 白英爱

## Lesson 3

**L3-1**

| | |
|---|---|
| **Noun:** | 九月，月，星期，星期四，天，生日，岁，饭，菜 |
| **Measure Word:** | 号，点 |
| **Pronoun:** | 怎么样，我们 |
| **Numeral:** | 十二，十八，半 |
| **Verb:** | 吃，谢谢，喜欢，见，再见 |
| **Adjective:** | 大 |
| **Adverb:** | 多 |
| **Conjunction:** | 还是，可是 |
| **Time Word:** | 今年，晚上 |
| **Others:** | 太…了 |
| **Proper Noun:** | 英国 |

**L3-2**

| | |
|---|---|
| **Noun:** | 事（儿），晚饭，同学，朋友 |
| **Measure Word:** | 刻 |
| **Pronoun:** | 为什么 |
| **Verb:** | 认识 |
| **Adjective:** | 忙 |
| **Adverb:** | 很，还 |
| **Conjunction:** | 因为 |
| **Time Word:** | 现在，今天，明天 |

## Lesson 4

**L4-1**

| | |
|---|---|
| **Noun:** | 周末，电视，音乐，书，时候，电影，外国 |
| **Pronoun:** | 有的 |
| **Verb:** | 打球，看，唱歌，跳舞，听，去，请客 |
| **Adjective:** | 对 |
| **Adverb:** | 常常 |
| **Conjunction:** | 那，所以 |
| **Time Word:** | 昨天 |

L4-2

**Noun:** 别人
**Verb:** 觉得，睡觉，找
**Modal Verb:** 想
**Adjective:** 小，不错，有意思
**Adverb:** 只
**Others:** 好久，算了

## Lesson 5

L5-1

**Noun:** 学校，茶，咖啡，可乐，水
**Measure Word:** 点（儿），瓶，杯
**Pronoun:** 哪儿
**Verb:** 进，进来，来，介绍，坐，喝，要，对不起，给
**Modal Verb:** 可以
**Adjective:** 高兴，漂亮
**Adverb:** 快
**Preposition:** 在
**Particle:** 呀，吧
**Others:** 一下
**Proper Noun:** 高小音

L5-2

**Noun:** 图书馆
**Verb:** 玩（儿），聊天（儿），回家
**Adverb:** 一起，才
**Particle:** 了

## Lesson 6

### L6-1

**Noun:** 时间，问题，课，年级，空儿，办公室
**Measure Word:** 位，节
**Pronoun:** 您，哪
**Verb:** 打电话，在，开会，考试，到，行，等
**Modal Verb:** 要
**Adjective:** 方便，客气
**Adverb:** 就，别
**Preposition:** 给
**Conjunction:** 要是
**Time Word:** 下午，上午，以后
**Others:** 喂
**Proper Noun:** 常老师

### L6-2

**Noun:** 中文
**Verb:** 帮，准备，练习，说，见面，回来
**Modal Verb:** 得
**Preposition:** 跟
**Conjunction:** 但是
**Particle:** 啊
**Others:** 下个

## Lesson 7

### L7-1

**Noun:** 字，笔，纸，语法，生词，汉字
**Measure Word:** 枝，张
**Pronoun:** 怎么，哪里
**Verb:** 说话，复习，写，教，懂，预习，学
**Adjective:** 慢，容易，多，难
**Adverb:** 真
**Particle:** 得
**Others:** 上个，第

L7-2

Noun: 功课，课文，录音
Pronoun: 这么，大家
Verb: 上课，开始，念，学习
Adjective: 早，晚，帅，酷
Adverb: 平常
Time Word: 早上

## Lesson 8

L8-1

Noun: 日记，早饭，教室，发音，电脑，餐厅，午饭，宿舍
Measure Word: 篇
Pronoun: 那儿
Verb: 起床，洗澡，上网，告诉，知道
Adjective: 累，新
Adverb: 一边，正在，已经
Time Word: 中午，以前

L8-2

Noun: 信，学期，专业，音乐会
Measure Word: 封
Verb: 希望，用，笑，祝
Modal Verb: 会，能
Conjunction: 除了…以外
Time Word: 最近，后来

## Lesson 9

L9-1

Noun: 商店，东西，售货员，衣服，衬衫，颜色，裤子，号，长短，钱
Measure Word: 件，条，块，毛，分
Pronoun: 多少
Numeral: 百
Verb: 买，穿，试，找（钱）
Adjective: 黄，红，中，便宜，合适
Adverb: 一共
Conjunction: 如果…的话
Others: 不用

L9-2

| | |
|---|---|
| **Noun:** | 鞋，大小，咖啡色，样子，信用卡 |
| **Measure Word:** | 双，种 |
| **Pronoun:** | 它，这儿 |
| **Verb:** | 换，刷卡，收，付钱 |
| **Adjective:** | 一样，黑 |
| **Adverb:** | 挺，再 |
| **Conjunction:** | 虽然，不过 |

## Lesson 10

L10-1

| | |
|---|---|
| **Noun:** | 寒假，飞机，票，（飞）机场，公共汽车，地铁，路，线，出租汽车 |
| **Measure Word:** | 站 |
| **Verb:** | 坐，走，下车，打车，开车，送 |
| **Adjective:** | 绿，蓝，麻烦 |
| **Adverb:** | 先，然后 |
| **Conjunction:** | 或者 |
| **Others:** | 最后 |

L10-2

| | |
|---|---|
| **Noun:** | 电子邮件，城市，高速公路，手机，新年 |
| **Pronoun:** | 每，自己 |
| **Verb:** | 让，花，出去，发短信 |
| **Adjective:** | 紧张，快乐 |
| **Adverb:** | 特别 |
| **Others:** | 不好意思 |

# Vocabulary Index (How About You?)

The How About You? vocabulary index is sequenced according to the order of the corresponding images, horizontally from left to right. Exercises that do not include images corresponding to vocabulary items (e.g., in Lesson 1: Dialogue 1) are omitted.

| English | Simplified | Traditional | Pinyin | Part of Speech |
|---|---|---|---|---|
| **L1: Dialogue 2** | | | | |
| Mexico | 墨西哥 | | *Mòxīgē* | pn |
| India | 印度 | | *Yìndù* | pn |
| Canada | 加拿大 | | *Jiānádà* | pn |
| Britain | 英国 | 英國 | *Yīngguó* | pn |
| **L2: Dialogue 2** | | | | |
| soldier | 军人 | 軍人 | *jūnrén* | n |
| teacher | 老师 | 老師 | *lǎoshī* | n |
| nurse | 护士 | 護士 | *hùshi* | n |
| **L3: Dialogue 1** | | | | |
| British food | 英国菜 | 英國菜 | *Yīngguó cài* | n |
| Chinese food | 中国菜 | 中國菜 | *Zhōngguó cài* | n |
| American food | 美国菜 | 美國菜 | *Měiguó cài* | n |
| **L4: Dialogue 1** | | | | |
| read books | 看书 | 看書 | *kàn shū* | vo |
| watch movies | 看电影 | 看電影 | *kàn diànyǐng* | vo |
| play ball | 打球 | | *dǎ qiú* | vo |
| listen to music | 听音乐 | 聽音樂 | *tīng yīnyuè* | vo |
| **L4: Dialogue 2** | | | | |
| sleep | 睡觉 | 睡覺 | *shuì jiào* | vo |

| English | Simplified | Traditional | Pinyin | Part of Speech |
|---|---|---|---|---|
| go shopping | 逛街 | | *guàng jiē* | vo |
| draw, paint | 画画儿 | 畫畫兒 | *huà huàr* | vo |
| play chess | 下棋 | | *xià qí* | vo |
| **L5: Dialogue** | | | | |
| fruit juice | 果汁 | | *guǒzhī* | n |
| Coca-Cola | 可口可乐 | 可口可樂 | *Kěkǒukělè* | pn |
| mineral water | 矿泉水 | 礦泉水 | *kuàngquánshuǐ* | n |
| Sprite | 雪碧 | | *Xuěbì* | pn |
| **L5: Narrative** | | | | |
| school | 学校 | 學校 | *xuéxiào* | n |
| library | 图书馆 | 圖書館 | *túshūguǎn* | n |
| home | 家 | | *jiā* | n |
| **L6: Dialogue 1** | | | | |
| home | 家 | | *jiā* | n |
| office | 办公室 | 辦公室 | *bàngōngshì* | n |
| library | 图书馆 | 圖書館 | *túshūguǎn* | n |
| **L6: Dialogue 2** | | | | |
| Japanese language | 日语 | 日語 | *Rìyǔ* | pn |
| Spanish language | 西班牙语 | 西班牙語 | *Xībānyáyǔ* | pn |
| French language | 法语 | 法語 | *Fǎyǔ* | pn |
| **L7: Dialogue 2** | | | | |
| Chinese textbook | 中文课本 | 中文課本 | *Zhōngwén kèběn* | n |
| Chinese workbook | 中文练习本 | 中文練習本 | *Zhōngwén liànxíběn* | n |
| Chinese dictionary | 中文字典 | | *Zhōngwén zìdiǎn* | n |

| English | Simplified | Traditional | Pinyin | Part of Speech |
|---|---|---|---|---|
| **L8: Diary Entry** | | | | |
| classroom | 教室 | | *jiàoshì* | n |
| dormitory | 宿舍 | | *sùshè* | n |
| dining room, cafeteria | 餐厅 | 餐廳 | *cāntīng* | n |
| **L8: Letter** | | | | |
| business management | 工商管理 | | *gōngshāng guǎnlǐ* | n |
| chemistry | 化学 | 化學 | *huàxué* | n |
| mathematics | 数学 | 數學 | *shùxué* | |
| **L9: Dialogue 1** | | | | |
| sweater | 毛衣 | | *máoyī* | n |
| coat | 外套 | | *wàitào* | n |
| suit | 西装 | 西裝 | *xīzhuāng* | n |
| **L9: Dialogue 2** | | | | |
| blue | 蓝色 | 藍色 | *lánsè* | n |
| green | 绿色 | 綠色 | *lǜsè* | n |
| pink | 粉红色 | 粉紅色 | *fěnhóngsè* | n |
| **L10: Dialogue** | | | | |
| walk | 走路 | | *zǒu lù* | vo |
| ride a bicycle | 骑自行车 | 騎自行車 | *qí zìxíngchē* | vo |
| take a bus | 坐公共汽车 | 坐公共汽車 | *zuò gōnggòng qìchē* | vo |
| **L10: Email** | | | | |
| ride a motorcycle | 骑摩托车 | 騎摩托車 | *qí mótuōchē* | vo |
| drive a car | 开车 | 開車 | *kāi chē* | vo |
| take the subway | 坐地铁 | 坐地鐵 | *zuò dìtiě* | vo |

# Appendix 1: Lesson Texts in Traditional Characters

## Lesson 1

**Dialogue 1**

Exchanging Greetings

At school, Wang Peng and Li You meet each other for the first time.

王朋：你好[a]！
李友：你好！
王朋：請問[b]，你[c]貴姓？
李友：我姓[1]李。你呢[2]？
王朋：我姓王。李小姐[d]，你叫[3]什麼名字？
李友：我叫李友。王先生，你叫什麼名字？
王朋：我叫王朋[4]。

**Dialogue 2**

Where Are You From?

Wang Peng and Li You start chatting after bumping into each other on campus.

李友：王先生，你是[5]老師嗎[6]？
王朋：我不[7][a]是老師，我是學生。李友，你呢？
李友：我也[8]是學生。你是中國人嗎？
王朋：是[b]，我是北京人。你是美國人嗎？
李友：是，我是紐約人。

## Lesson 2

**Dialogue 1**

Looking at a Family Photo

Wang Peng is in Gao Wenzhong's room and points to a picture on the desk.

王朋：高文中，那是你的[1]照片嗎？

They walk toward the picture and stand in front of it.

高文中：是。這是我爸爸，這是我媽媽。
王朋：　這[a]個[2]女孩子是誰[3]？
高文中：她是我姐姐。
王朋：　這個男孩子是你弟弟嗎？
高文中：不是，他是我大哥的兒子[b]。
王朋：　你大哥有[4]女兒嗎？
高文中：他沒有女兒。

**Dialogue 2**

Discussing Family

Li You and Bai Ying'ai are chatting about their family members and what each of them does.

李友：　白英愛，你家[a]有[5]幾口[b]人？
白英愛：我家有六口人，我爸爸、我媽媽、一[c]個哥哥、兩[6]個妹妹和[d]我[e]。李友，你家有幾口人？
李友：　我家有五口人：爸爸、媽媽、大姐、二姐和我。你爸爸媽媽做什么工作？
白英愛：我爸爸是律師，媽媽是英文老師，哥哥、妹妹都[7]是大學生。
李友：　我媽媽也是老師，我爸爸是醫生。

## Lesson 3

**Dialogue 1**

Out for a Birthday Dinner

Gao Wenzhong is talking to Bai Ying'ai about a special day coming up.

高文中：　白英愛，九月十二[1a]號[2]是星期幾[2]？
白英愛：　是星期四。
高文中：　那天[b]是我的[3]生日。
白英愛：　是嗎？你今年多大[c]？
高文中：　十八歲[d]。
白英愛：　我星期四請你吃飯[4]，怎麼樣？
高文中：　太好了[e]。謝謝，謝謝[f]。
白英愛：　你喜歡吃中國菜還是[5]美國菜？
高文中：　我是英國人，可是我喜歡吃中國菜。
白英愛：　好，我們吃中國菜。
高文中：　星期四幾點？
白英愛：　七點半怎麼樣？
高文中：　好，星期四晚上見。
白英愛：　再見！

**Dialogue 2**

Dinner Invitation

Bai Ying'ai asks Wang Peng about his plans for tomorrow.

王朋：　白英愛，現在幾點？
白英愛：五點三刻。
王朋：　我六點一刻有事兒。
白英愛：你今天很忙[a]，明天忙不忙[6]？
王朋：　我今天很忙，可是明天不忙。有事兒嗎？
白英愛：明天我請你吃晚飯，怎麼樣？
王朋：　你為什麼請我吃飯？
白英愛：因為明天是高文中的生日。
王朋：　是嗎？好。還[7]請誰？
白英愛：還請我的同學李友。
王朋：　那太好了，我認識李友，她也是我的朋友。明天幾點？
白英愛：明天晚上七點半。
王朋：　好，明天七點半見。

## Lesson 4

**Dialogue 1**

Discussing Hobbies

Gao Wenzhong asks Bai Ying'ai about her weekend plans and wants to invite her to a movie; however . . .

高文中：白英愛，你週末喜歡做什麼[1]？
白英愛：我喜歡打球、看電視[a]。你呢？
高文中：我喜歡唱歌、跳舞，還喜歡聽音樂。你也喜歡看書，對不對？
白英愛：對，有的時候也喜歡看書。
高文中：你喜歡不喜歡[2]看電影？
白英愛：喜歡。我週末常常看電影。
高文中：那[3]我們今天晚上去看[4]一個外國電影，怎麼樣？我請客。
白英愛：為什麼你請客？
高文中：因為昨天你請我吃飯，所以今天我請你看電影。
白英愛：那你也請王朋、李友，好嗎[5]？
高文中：……好。

Dialogue 2

Let's Play Ball

Wang Peng visits Gao Wenzhong and invites him to play ball over the weekend.

王朋： 小高[a]，好久不見[b]，你好嗎[c]？
高文中：我很好。你怎麼樣？
王朋： 我也不錯。這個週末你想[6]做什麼？想不想去打球？
高文中：打球？我不喜歡打球。
王朋： 那我們去看球，怎麼樣？
高文中：看球？我覺得看球也沒有意思[d]。
王朋： 那你這個週末想做什麼？
高文中：我只想吃飯、睡覺[7][e]。
王朋： 算了，我去找別人。

## Lesson 5

Dialogue

Visiting a Friend's Place

Wang Peng and Li You visit Gao Wenzhong and meet his sister, Gao Xiaoyin.
(The doorbell rings.)

高文中： 誰呀？
王朋： 是我，王朋，還有李友。
高文中： 請進，請進，快進來！來，我介紹一下[1]，這是我姐姐，高小音。
李友和王朋：小音，你好。認識你很高興。
高小音： 認識你們我也很高興。
李友： 你們家很大[2]，也很漂亮。
高小音： 是嗎？[a]請坐，請坐。
王朋： 小音，你在[3]哪兒[b]工作？
高小音： 我在學校工作。你們想喝點兒[1]什麼？喝茶還是喝咖啡？
王朋： 我喝茶吧[4]。
李友： 我要一瓶可樂，可以嗎？
高小音： 對不起，我們家沒有可樂。
李友： 那給我一杯水吧。

Narrative

At a Friend's Place

Gao Xiaoyin, Wang Peng, and Li You visited Gao Wenzhong's place.

昨天晚上，王朋和李友去高文中家玩兒。在高文中家，他們認識了[5]高文中的姐姐。她叫高小音，在學校的圖書館工作。她請王朋喝[a]茶，王朋喝了[5]兩杯。李友不喝茶，只喝了一杯水。他們一起聊天兒、看電視。王朋和李友晚上十二點才[6]回家。

## Lesson 6

### Dialogue 1
Calling Your Teacher

李友給[1]常老師打電話……

常老師：喂？

李友：　喂，請問，常老師在嗎？

常老師：我就是。您[a]是哪位？

李友：　老師，您好。我是李友。

常老師：李友，有事兒嗎？

李友：　老師，今天下午您有時間[b]嗎？我想問[c]您幾個問題。

常老師：對不起，今天下午我要[2]開會。

李友：　明天呢？

常老師：明天上午我有兩節[d]課，下午三點要給二年級考試。

李友：　您什麼時候[e]有空兒？

常老師：明天四點以後[f]才有空兒。

李友：　要是[g]您方便，四點半我到您的辦公室去，行嗎？

常老師：四點半，沒問題[h]。我在辦公室等你。

李友：　謝謝您。

常老師：別[3]客氣。

### Dialogue 2
Calling a Friend for Help

李友給王朋打電話……

李友：喂，請問，王朋在嗎？

王朋：我就是。你是李友吧[a]？

李友：王朋，我下個星期[4]要考中文，你幫我準備一下，跟我練習說中文，好嗎？

王朋：好啊，但是你得[5]請我喝咖啡。

李友：喝咖啡，沒問題。那我什麼時候跟你見面？你今天晚上有空兒嗎？

王朋：今天晚上白英愛請我吃飯。

李友：是嗎？白英愛請你吃飯？

王朋：對。我回來[6]以後給你打電話。

李友：好，我等你的電話。

## Lesson 7

### Dialogue 1

How Did You Do on the Exam?

王朋跟李友說話……

王朋：李友，你上個星期考試考得[1]怎麼樣？

李友：因為你幫我復習，所以考得不錯。但是我寫中國字寫得太[2]慢了！

王朋：是嗎？以後我跟你一起練習寫字，好不好[a]？

李友：那太好了！我們現在就[3]寫，怎麼樣？

王朋：好，給我一枝筆[4]、一張紙。寫什麼字？

李友：你教我怎麼寫"懂"字吧。

王朋：好吧。

李友：你寫字寫得真[2]好，真快。

王朋：哪裡，哪裡[b]。你明天有中文課嗎？我幫你預習。

李友：明天我們學第七[5]課。第七課的語法很容易，我都懂，可是生詞太多，漢字也有一點兒[6]難。

王朋：沒問題，我幫你。

### Dialogue 2

Preparing for Chinese Class

李友跟白英愛說話……

李友：白英愛，你平常來得很早，今天怎麼[7]這麼晚？

白英愛：我昨天預習中文，早上[a]四點才[3]睡覺，你也睡得很晚嗎？

李友：我昨天十點就[3]睡了。因為王朋幫我練習中文，所以我功課做得很快。

白英愛：有個中國朋友真好。

上中文課……

常老師：大家早[b]，現在我們開始上課。第七課你們都預習了嗎？

白英愛和李友：預習了。

常老師：李友，請你念課文。……念得很好。你昨天晚上聽錄音了吧？

李友：我沒聽。

白英愛：但是她的朋友昨天晚上幫她學習了。

常老師：你的朋友是中國人嗎？

李友：　　　是。
白英愛：　　他是一個男的[8]，很帥[c]，很酷，叫王朋。[9]

Lesson 8

Diary Entry

A Typical School Day

李友的一篇日記

十一月三日星期二

今天我很忙，很累。早上七點半起床[1]，洗了澡以後就[2]吃早飯。我一邊吃飯，一邊[3]聽錄音。九點到教室去上課[4]。

第一節課是中文，老師教我們發音、生詞和語法，也教我們寫字，還給了[5]我們一篇新課文[6]，這篇課文很有意思。第二節是電腦[a]課，很難。

中午我和同學們一起到餐廳去吃午飯。我們一邊吃，一邊練習說中文。下午我到圖書館去上網。四點王朋來找我打球。五點三刻吃晚飯。七點半我去白英愛的宿舍跟她聊天(兒)。到那兒的時候，她正在[7]做功課。我八點半回家。睡覺以前，高文中給我打了一個電話，告訴我明天要考試，我說我已經知道了。

Letter

Writing to a Friend

一封信

這是李友給高小音的一封信。

小音：

你好！好久不見，最近怎麼樣？

這個學期我很忙，除了專業課以外，還[8]得學中文。我們的中文課很有意思。因為我們的中文老師只會[9]說中文，不會說英文，所以上課的時候我們只說中文，不說英文。開始我覺得很難，後來[a]，王朋常常幫我練習中文，就[10]覺得不難了[b]。

你喜歡聽音樂嗎？下個星期六，我們學校有一個音樂會，希望你能[9]來。我用中文寫信寫得很不好，請別笑我。祝

好！

你的朋友
李友
十一月十八日

**Lesson 9**

## Dialogue 1

Shopping for Clothes

李友在商店買東西，售貨員問她……

售貨員：小姐，您要[1]買什麼衣服？
李友：　我想買一件[2]襯衫。
售貨員：您喜歡什麼顏色的[3]，黃的還是紅的？
李友：　我喜歡穿[a]紅的。我還想買一條[2]褲子[b]。
售貨員：多[4]大的？大號的、中號的、還是小號的？
李友：　中號的。不要太貴的，也不要太便宜[c]的。
售貨員：這條褲子怎麼樣？
李友：　顏色很好。如果長短合適的話，我就買。
售貨員：您試一下。

Li You checks the size on the label and measures the pants against her legs.

李友：　不用試。可以。
售貨員：這件襯衫呢？
李友：　也不錯。一共多少錢？
售貨員：襯衫二十一塊五，褲子三十二塊九毛九，一共是五十四塊四毛九分[5]。
李友：　好，這是一百塊錢。
售貨員：找您四十五塊五毛一。
李友：　謝謝。

## Dialogue 2

Exchanging Shoes

王朋想換一雙鞋，他問售貨員……

王朋：　對不起，這雙鞋太小了。能不能換一雙？
售貨員：沒問題。您看，這雙怎麼樣？
王朋：　也不行，這雙跟那雙一樣[6]大。
售貨員：那這雙黑的呢？
王朋：　這雙鞋雖然大小合適，可是[7]顏色不好。有沒有咖啡色的？
售貨員：對不起，這種鞋只有黑的。
王朋：　這雙鞋樣子挺好的[a]，就是它吧[b]。你們這兒可以刷卡嗎？
售貨員：對不起，我們不收信用卡。不過，這雙的錢跟那雙一樣，您不用再付錢了。

## Lesson 10

**Dialogue**

Going Home for Winter Vacation

李友跟王朋說話……

王朋：李友，寒假你回家嗎？

李友：對，我要回家。

王朋：飛機票你買了嗎[1]？

李友：已經買了。是二十一號的。

王朋：飛機是幾點的？

李友：晚上八點的。

王朋：你怎麼去[a]機場？

李友：我想坐公共汽車或者[2]坐地鐵。你知道怎麼走[a]嗎？

王朋：你先坐一路汽車，坐三站下車，然后換地鐵。先坐紅線，再[3]換綠線，最後換藍線。

李友：不行，不行，太麻煩了。我還是[4]打車[b]吧。

王朋：出租汽車太貴，我開車送你去吧。

李友：謝謝你。

王朋：不用客氣。

**Email**

Thanks for the Ride

李友給王朋寫電子郵件[a]：

Date: 12月20日

From: 李友

To: 王朋

Subject: 謝謝!

王朋：

謝謝你那天開車送我到機場。不過，讓你花那麼多時間，真不好意思。我這幾天每天都[5]開車出去看老朋友。這個城市的人開車開得特別快。我在高速公路上開車，真有點兒緊張。可是這兒沒有公共汽車，也沒有地鐵，只能自己開車，很不方便。

有空兒的話打我的手機或者給我發短信，我想跟你聊天兒。

新年快要到了[6]，祝你新年快樂！

李友

# Appendix 2: Lesson Texts in English

## Lesson 1

### Dialogue 1

Exchanging Greetings

**At school, Wang Peng and Li You meet each other for the first time.**

Li You: How do you do?
Wang Peng: What's your family name, please? (lit. Please, may I ask . . . your honorable family name is . . . ?)
Li You: My family name is Li. What's yours?
Wang Peng: My family name is Wang. Miss Li, what's your name?
Li You: My name is Li You. Mr. Wang, what's your name?
Wang Peng: My name is Wang Peng.

### Dialogue 2

Where Are You From?

**Wang Peng and Li You start chatting after bumping into each other on campus.**

Li You: Mr. Wang, are you a teacher?
Wang Peng: I'm not a teacher, I'm a student. How about you, Li You?
Li You: I'm a student, too. Are you Chinese?
Wang Peng: Yes, I'm from Beijing (lit. I'm a Beijinger). Are you American?
Li You: Yes, I'm from New York (lit. I'm a New Yorker).

## Lesson 2

### Dialogue 1

Looking at a Family Photo

**Wang Peng is in Gao Wenzhong's room and points to a picture on the desk.**

Wang Peng: Gao Wenzhong, is that picture yours?

**They walk toward the picture and stand in front of it.**

Gao Wenzhong: Yes. This is my dad. This is my mom.
Wang Peng: Who's this girl?
Gao Wenzhong: She's my older sister.
Wang Peng: Is this boy your younger brother?
Gao Wenzhong: No, he's my eldest brother's son.
Wang Peng: Does your eldest brother have any daughters?
Gao Wenzhong: He doesn't have any daughters.

### Dialogue 2

Discussing Family

**Li You and Bai Ying'ai are chatting about their family members and what each of them does.**

Li You: Bai Ying'ai, how many people are there in your family?
Bai Ying'ai: There are six people in my family: my dad, my mom, an older brother, two younger sisters, and me. Li You, how many people are there in your family?
Li You: There are five people in my family: my dad, my mom, my oldest sister, my second oldest sister, and me. What do your dad and mom do?
Bai Ying'ai: My dad is a lawyer. My mom is an English teacher. My older brother and younger sisters are all college students.
Li You: My mom is also a teacher. My dad is a doctor.

## Lesson 3

**Dialogue 1**

Out for a Birthday Dinner

**Gao Wenzhong is talking to Bai Ying'ai about a special day coming up.**

Gao Wenzhong: Bai Ying'ai, what day is September 12?
Bai Ying'ai: Thursday.
Gao Wenzhong: That (day) is my birthday.
Bai Ying'ai: Really? How old are you this year?
Gao Wenzhong: Eighteen.
Bai Ying'ai: I'll treat you to a meal on Thursday. How's that?
Gao Wenzhong: That would be great. Thank you very much!
Bai Ying'ai: Do you like Chinese food or American food?
Gao Wenzhong: I'm an Englishman, but I like Chinese food.
Bai Ying'ai: All right. We'll have Chinese food.
Gao Wenzhong: Thursday at what time?
Bai Ying'ai: How about seven-thirty?
Gao Wenzhong: All right. See you Thursday evening.
Bai Ying'ai: See you.

**Dialogue 2**

Dinner Invitation

**Bai Ying'ai asks Wang Peng about his plans for tomorrow.**

Wang Peng: Bai Ying'ai, what time is it now?
Bai Ying'ai: A quarter to six.
Wang Peng: I have something to do at a quarter after six.
Bai Ying'ai: You're busy today. Are you busy tomorrow?
Wang Peng: I'm busy today, but I won't be tomorrow. What's up?
Bai Ying'ai: I'd like to invite you to dinner tomorrow. How about it?
Wang Peng: Why are you inviting me to dinner?
Bai Ying'ai: Because tomorrow is Gao Wenzhong's birthday.
Wang Peng: Really? Great. Who else are you inviting?
Bai Ying'ai: I'm also inviting my classmate Li You.
Wang Peng: Awesome. I know Li You. She's my friend, too. What time tomorrow?
Bai Ying'ai: Seven-thirty tomorrow evening.
Wang Peng: OK, I'll see you tomorrow at seven-thirty.

## Lesson 4

**Dialogue 1**

Discussing Hobbies

**Gao Wenzhong asks Bai Ying'ai about her weekend plans and wants to invite her to a movie; however . . .**

Gao Wenzhong: Bai Ying'ai, what do you like to do on weekends?
Bai Ying'ai: I like to play ball and watch TV. How about you?
Gao Wenzhong: I like to sing, dance, and listen to music. You like to read, right?
Bai Ying'ai: Yes, sometimes I like to read as well.
Gao Wenzhong: Do you like to watch movies?
Bai Ying'ai: Yes, I do. I often watch movies on weekends.
Gao Wenzhong: Then let's go see a foreign movie this evening. OK? My treat.
Bai Ying'ai: Why your treat?
Gao Wenzhong: Because you treated me to dinner yesterday, today I'm treating you to a movie.
Bai Ying'ai: Then invite Wang Peng and Li You as well, OK?
Gao Wenzhong: . . . OK.

**Dialogue 2**

Let's Play Ball

**Wang Peng visits Gao Wenzhong and invites him to play ball over the weekend.**

Wang Peng: Gao Wenzhong, long time no see. How are you?

Gao Wenzhong: I'm fine. How about yourself?

Wang Peng: I'm fine, too. What would you like to do this weekend? Would you like to play ball?

Gao Wenzhong: Play ball? I don't like playing ball.

Wang Peng: Then let's watch a ball game. How's that?

Gao Wenzhong: Watch a ball game? I don't think watching a ball game is much fun, either.

Wang Peng: Then what do you want to do this weekend?

Gao Wenzhong: I only want to eat and sleep.

Wang Peng: Never mind. I'll ask somebody else.

## Lesson 5

**Dialogue**

Visiting a Friend's Place

**Wang Peng and Li You visit Gao Wenzhong and meet his sister, Gao Xiaoyin.**
**(The doorbell rings.)**

Gao Wenzhong: Who is it?

Wang Peng: It's me, Wang Peng. Li You is here, too.

Gao Wenzhong: Please come in. Let me introduce you to one another. This is my sister, Gao Xiaoyin.

Wang Peng and Li You: How do you do, Xiaoyin! Pleased to meet you.

Gao Xiaoyin: Pleased to meet you, too.

Li You: Your home is very big, and very beautiful, too.

Gao Xiaoyin: Really? Have a seat, please.

Wang Peng: Xiaoyin, where do you work?

Gao Xiaoyin: I work at a school. What would you like to drink? Tea or coffee?

Wang Peng: I'll have tea.

Li You: I'd like a bottle of cola.

Gao Xiaoyin: I'm sorry. We don't have cola.

Li You: Then please give me a glass of water.

**Narrative**

At a Friend's Place

**Gao Xiaoyin, Wang Peng, and Li You visited Gao Wenzhong.**

Last night, Wang Peng and Li You went to Gao Wenzhong's home for a visit. At Gao Wenzhong's home they met Gao Wenzhong's older sister. Her name is Gao Xiaoyin. She works at a school library. She offered tea to Wang Peng. Wang Peng had two cups. Li You doesn't drink tea. She only had a glass of water. They chatted and watched TV together. Wang Peng and Li You didn't get home until twelve o'clock.

## Lesson 6

### Dialogue 1

Calling Your Teacher

**Li You is on the phone with her teacher . . .**

| | |
|---|---|
| Teacher Chang: | Hello? |
| Li You: | Hello, is Teacher Chang there? |
| Teacher Chang: | This is she. Who is this, please? |
| Li You: | Teacher, how are you? This is Li You. |
| Teacher Chang: | Hi, Li You. What's going on? |
| Li You: | Teacher, are you free this afternoon? I'd like to ask you a few questions. |
| Teacher Chang: | I'm sorry. This afternoon I have to go to a meeting. |
| Li You: | What about tomorrow? |
| Teacher Chang: | Tomorrow morning I have two classes. Tomorrow afternoon at three o'clock I have to give an exam to the second-year class. |
| Li You: | When will you be free? |
| Teacher Chang: | I won't be free until after four o'clock tomorrow. |
| Li You: | If it's convenient for you, I'll go to your office at four-thirty. Is that all right? |
| Teacher Chang: | Four-thirty? No problem. I'll wait for you in my office. |
| Li You: | Thank you. |
| Teacher Chang: | You're welcome. |

### Dialogue 2

Calling a Friend for Help

**Li You and Wang Peng are talking on the phone . . .**

| | |
|---|---|
| Li You: | Hello, is Wang Peng there? |
| Wang Peng: | This is he. Is this Li You? |
| Li You: | Hi, Wang Peng. Next week I have a Chinese exam. Could you help me prepare by practicing speaking Chinese with me? |
| Wang Peng: | Sure, but you have to take me out for coffee. |
| Li You: | Take you out for coffee? No problem. So, when can I see you? Are you free this evening? |
| Wang Peng: | Bai Ying'ai is taking me out to dinner this evening. |
| Li You: | Is that so? Bai Ying'ai is taking you out to dinner? |
| Wang Peng: | That's right. I will call you when I get back. |
| Li You: | OK. I'll wait for you to call. |

## Lesson 7

**Dialogue 1**

How Did You Do on the Exam?

**Wang Peng is talking with Li You . . .**

Wang Peng: How did you do on last week's exam?

Li You: Because you helped me review, I did pretty well, but I'm too slow at writing Chinese characters.

Wang Peng: Really? I'll practice writing characters with you from now on. How's that?

Li You: That would be great! Let's do it right now, OK?

Wang Peng: OK. Give me a pen and a piece of paper. What character should we write?

Li You: Why don't you teach me how to write the character "dǒng" (to understand)?

Wang Peng: OK.

Li You: You write characters really well, and very fast, too.

Wang Peng: I'm flattered. Do you have Chinese class tomorrow? I'll help you prepare.

Li You: Tomorrow we'll study Lesson 7. The grammar for Lesson 7 is easy; I understand all of it. But there are too many new words, and the Chinese characters are a bit difficult.

Wang Peng: No problem. I'll help you.

**Dialogue 2**

Preparing for Chinese Class

**Li You is talking with Bai Ying'ai . . .**

Li You: Bai Ying'ai, you usually arrive very early. How come you got here so late today?

Bai Ying'ai: Yesterday I was preparing for Chinese. I didn't go to bed till four o'clock in the morning. Did you go to bed very late, too?

Li You: No, yesterday I went to bed at ten. Because Wang Peng helped me practice Chinese, I finished my homework very quickly.

Bai Ying'ai: It's so great to have a Chinese friend.

**In Chinese class . . .**

Teacher Chang: Good morning, everyone. Let's begin. Have you all prepared for Lesson 7?

Bai Ying'ai and Li You: Yes, we have.

Teacher Chang: Li You, would you please read the text aloud? . . . You read very well. Did you listen to the audio recording last night?

Li You: No, I didn't.

Bai Ying'ai: But her friend helped her study yesterday evening.

Teacher Chang: Is your friend Chinese?

Li You: Yes.

Bai Ying'ai: He's a very cool and handsome guy. His name is Wang Peng.

## Lesson 8

**Diary Entry**

A Typical School Day

### An Entry from Li You's Diary

November 3, Tuesday

I was very busy and tired today. I got up at seven-thirty this morning. After taking a shower, I had breakfast. While I was eating, I listened to an audio recording. I went to class at nine o'clock.

We had Chinese for first period. The teacher taught us pronunciation, new vocabulary, and grammar. The teacher also taught us how to write Chinese characters, and gave us a new text. The text was very interesting. Second period was computer science. It was very hard.

At noon I went to the cafeteria with my classmates for lunch. As we ate, we practiced speaking Chinese. In the afternoon I went to the library to use the Internet. At four o'clock, Wang Peng came looking for me to play ball. I had dinner at a quarter to six. At seven-thirty, I went to Bai Ying'ai's dorm for a chat. When I got there, she was doing her homework. I got home at eight-thirty. Before I went to bed, Gao Wenzhong called. He told me there'd be an exam tomorrow. I said I already knew.

**Letter**

Writing to a Friend

### A Letter

**This is a letter Li You wrote to Gao Xiaoyin.**
Xiaoyin:

How are you? Long time no see. How are things recently?

I've been busy this semester. Besides the classes required for my major, I also need to study Chinese. Our Chinese class is really interesting. Because our Chinese teacher only speaks Chinese and can't speak any English, we only speak Chinese in class; no English. In the beginning, I felt it was very difficult. Wang Peng often helped me practice Chinese, and it doesn't feel so hard anymore.

Do you like listening to music? Next Saturday there'll be a concert at our school. I hope you can come. I don't write well in Chinese. Please don't poke fun at me. Wishing you all the best.

Your friend,
Li You
November 18

## Lesson 9

**Dialogue 1**

Shopping for Clothes

**Li You is shopping at a store and the salesperson asks her . . .**

Salesperson: Miss, what are you looking to buy?
Li You: I'd like to buy a shirt.
Salesperson: What color would you like? Yellow or red?
Li You: I'd like one in red. I'd also like to buy a pair of pants.
Salesperson: What size? Large, medium, or small?
Li You: Medium. Something not too expensive, but not too cheap, either.
Salesperson: How about these pants?
Li You: The color is nice. If the size is right, I'll take them.
Salesperson: Please try them on.

**Li You checks the size on the label, and measures the pants against her legs.**

Li You: No need to try them on. They'll do.
Salesperson: And how about this shirt?
Li You: It's not bad either. How much altogether?
Salesperson: Twenty one dollars and fifty cents for the shirt, and thirty-two ninety-nine for the pants. Fifty-four dollars and forty-nine cents altogether.
Li You: OK. Here's one hundred.
Salesperson: Forty-five fifty-one is your change.
Li You: Thank you.

**Dialogue 2**

Exchanging Shoes

**Wang Peng wants to exchange a pair of shoes and he asks the salesperson . . .**

Wang Peng: Excuse me, this pair of shoes is too small. Can I exchange them for another pair?
Salesperson: No problem. How about this pair?
Wang Peng: No, they won't do either. This pair is the same size as the other one.
Salesperson: What about this pair in black?
Wang Peng: This pair is the right size, but it's not a good color. Do you have any in brown?
Salesperson: I'm sorry. We only have these shoes in black.
Wang Peng: These shoes look good. I'll take them. Can I use my credit card here?
Salesperson: I'm sorry, we don't take credit cards. But this pair is the same price as the other one. You won't need to pay again.

## Lesson 10

**Dialogue**

Going Home for Winter Vacation

**Li You is talking to Wang Peng...**

Wang Peng: Are you going home for winter break?
Li You: Yes, I am.
Wang Peng: Have you booked a plane ticket?
Li You: Yes, for the twenty-first.
Wang Peng: When is the plane leaving?
Li You: Eight p.m.
Wang Peng: How are you getting to the airport?
Li You: I'm thinking of taking the bus or the subway. Do you know how to get there?
Wang Peng: You first take Bus No. 1. Get off after three stops. Then take the subway. First take the red line, then change to the green line, and finally change to the blue line.
Li You: Oh no. That's too much trouble. I'd better take a cab.
Wang Peng: It's too expensive to take a cab. I'll take you to the airport.
Li You: Thank you so much.
Wang Peng: Don't mention it.

**Email**

Thanks for the Ride

**Li you writes an email to Wang Peng:**

Date: December 20
From: Li You
To: Wang Peng
Subject: Thank you!

Wang Peng:
Thank you for driving me to the airport the other day. But I feel very bad for taking up so much of your time. The past few days I've been driving around to see old friends. People in this city drive very fast. I'm really nervous driving on the highway. But there are no buses or subway here; I have to drive. It's very inconvenient. When you have time, please call me on my cell or send a text message. I'd like to chat with you.

New Year is almost here. Happy New Year!

Li You